SMOKE COOKING

SMOKE COOKING

MATT KRAMER and ROGER SHEPPARD

HAWTHORN BOOKS, INC.   Publishers   New York

SMOKE COOKING

Library of Congress Catalog Card Number: 67-14855

ISBN: 0-8015-6896-

3 4 5 6 7 8 9 10

Designed by Gene Gordon

CONTENTS

SMOKE COOKING

1

About Smoke Cooking

Smokehouses have been used for centuries in the preservation of meat. Yet smoke does not preserve meat.

Is it only a myth then, that keeps smoke cooking alive?

Not at all. Smoke does two wonderful things for meat. It adds color—usually a cheery red—and it bestows a taste that is universally liked.

How to describe the taste? Some say it's as if a wine sauce were added, imparting a tartness not previously there. Others say it makes meat sweeter. Well, tastes vary from person to person, and anyone's taste can be questioned. There is no question, however, that smoke alters the taste, and for the better.

Surprisingly, a whole new generation is just discovering this. To them it is a new treat, a discovery to be shared with others. For many the first introduction came at the barbecue grills that have appeared in thousands of back yards in recent years. Barbecuing has inconveniences, but it also has its reward: a superb taste, not the least part of which is smokiness.

Modern smoke cooking is essentially barbecuing, but there is a difference: a cover. And what a difference this cover makes. It takes the trouble out of barbecuing, and it enables you to control the amount of smokiness you want. It makes the barbecue into an oven that retains heat, yet allows a constant flow of fresh air past the meat. Most modern smokers are portable barbecue stands with covers a foot or more high.

Usually charcoal is burned. The fire is built on the usual grate. The meat is placed on the usual grill. The difference comes in a draft control under the grate and in the lid.

Other cooking equipment is more demanding. A cook must remove the food at just the right moment, or it will be irretrievably
damaged. Place a roast in a non-smoke oven, and you will have
trapped just so much oxygen and moisture along with it. The heat
vaporizes the moisture, which can be replaced only by the moisture
that comes out of the meat. If the roast is in there a little too long,
it is a little too dry.

In a smoker, air is drawn in constantly from the draft below the
coals. As it moves upward, much of the oxygen is given up to the
coals. Not enough is left to allow the curse of the barbecue—flaming
fat. Even the fattest meats drip freely onto the coals without a flame
rising to char the meat. Smoke is created, of course, and it billows
around inside, mingling with smoke from the hardwood chips you
have placed on the coals. Finally it escapes through a hole in the
lid. This constant stream of air, continually bringing more moisture
into the oven, is the reason why timing is less critical and the meat
juicier.

Because of the lid, there is heat above the meat as well as below
it. You don't need to turn meat on the grill. It will cook on both
sides at once. Some persons, however, like to see grill marks on their
meat. When you serve them, turn up the side of the meat that was
resting on the grill.

It took us a while to recognize the remarkable things a smoke
oven accomplishes. Our first trials were with hamburger patties.
For the first time in our back-yard cooking experience, we didn't
have to fight the flames that flare when hamburger fat drips onto
the coals of a barbecue. We were pleased too that, once the hamburgers were done, we could shut off the draft and preserve the
charcoal for next time.

It was some time before we realized it was no accident that our
hamburgers were tasting better than they had before. They were
juicier and had more flavor. That's when we began trying steaks
and eventually roasts.

It is seldom now that either of our families has meat cooked in
anything but the smoker. Because of the constant supply of air, and
therefore humidity, the meat emerges juicier. Even cuts of meat
that are not particularly enhanced by smoke flavor go into our
smokers. That's because we can cook them without imparting
smokiness. This is one of the ways in which it's more versatile than

a barbecue. It's nearly impossible to barbecue meat without a smoke taste, for the meat must be over the coals and, when fat drips down, smoke comes back up. In a smoke oven, however, the meat can be placed to one side—not directly over the coals—and yet be cooked in the trapped heat, emerging juicier, with more flavor, and more tender than when cooked any other way.

Mostly, however, we want smoke. Meat cooked in a smoker has greater aroma than meat cooked in a conventional oven. The Food and Container Institute's research concludes that the aroma of cooked meat is more important than the flavor or taste. Nothing can compete with a smoke oven when it comes to a mouth-watering aroma.

Smoke cooking also increases menu variety. Before refrigeration came along, meat smoking was as common as salt. All farms had smokehouses. They have not disappeared completely, but the practitioners have become as scarce as mules. Along the way some delicious eating disappeared. Smoked foods have been provided by commercial producers since the advent of refrigeration, but they are usually only the traditional items—ham, bacon, sausage, some fish, and cheese.

Now the delicacies can be prepared at home in what to the new generation is a whole new way of cooking.

Actually, smoke cooking has been with us so long that its origins are lost. It was an integral part of preserving meat before refrigeration came along.

It was Henry Ford, the automotive genius, who brought it back. In the early 1920s, Ford cars used much wood—for the floorboards, roof struts, wheel spokes. Ford noticed that the sawed-off board ends were going to waste. He immediately set out to find some way of using them. One day it came to him: charcoal.

He found, however, that industrial users of charcoal already had their own supply. He would have to create a new market. So he shipped the charcoal to his automobile distributors with instructions to promote it.

Right away there was another problem. The wood trimmings were of odd shapes, unchanged in conversion to charcoal. The pieces did not fit together well. It took too much space to ship them.

So he changed the shape. The charcoal was ground and the powder fed to powerful presses, where, with the aid of cornstarch binder, semiround hunks of charcoal were produced. They were uniform in size, nestled together well, and burned without harmful fumes. Thus Henry Ford, the world's first mass producer of automobiles, became the first mass producer of the now familiar charcoal briquet.

It all seemed a dismal failure at the time, even though the briquet was superior to the previously used charcoal. It was concentrated charcoal, less liable to damage, more portable, longer burning and capable of higher heat.

At the time, however, the country was switching from wood and coal stoves to gas and electricity. It was considered a step backward to take charcoal into the house, and almost no one could conceive of taking charcoal into the back yard for cooking. Who would cook outdoors, when he had a new electric stove?

It took another generation and a more affluent society to adopt the briquet. Henry Ford did not profit from it. He was dead by the time the public was ready for his new product. But new companies have flourished for, when the new generation discovered briquets, it was with a where-have-you-been-all-my-life enthusiasm. First it was barbecuing, and from coast to coast the smell of cooking—and sometimes charring—meat rose from back yards, parks and camp grounds.

Later smoke cookers were developed, in part because charring was almost impossible in them, and in part because they were more versatile. The sale of briquets mounted. Whereas industry once took the entire charcoal output of the United States, by 1963 the back yards and picnics were taking 200,000 tons compared to industry's 150,000 tons annually.

The kind of cooking done in the smokers may be called hot smoking in contrast to the ancient way of cold smoking as part of the food preservation process.

In hot smoking the smokiness is implanted while the meat is cooked quickly at temperatures of 250° and more. In the age-old method meat was smoked for days, and at temperatures of 90° or less. There is confusion over this. Many persons think the old way must be used, even in the new cookers. Some, for example, insist that fish must be brined before being smoked. There is still a place for brining, but it is not essential in the new cookers.

In the old days—and still today if you want to corn beef or smoke a batch of fish—it was the salt that preserved the food. The meat sometimes would be in the brine for days before it would go into the smokehouse. The days in the smokehouse would dehydrate it, and thus help preserve it. The smoke would add color and flavor.

It was believed too that long smoking was necessary for smoke to penetrate the meat. Actually the smoke penetrates quite rapidly. It varies with the density of meat. Ground meats, for example, smoke readily. A cut of meat takes longer. Most fish, especially white-meated fish, take on a smoky taste quickly.

Thus modern smoke cooking can be fast. Ground chuck steaks, which can become a delicacy in a smoker—more of that later—can be done in ten minutes. Even more surprising is the fact that the same steaks can be left in the smoker thirty minutes and still be edible. They will, of course, be well done, but they will not be burned unless you have managed to put in enough coals to signal ships.

There is another strange fact about smoke cooking at home. To the authors' knowledge, there is no other book on the subject, despite its ages-old history. At least the Library of Congress lists none, and we have been unable to find one elsewhere.

So it is time for such a book to be written. We intend in the following chapters to describe smokers which can be made or bought, how to use them for basic recipes, and also how to prepare exotic food. Most of the recipes will be for hot smoking, but you will also find a chapter on curing meat.

For convenience the recipes are divided into generic chapters. You will find ground-meat recipes in one chapter, beef in another, fish in still another, and so on.

2

Kinds of Smokers

If all the smokers made in this world were lined up end to end, you would scarcely believe they were designed with the same use in mind. Some are shaped like a storage tank, some like a balloon. There are squares, oblongs and ovals. They are made of sheet metal, enameled steel, cast iron, aluminum, clay, masonry, wood and even paper.

Perhaps even stranger, they all work, principally because over the centuries man has spent so much time improving anything connected with eating.

There is a smoker for every purpose. For the person who likes plug-in appliances there is an electric smoker. Essentially it is a sheet-metal box with racks in the upper part for meat or fish and an electric coil at the bottom, which chars wood chips or sawdust on a special tray.

An angler who wants to smoke a few fish for lunch on the river-bank can carry a smoker about the size of a shoebox. It can also be used in a fireplace, or even in an apartment room. If it is used in an apartment without a fireplace, some smoke will escape into the room—but it is aromatic anyway. This smoker is of light sheet metal. It uses a chemical fuel to heat a compartment where hardwood sawdust has been placed. The heat chars the sawdust and the smoke rises to the fish on the rack above.

Not everyone wants such a specialized smoker. There are many all-purpose smokers available, most of them burning wood or charcoal.

Smokers divide generally into two classes—those used for cold

14

smoking and those for hot smoking. Cold smokers usually are tall, hot smokers short.

Cold smoking is so called because the fish or meat placed in the smoking chamber will be subjected to smoke for hours, sometimes days, at low temperatures. It never gets hot but it does impart a smoky flavor to meat you want to preserve.

Hot smoking is cooking over coals with the temperature at more conventional levels, mostly from 250° to 450°. It is in fact roasting, which has otherwise almost disappeared from the Western world. These days a housewife turns on the electricity, puts meat in the oven and calls it roasting. Actually, roasting is the cooking of meat over open coals or a flame. Originally a spit was used to turn the meat and keep it from charring. The spit is not needed in a smoke oven, because the lid traps heat and so all sides are cooked. The essential remains, though: the free flow of heat and air past the meat. The flesh does not tend to dry as much, and there is the advantage that a smoky flavor can be introduced when wanted.

Some smokers can be used for both hot and cold methods. Generally speaking, though, the cold smoker is large, fixed in place, and uses wood rather than charcoal. The cold smoker frequently has an offset firebox, which is sometimes a number of feet from the smoking chamber. A tube or pipe will carry the smoke to the chamber. A chamber door is opened—or sometimes a vent at the top of the chamber—to create any needed draft. By the time smoke travels through the pipe to the chamber, much of the heat has dissipated. A smoldering fire can be kept going for days without the temperature inside the smoking chamber ever getting above 100°. Some of these chambers are taller than a man. The larger ones may not have an offset firebox. Instead, the fire is built on the floor of the smoking chamber itself. Wherever the fire, it usually is uneconomic to use one for hot smoking. It is designed to hold scores of fish or pounds of meat, and it would be ridiculous to heat one just to hot-smoke a fish fillet for dinner.

Hot smokers, on the other hand, are usually light enough in weight to be portable. They seldom stand higher than a man's belt. Usually they are designed to burn charcoal, and the firebox is merely the bottom of the smoking chamber.

It is not necessary to have a smoker to achieve a smoky taste in your food. An open fire will do it. Everyone who has barbecued steaks knows it is almost impossible to prevent a slightly smoky taste when cooking over open coals. The fat drips onto the coals, where it bursts into flame. This smudges the meat. If the meat is not charred, it is at least smoky. Even if the cook successfully combats flame, the dripping fat becomes smoke, which rises to impregnate the meat.

It is more efficient to use an enclosure—a smoke oven. The amount of air going into the enclosure can be controlled by the vents, which are so designed that there is enough air flow to keep the coals going, but not enough to allow any flame when drippings fall.

Some outdoor barbecues have a cover that converts them to smokers. Put on the vented lid and you have created a smoke oven. Almost all smoke ovens become barbecue grills when the lid is simply pulled back.

If you do not have a smoker, you may boggle at the choices before you. Perhaps our preferences may help you.

Roger's favorite is a three-foot-high smoker. It weighs more than a hundred pounds, and therefore is not easily moved. It doesn't need to be, though, as he keeps it on a roofed balcony, handy to dining room and kitchen. It is a handsome ceramic piece, beautifully proportioned and with a semiglaze finish. The points that will interest you, however, are the dimensions. The grill is round, 18 inches in diameter, which means it can hold eight hamburgers, or a twenty-pound turkey, or the biggest roast you can find. It is 11 inches from the grill to the top of the rounded dome and 11 inches from the grill to the grate. It heats quickly and, once the coals are going, ground round steaks can be done in ten minutes, fish fillets in five. By lighting only a few charcoal lumps, the smoker also can be used for the cold process.

Matt's favorite is made of sheet metal; it looks like two old-fashioned galvanized washtubs. The bottom part is in the normal position for a washtub (except that it stands on short legs). The top is turned upside down and fits onto the lower part to form a lid. It stands only 2 feet high and weighs only a few pounds, which means it can be moved easily from patio to covered back porch whenever rain threatens. The grill is round, 18 inches in diameter. It is only 6 inches from the bottom of the firebox to the grill, and 11 inches from the grill to the top of the lid. It does everything Roger's does except look pretty.

The things you should look for when buying a smoker:

—An easy-to-use draft control under the charcoal grate.

—A damper control on the top of the oven.

—A tight-fitting lid. This will extinguish the coals in minutes when the damper is closed, thereby saving fuel.

—Enough clearance between the grill and top cover to hold a turkey or big roast. Eight inches may do. Ten is better.

—Sufficient length. Is it long enough to hold a turkey? And don't conclude that you will never want to smoke a turkey. Smoked turkey is a great delicacy. Besides, if you get a smoker large enough to take a turkey, it will probably take anything else you want to cook too.

Most manufactured smokers come on wheels, and that is helpful if the smoker is made of cast iron or is otherwise heavy. And it is desirable to be able to move the smoker.

Of course, if you live where the weather is mild, you may want to do as we do—keep it on a covered balcony or porch where it can be used the year round without any worry about the weather. If you don't have a covered porch, try your carport or garage. The smoker takes little space and, with the garage door open, the smoke is whisked away.

3

Make Your Own Smoker

The trouble with most do-it-yourself projects is that they require skill. If you have skill, you probably do not need advice on how to make a smoker. You either have an idea already, or will as soon as you see a few examples.

So what we will present here is six easy smokers for the unskillful. At least two of them will be within your power because you don't even have to know how to operate a screwdriver to make them. And there's an outside chance you can make the others too. Also, we will tell you how to have a sheet-metal shop make smokers for use in your fireplace or on a hibachi.

A Cardboard Oven

This one is eminently practical, although you might not believe it when we tell you it is made of cardboard. Certainly cardboard burns, and certainly the whole thing can go up in flames. But it won't if you come close to following instructions.

Get a corrugated cardboard box—the kind in which bottles and canned goods are packed, or cigarettes or toilet paper if you want a really large box.

The size will depend on what you want to cook. If it is a few hamburgers for a picnic, you won't need a large box. A foot high and two feet square will do it.

Cut the bottom out of the box, but leave the top flaps. You will use them to regulate the draft. Scrape a shallow depression in the ground, and dig a shallow channel, about 18 inches long, leading

18

from the depression. Build your charcoal fire in the depression. After the flames have subsided and the coals are glowing evenly, center your cardboard box over the charcoal. The channel leading from the charcoal pit should extend far enough to pass beyond the side of the box. That will enable air to reach the charcoal and keep the coals going. Bank dirt around the rest of the box to close off any air leaks.

Punch small holes in the sides of the box and push sticks through from one side to the other to hold the cooking grill. If you don't have a grill that will fit inside the box, you can make one in a minute by buying hardware cloth. Trim it to fit your box and you're in business. See Figure 1.

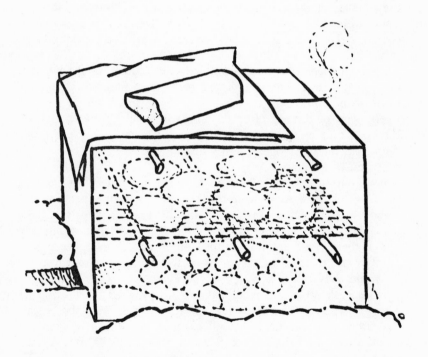

1—The cardboard oven, the simplest smoke cooker to make. Wooden rods poked through the sides of a carton support the grill and the top. Air enters the oven through the ditch at the bottom left.

If no store is handy, you can still cook hamburgers by pushing several sticks or long twigs through the box, close enough together to keep a hamburger patty from falling through. If the sticks are about four inches from the coals, you won't have to worry about their igniting as long as you use only a dozen or so charcoal briquets. You can use a dozen briquets safely even if the box is only about a foot square. If you are cooking only a couple of hamburgers, you can keep the coals fairly close together. If there are more patties to cook, you will have to spread the coals in order to get heat under each patty. You may even have to get a larger box in order to keep the coals from getting too close to the side of the box. A shallow box is best. It enables you to keep the heat on top of the patty closer to the temperature on the bottom. Because of the coolness of the ground, it is difficult to get the temperature in a box up to 300°. So the meat tends to cook more slowly than in a commercial smoker. It may take a half hour to cook hamburger steaks.

Drippings from the hamburger will create some smoke when it falls on the coals, but you should have some hardwood chips or sawdust to spread over the coals to provide wood smoke.

The flaps of the box often do not fit together tightly enough by themselves to create a good smoke oven. They allow too much draft, and the dripping fat may cause flames. A way to reduce the draft must be found.

It may be necessary sometimes to punch holes near the top and push two or three sticks from one side to the other. Then you can weight the top with rocks—several small ones or perhaps one large one. The sticks will keep the weighted flaps from falling into the box. If there is still a gap because the flaps do not meet, get a piece of plywood, a board or weighted or wet newspaper to cover the hole and thus create a better smoke oven.

If you fish often and would like to smoke your catch while it's fresh, a large cardboard box may be the answer. With the bottom cut out it can be folded flat and carried on the floor of your car trunk. Hardware cloth grills will lie flat inside the box. Rather than get a new box every time, you may want to keep the same one. In that case it will be easier to get quarter-inch doweling to shove through the sides of the box instead of cutting fresh switches every time. The strength of the box is restored, of course, when you put the flattened box into its original shape and shove the sticks through from one side to the other. You can have several layers of grill by pushing sticks through at varying levels.

Grills are not necessary for smoking fish. They are handy for some fish, but other fish can be split open and stretched over the stick while the smoking goes on. Perhaps even better is the hook system. You can make hooks from coat hangers or other strong wire. One hooked end is shoved through the gills and the other is hooked over a stick inside the box. Many fish can be loaded into a smoker box with this system.

A low fire and sawdust or wood chips should be used in smoking fish. See Chapter 9.

Wire Frame Smoker

If you have a barbecue, it can be converted into a smoker with wire and a piece of canvas. First bend a length of wire to fit around the inside rim of the barbecue bowl. Twist other lengths of wire onto that at intervals, arching these from one side of the bottom wire to the other, creating a dome. The top should be about a foot above the grill. Drape canvas over this and cut a small hole in the top for a draft. You can use another small piece of canvas, or a light piece of wood, or even your hat if you wish, to go over the hole and so regulate the draft. You may have to prop a small section of the draped canvas top up a bit to allow air to get in at the bottom, or cut another flap down low to allow the air to get in to keep the coals alive.

Five-Gallon Can

A 5-gallon can—or a 50-gallon can for that matter—can be converted into a smoker quickly. The inside must be clean so that the meat will not be tainted with undesirable smoke. Also, the can must have a removable lid.

Cut a hole about 1½ inches in diameter in the bottom of the five-gallon can. Using a quarter-inch drill, put three holes in the side of the can, about three inches from the bottom, spacing the holes equidistant from each other around the side. Put inch-long bolts through the holes, securing them with nuts on the inside. Cut heavy hardware cloth or extruded metal to fit inside the can and place it on the protruding bolts. That will be your grate.

About four inches from the top of the can, drill three holes exactly as you did for the bottom. Insert bolts and install a grill. Hardware cloth may be used for that too.

The removable lid can be left ajar to provide the draft. If you do not have a lid, make one by using a piece of plywood large enough to cover the top. Use a stick to prop the lid for the draft.

Lift the can off the ground by setting it on three bricks so that it will have a free draft through the hole in the bottom.

Masonry Smoker

A permanent smoker can be built of masonry in the back yard. Mortared rocks or bricks will make a smoker that will outlast your generation. If you lack the skill, though, try this mortarless smoker:

Dig a trench about a foot wide and five feet long. It should be about 18 inches deep at one end and slope up to about 10 inches deep at the other. The lower end of the trench will be for your firebox. Place a foot-square concrete stepping stone on the bottom of that end. If you can't find a stepping stone of the right size, you can use bricks. The fire will be built on it. Use more stepping stones or bricks to line the sides of the trench above the stepping stone on which the fire will be built. Now you have a one-foot-square firebox, lined with masonry on the bottom and three sides. The top you will leave open for now, so that you can place fuel on the fire and to provide the necessary draft. To carry smoke up the sloping ditch, place a row of 8-inch-wide concrete drain tiles along the ditch. Lay each tile on its side, butting the open ends together, so that they make a continuous pipe to carry smoke from the firebox to the other end of the ditch. Where the tiles butt together, wrap a piece of asphalt paper around the joint. That will keep dirt from sifting in. Cover the drain tile with dirt, being careful not to let dirt spill into the firebox area. Do not close the other end of the ditch either. Leave about a 6-inch air space beyond the last drain tile.

Above that air space stack some large flue tiles for a chimney. It should be about 4 feet high. The tiles are usually rectangular and a foot high, so you will need four of them. You stack them with the open ends at top and bottom, so that they form a vertical column. You do not need mortar in the joints. The weight will keep them in place.

A plywood lid can be cut to fit over the top flue tile. Put a handle on the top side. A screen-door handle is easily attached with two screws. Or any piece of wood can be screwed onto the plywood for a handle. A sheet of metal also can be used for a lid. Do not close the top entirely when using the smoker, or you'll kill the draft.

Meat can be hung in the smoker from a hook attached to the bottom of the lid. Or hardware cloth or metal grills—if you find some of the right size—can be used to hold the meat. Insert the grill between the topmost flue tiles and, if you want, in the next layer down too. It is a good idea to build a fire or two in the smoker before cooking meat in it. That will enable you to learn how big a fire to build, and how much of an opening to leave at the top of the chimney. Put an oven thermometer in the smoker, about a foot from the top, to learn how hot it gets with varying draft openings. See Figure 2.

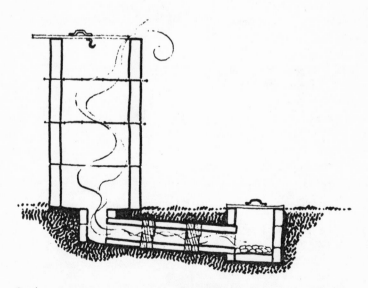

2—*A permanent masonry smoker. The firebox is at the right, connected by a brick tunnel to the stack of four flue tiles that contain the grill.*

The Old Smokehouse

If you want to smoke large quantities of fish or meat, you will probably want an old-fashioned smokehouse—the kind that once was found on almost every farm. Almost any small shack will do, providing it is not too drafty. It should have a door and a dirt, concrete or brick floor on which a small fire can be built, and you must be able to stretch racks from one side to the other—or install hooks from the roof—to hold the meat or fish.

If you have to start from scratch, have it built about 4 feet square and about 7½ to 8 feet high.

The use is easy. Build a hardwood fire on the floor and leave the door cracked open for draft. Experience will show you how wide the crack needs to be for varying degrees of heat. This is a slow process, so keep the fire small and let it smolder for one, two and sometimes several days.

See Chapter 16 on curing.

Fireplace Smoke Oven

Not many stores sell smoke ovens designed to fit in fireplaces. But if the fireplace is the only place you can smoke-cook, here are plans for three fireplace models. They can be made at any sheet-metal shop if you don't have the talent, time or tools to do the job.

The first model is like a bread box (Figure 3). The front door

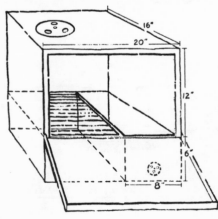

3—A fireplace smoker can be made from sheet metal. The fire occupies the space at the bottom right of the oven, and the meat sits beside it on the grill.

swings down to reveal the grate and the grill. There is enough room to roast a turkey if the bird is placed in the end away from the charcoal grate. The door opens down to allow accumulated smoke to go up the fireplace chimney rather than into the room. Note that the grate is in a position to receive more charcoal or green wood without making you remove the meat from the grill. This is a convenience not found in all smoke ovens. Also, both hands are free to baste or turn the meat because the open door is held in position on a hinge. The grill or rack is off to one side, which makes it almost impossible to burn the meat or to have fat drip into the fire.

Hibachi Smoke Oven

The next two models fit on the popular cast-iron hibachis illustrated in Figure 4. These ovens use the cast-iron hibachi as the grate. They not only will work perfectly in your fireplace but also will fit into your car trunk for use on camping trips.

Take the hibachi to the sheet-metal shop for accurate measurements to fit the oven to the grill. About 18- or 20-gauge sheet metal is heavy enough.

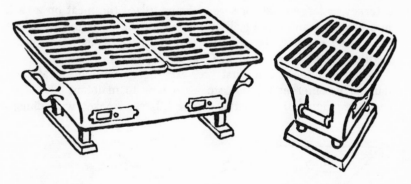

4—Hibachis, which form the base for the hibachi smoke oven.

The oven for the single hibachi (Figure 5) does not need a grill to hold the broiling pan. One half of the oven bottom is completely closed so the pan with a meat rack can rest right on the oven

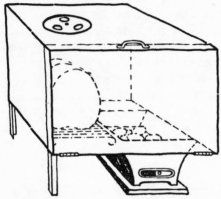

5—*A single hibachi smoker, with the charcoal placed in the hibachi.*

bottom. A removable shelf can also be built in the oven to increase the capacity and make it possible to smoke two layers of meat or fish.

The oven for the double-grill hibachi is entirely open at the bottom except for a 3-inch shelf on each side. It will fit snugly over both grates. The grills will then be placed inside the oven. This will allow use of the grills with the door closed or open if you want to broil food directly over the coals. If you want to roast a turkey or large roast for several hours, place the meat on a rack in a broiling pan on the grill at one end of the oven and build the fire in the grate at the opposite end. This is the indirect smoke-roasting method discussed in Chapter 4.

When you build your first fire, experiment with the draft and damper in different positions to learn how to maintain 300°–350° readings. Figure 6 shows the double hibachi smoker with dimensions.

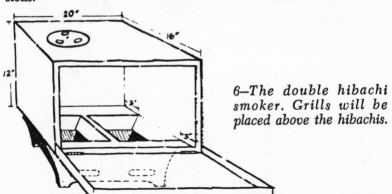

6—*The double hibachi smoker. Grills will be placed above the hibachis.*

An Old Roaster Oven

A simple smoke oven, small and light, can be made at little expense out of an old roaster. One can easily be found in thrift shops and second-hand stores. (Figure 7 shows an example of a roaster oven smoker.) Punch or drill four or five holes at one end of the bottom half for a draft. Drill a similar cluster of holes in the opposite end of the top half for a damper. Form a grate out of a piece of heavy hardware cloth or a small metal pan that will fit in about one third of the roaster bottom. If a metal pan is used, drill holes for draft.

The grill rack for the opposite end can be made from more hardware cloth, bent to form short one-inch-high legs. Or you can use a small cake-cooling rack. Use an aluminum foil drip pan under the rack.

A small piece of sheet metal or a brick can be used over the damper holes to control the temperature.

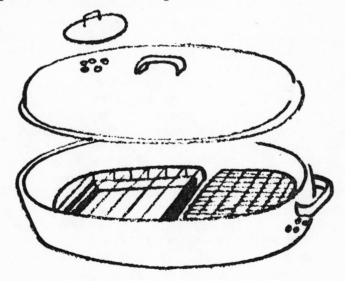

7—An old roaster can easily be converted into a simple smoke oven.

4

How to Use Your Smoker

From the time man struck two rocks together and saw the spark touch off a flame in the grass, there has been a gradual improvement in the ways of starting a fire. This is fortunate, for igniting charcoal is not the easiest thing in the world. It takes a temperature of 650°, and even if you get one piece of charcoal going, you don't want to sit back and wait while the heat spreads slowly to the rest of the charcoal. That's why it's best to use such improvements as the liquid starters that are available wherever charcoal is sold.

There are several ways to use it. Probably the most satisfactory for all smokers is to pile the charcoal in a pyramid, sprinkle the fluid on generously and touch a match to it (See Figure 8). The flame will spread slowly over the mass, burn several minutes, and then die, leaving glowing spots on the charcoal. Preferably there will be at least one glowing spot on each charcoal chunk. If not, the heat will spread eventually to the unlit chunks.

Leave the lid off the smoker until all the charcoal is glowing. The quickest way to get the charcoal going is to give it the greatest possible exposure to oxygen. If the wind is blowing and reaches into your firebox, you may spread the chunks out more. The passage of oxygen over the charcoal will make for an even quicker spread of heat. Where the breeze is not a factor, it's probably best to pile the charcoal in a pyramid. As the coals begin to glow, the heat creates its own draft and speeds the process.

If an electric starter is used, put a layer of charcoal under the element. Pile other chunks on top of it. As the element gets hot, it creates an updraft that carries heat to the briquets (Figure 9).

*8—Charcoal piled in a pyra-
mid—best method for starting
a fire.*

*9—The electric starter is in the shape of a loop, which can be built
into the pyramid of charcoal.*

There are other aids in starting charcoal, including wired and battery-powered blowers, torches and bellows. If you have none of these, you can still get the coals going by building a fire of shavings atop the briquets. This will take longer, because you can't get spots of heat started on all the briquets at once. But the heat will spread, especially if you are able to start the fire where there is a breeze. Note too that the wind action on charcoal is just the reverse of a wood fire. Wood ignites on the leeward side of the fire as the heat is blown to it. A charcoal fire advances into the breeze, seeking the oxygen.

With ignition aids the coals can be ready to use in twenty to thirty minutes. It's always best to wait until all the charcoal is glowing well. You should see no black, but only growing red or a light gray where a coating of ash has formed. This means volatile matter has burned away and combustion is well along.

If your smoker is new to you, build a fire or two in it before you try to cook. You should have an oven thermometer. Put it on the grill after the charcoal is going good, put on the lid and wait a few minutes to take a reading. First try it directly over the coals. Next move it to the side, put on the lid and wait a few minutes. Note any difference in temperatures.

For the first fire, put in enough charcoal so that the lumps, when spread an inch or so apart, will cover the bottom of the grate. Vary the draft opening and note its effect on the oven temperature. That way you will learn the opening needed to maintain 350°, 250° or 150°. The temperature you will be using most is around 300°—a common reading for hot-smoking meat. Note how long the coals last at 300°. That will tell you whether you can do a roast without adding fresh fuel. It's best to have more charcoal in the smoker than needed: you don't need the draft wide open; you can trim it to control the heat; you can cook longer that way, and can turn up the heat if you have miscalculated. If there are too few coals, you will need to open the draft all the way; you may not achieve the temperature you want; the wide-open draft will consume your coals; and in the end you'll have to add more coals anyway.

With plenty of coals, you may find the thermometer registers 400° when you want 300°. In that case, close the draft a bit until the temperature sinks. Don't worry if you have meat in the oven, since there is great latitude in smoke cooking, and you won't ruin the roast.

Both the top and bottom controls can be used, but for convenience the top one alone will do the job, for it regulates the amount of air passing through the oven. Close it and the fire dies. The bottom control can be a help, however, in regulating for the lower readings.

There are two basic ways to cook in the smoker: directly and indirectly.

The direct method is used for most flat cuts, steaks, chops, ground beef, shish kabobs, fillets and fish steaks. The food is placed directly over the coals. The coals are spread, if necessary, to get some under each piece of meat. Occasionally, dripping fat will flare when the

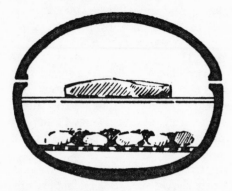

10—*The direct method of smoking. Meat is placed directly above the coals. This method is used for most flat cuts of meat or fish.*

meat is first placed over the coals. Put the lid on, and the flame will soon subside. There will be no blackened meat, because no flame can last long when the cover is in place. See Figure 10.

The indirect method is slower and is used mostly with roasts, fowl, ham and the larger cuts of meat. Unlike the direct method, no drippings fall onto the coals to cause smoke. Of course, any cooking in the smoker involves indirect heat, for the hot air, trapped by the lid, cooks the top of the meat as well as the bottom. However, you do apply greater heat to the bottom when you place the meat directly over the coals. Ground-beef patties, for example, are usually done in ten minutes by the direct method at 300°, while it takes twenty minutes by the indirect method.

There are several indirect methods. In one, put the charcoal on the left side of the grate, and the meat on the right side. That makes for slower cooking, which is desirable for the larger cuts of meat.

11—*The first indirect method of smoking, which provides the slower cooking necessary for larger cuts of meat. A drip pan below the meat catches juices.*

There is less shrinkage, more flavor and more juice. You can also place a drip pan below the meat to catch any escaped juices for basting or sauce. A temperature of 300° to 325° is best for the roasts and large birds. See Figure 11.

Occasionally you may cook a very large bird or roast and find the heat subsiding after several hours. The smoke oven obviously needs more charcoal. Get the coals glowing before putting them in the oven. That way the temperature of the oven will not be lowered by the addition of unlit charcoal. Also, the coals will glow sooner if started outside the smoker.

Ignite them on a shovel, a patch of concrete or even a metal garbage can lid. If they are on a shovel or a lid, once they are glowing, pick it up and dump the coals directly into the oven. If they are on concrete or the ground, use tongs to place them in an empty can—a two-pound coffee can is handy—pick up the can with tongs or pliers and dump the coals into the oven. If you punch holes in the bottom and sides of the two-pound can, light the charcoal in it. The holes admit air, and the can becomes a flue.

Some grills have a hinged portion, so that more coals can be added without your having to remove the grill. With others, both the roast and the grill will have to be removed momentarily while coals are added.

Actually there aren't many times when it's necessary to replenish the coals. It's not like cooking in an open barbecue where coals are consumed in an hour or so. With no draft control, a mass of briquets in a barbecue will burn out quickly, producing heat upwards of 700°. That is why a back-yard chef discovers the meat has burned while his back was turned. The controls of a smoker, however, ensure an even heat, and the coals will last up to three hours, sometimes longer.

In addition to the oven thermometer, a meat thermometer is a desirable guide. The bottom of this thermometer is pointed, so that the rod can be plunged into the meat. You can tell if a roast is done by cutting into it. But it is easier and safer to read the internal temperature instead of slashing the meat with a knife to peek at the texture. Poke the sharp end of the thermometer to the center of the meat, but make sure it doesn't touch a bone, which would give too high a reading.

Throw on some hardwood chips or sawdust as soon as the meat

or fish goes into the oven. At this time no film has formed to prevent the smoke flavor from penetrating the food. Smoke is like garlic in that it's a matter of individual taste. Too much for some is not enough for others.

For a start, try this: For six ground-beef patties, put on a handful of wet hardwood sawdust or a half dozen pieces of wet wood about a ½-inch square and 3 inches long. For two patties, use only two pieces of wood or a third of a handful of sawdust. If a roast or large fowl is being cooked, more sawdust or wood chips will need to be added from time to time. A few trials will help to determine how much smoke is desirable.

Remember that drippings on the coals will cause a smoke taste entirely different from that of wood. If you want only a wood-smoke flavor, try one of the three methods of indirect roasting.

One already mentioned: coals on one side of the grate, meat on the opposite side, so that no coals are below the meat.

If your smoker is small, you may need a hotter fire than can be managed that way. In that case, try a circle fire: Arrange the coals around the outside of the grate so they encircle the bottom but leave an empty space in the middle. The meat can go on the grill above the empty space (see Figure 12).

Or you can build the fire as usual, put a drip pan on the grill and place the meat on a rack over the drip pan. This keeps the

12—The circle method, a space-saving indirect technique. Coals do not go directly below the meat, but are placed in a circle leaving space in the center.

drippings from falling on the coals. The rack keeps the meat from simmering in the juices that collect in the pan and also permits the heat and smoke to circulate around the meat. We use this method often for basting and for cooking vegetables with a roast (see Figure 13).

13—Another indirect method, similar to that in Figure 11 except that the roast is on a rack over a pan. This makes it easy to recapture the juices for basting and permits vegetables to be cooked in the pan if desired.

On occasion we use still another method, for fish. In the first place we don't build as big a fire as for meat—200° to 250° is best for most fish, compared to the 300° to 350° for red meat. The flesh of fish is more delicate and more easily overcooked.

Place aluminum foil on a shallow pan or cookie sheet with edges, and butter the foil. The shallow container makes it easy to lift the fish in and out of the smoke oven without tearing the foil. The fish fillets or slices go on the foil. They are sprinkled with lemon juice, salt, pepper and any special seasoning, such as oil and vinegar, Worcestershire sauce, store-bought Italian dressing (which we prefer) and others. The whole goes on the grill, directly over the coals. A half dozen hardwood chips are thrown on the coals just in advance. The fish cooks in the butter and its own juices, and also takes on a smoky flavor from the wood. It is a shortcut, enabling you to have both smoked fish and a spicy, seasoned dish without preparing a separate sauce. It works because fish, even though exposed on only one side, takes on a smoky flavor so quickly.

Cleaning the Grill

The grill occasionally needs cleaning, but this does not mean hauling a greasy, black circle of wire to the kitchen sink. We clean ours in the smoker.

When the briquets are lit, place the grill over them at once. By the time the briquets are ready to use, the grill will be hot. Much of the grease will have dripped or burned away, but take a stiff wire brush—a handle about a foot long enables the hand to avoid the heat—and scrub the wires to remove any that remains. The heat of the oven, of course, kills any dangerous bacteria on the grill, which, being metal, gets even hotter than the meat.

Or you can put the grill in a tub, cover it with water, and put in a good cleaner, such as trisodium phosphate, then let it soak for a half hour before scrubbing the wires.

In the years we have used smokers, we have never found occasion to clean anything but the grill and the utensils we use. Some soot coats the inside of the smoker, but it's harmless and doesn't fall on the food, and we've found no reason to scrape it off.

Utensils

As for utensils, pancake turners or spatulas are helpful in getting meat off the grill. You need one wide enough to handle hamburgers, and one with at least a five-inch-long blade to handle steaks and chops. If the pancake turner is strong it can be used to remove roasts and fowl from the oven. Otherwise you will need wooden spoons or other strong, fairly flat utensils—one on each side of the roast or bird in order to lift it to the board where you will let it cool until time for carving. Do not use forks. You might accidentally puncture the roast or bird and the juices would escape.

Tongs are handy. A couple might be in order—one to move coals and another to lift cuts of meat that are awkward for spatula or fork.

Occasionally it's necessary to empty ashes from the smoker. Some tool—a small shovel, perhaps—may be helpful if your smoker is not easily portable. If the smoker is carried easily, wait until it's cool, remove the grill and grate and carry the bottom part of the smoker to wherever you dump ashes.

Don't let the ashes build up too high. They can cut the efficiency of the smoker by 90 percent if you let them plug the damper, the holes in the grate, or even on top of the grate, where they can smother the heat of the coals.

It's a good idea, before lighting the fire, to remove the grill and use the tongs to shake the grate a bit in order to dislodge ash from the last time the smoker was used.

Whenever cooking is completed, close the draft on top of the oven. This will stop the flow of air and extinguish the coals. The remaining charcoal chunks can be used the next time.

Small smokers can be used indoors. Make sure, however, that there is ample ventilation. Use the smoker in the fireplace or beside an open window. Do not use one in a closed room. Charcoal consumes oxygen, and when the oxygen level drops, so do you.

The barbecue may be a summer thing, but the smoker can be used the year round. Wind, the bane of the barbecue, never bothers the smoke oven once the lid is on. No wind can blow ashes around or cause the flame to flare.

Rain also is no concern. We live in Oregon, where rain is frequent, so we keep the smokers on covered porches. That's for our convenience, not the smokers'. If you keep yours outdoors, the rain will wash the cover for you.

We have even used smokers in subfreezing weather. At first it was an experiment to see whether the cold would cut the temperature inside the cooker. There was scarcely any effect. Charcoal, after all, is a very efficient fuel. The high heat from briquets— 650° and up—easily overcomes an outdoor freezing temperature.

Fuel and Smoke

The basic fuel for smoke cooking is charcoal. It is as convenient as it is effective. Like coal, it is essentially carbon—and good charcoal is about 85 percent carbon, a higher proportion than is found in some grades of coal. With this high carbon content, charcoal burns with an intense, glowing heat. Among its advantages over coal, charcoal is light and thus easy to carry.

Charcoal is made from wood. You can get some idea of the charcoal-making process yourself by covering a small pile of wood

almost entirely with a mound of dirt, and lighting the exposed area
of the wood. The flames will die out, but the wood under the dirt
will continue to smolder until it becomes black and porous.

The result is a fuel that is a vast improvement over wood, especially as fuel for the modern smoke cooker. Charcoal is self-sufficient
and enough to give wood an inferiority complex. If you get just one
spot of heat glowing on the surface, it will spread until the entire
charcoal chunk is red. It needs no help other than free access to
oxygen. Charcoal is smokeless, tasteless, flameless and remarkably
easy to work with.

Charcoal is sold either in chunks (its pure state) or, more com-
monly, pulverized and formed into briquets. Some purists prefer
the chunks, claiming that briquets transmit an artificial flavor from
the starch that is used to help bind the charcoal dust together. But
we have found that the briquets add no extra flavor. Furthermore,
they are denser than the original charcoal found in the chunks, and
they burn longer. You can buy briquets almost anywhere, and they
are more compact than the charcoal in chunks.

For your fire, then, you need charcoal. For smoke, you need
wood—wood chips or sawdust that you sprinkle on the glowing
coals to provide the smoke that flavors and colors meat. Be sure
the chips or sawdust that you use in the smoker are derived from
hardwood. (Hardwood means a tree with broad leaves, as opposed
to conifers with scale-like or needle-like leaves; hardwood trees
are usually deciduous—they lose their leaves in the autumn. Softwoods are the evergreens, plus larch and some of the cypress
varieties.)

You will find that alder, oak, willow, hickory, ash, maple, birch,
dogwood—any hardwood, including fruit and nut trees—will make
good chips or sawdust for smoke. Avoid mountain mahogany,
though, or any of the very dense woods, which are likely to be oily.

If you use chips rather than sawdust, they should be thin enough
so that you can drop them between the wires of your grate. Of
course the grate can be removed for the placement of the chips,
but it is more convenient to be able to drop them through the grate.

Keep the chips in a jar or can of water near the smoker. They
produce more smoke when wet.

Among smoke fanciers there is a debate on which wood produces
the best smoke. A devotee of the old ways—he uses a smokehouse

regularly—favors a combination: oak to keep the coals going, alder for a penetrating smoke, and vine maple to add tang.

Another will use only alder, and that only after all the bark has been removed. He says bark smoke is bitter. Another prefers green wood and would not think of removing the bark from the slender branches he cuts up. In fact, he prefers bark smoke.

Everyone seems to have a preference, and so we recommend experiments until you suit your own taste. We also recommend that you never try pine, fir or any of the softwoods—unless, of course, you enjoy a creosote flavor.

5

Hors d'Oeuvre

Hors d'oeuvre are unsuitably labeled. The French phrase is hard to spell, often incorrectly pluralized, and difficult to pronounce, and the literal meaning has nothing to do with tasty tidbits served before the main entry or the snacks served with cocktails.

Hors d'oeuvre literally translated means "outside the work." Hot or cold, this is hardly a term for smoked chicken livers, smoked pâté, brochettes of sweetbreads or smoked kibbi.

The Russians call their appetizers zakuski. The Italians have antipasto (before the pasta) and of course the Scandinavians enjoy smörgåsbord. The early Romans had gustatios, a term that still retains a sort of gusty flavor.

Regardless of what we call them, hors d'oeuvre have been around for centuries and are served in every corner of the world. From elaborate to simple, there are thousands of before-dinner snacks.

Only a few rules apply to correct serving of appetizers. Hot hors d'oeuvre should be hot (not barely warm), and cold hors d'oeuvre should be chilled a few hours in the refrigerator. They should be light and tasty. They should increase your appetite for the meal to follow. Or, if there is no formal meal, they should be heavy enough to satisfy your hunger.

Heavy hors d'oeuvre should not be served before a heavy meal. Try to achieve a contrast. Don't serve smoked meats before a smoked dinner. Better to serve sea food appetizers before a smoked turkey than smoked liver pâté. This is especially true if the choice of hors d'oeuvre on your table is limited to two or three. Don't worry, though, if you're going all out and want to prepare a dozen or more varieties.

Good food that has been well prepared deserves to be artfully presented. Arrange your hors d'oeuvre attractively. Provide sauces next to the items that are improved by dunking. Garnishes should be edible. Have plenty of toothpicks for serving bit-size pieces. Have forks if your preparations require them. Serve hot food on preheated plates. Serve appetizers from the smoke oven at intervals so you always have piping-hot snacks ready for your guests. Serve chilled items a plate at a time from the refrigerator so they won't get warm before they are eaten.

Canapés are snacks that are served on small slices of toasted or fried bread. Crackers and chips are also used as a vehicle for various spreads, plain and fancy. Keep them bite-size. The bread or cracker should be spread with butter before the spread is added. This not only improves the flavor, but helps to prevent the cracker from becoming soggy from the moisture in the paste or spread. Various tasty prepared butters can easily be made that will improve ordinary canapés.

Here are a few; you will find others in the chapter on marinades, sauces, bastes and butters.

BLUE CHEESE BUTTER. Cream equal parts of butter and blue cheese.

ANCHOVY BUTTER. Blend 4 teaspoons of anchovy paste, ½ teaspoon lemon juice and ½ cup of butter.

MUSTARD BUTTER. Blend 1 tablespoon prepared mustard with 1 cup of butter. Taste for flavor. Add more mustard if not sharp enough for your taste.

GARLIC BUTTER. Crush 4 cloves of garlic and blend with a stick of soft butter and a pinch of salt.

SMOKED SALMON BUTTER. Use smoked salmon and an equal weight of butter. Chop salmon fine, blend with soft butter and add ½ teaspoon white pepper for ½ pound of salmon butter. Run through an electric blender or force through a fine sieve.

When you are making canapés, spread toast or crackers first with any of the above butters. If you want to be fancy, put some into a pastry bag and decorate the crackers. Canapé surfaces brushed with aspic and allowed to chill are attractive.

There is an almost unlimited supply of good ready-to-eat foods that can be purchased for canapés and hors d'oeuvre. Olives, cheeses, pickles, cold vegetables, sardines, sausages, canned shrimp, caviar, nuts and anchovies are a few. The recipes that follow in this chapter are all from the smoke oven. Some are quick and easy to prepare, others require time and a little patience. None is difficult. In addition to these recipes you will find more in other chapters, as follows.

SAUSAGE (Chapter 12). Thin-sliced sausages, hot or cold, make fine appetizers. Tiny meat balls can be made of most of the sausage recipes. Smoke them and serve hot with or without a sauce.

GROUND MEAT (Chapter 6). Make small meat balls from some of the more highly seasoned meat mixtures. Serve with toothpicks. Can be kept hot in a sauce dish over a candle or in a chafing dish.

SKEWERED MEAT (Chapter 11). Small pieces of chicken, beef, pork, liver or any other meat of your choice can be marinated and cooked on skewers. Just make the meat pieces smaller than you would if the skewer recipe were intended as a main course. One-half- to ¾-inch-size cubes cook fast.

SEAFOOD (Chapter 9). Serve small skewered scallops, shrimp and oysters, or bite-size cubes of salmon, halibut and other firm-bodied fish. Serve plain or with a dipping sauce.

ORIENTAL (Chapter 15). Many of these recipes, if the meat cubes are made small, are perfect for hors d'oeuvre, especially the spicy marinated meats cooked on skewers. Try cooking single pieces on toothpicks with one small onion or mushroom.

SAUCES, MARINADES, BASTES AND BUTTERS (Chapter 14). Marinades and dipping sauces perk up jaded appetites. Small servings of hors d'oeuvre allow you more opportunity to experiment with your smoke oven than you would find practical with main courses; hors d'oeuvre are not nearly as expensive either. Try using leftovers with sauces. Let your imagination go, and enjoy yourself.

JEWISH-STYLE CHOPPED LIVER

1 pound chicken livers
1 large onion, chopped
2 hard-boiled eggs

⅓ cup chicken fat
1 teaspoon salt
¼ teaspoon black pepper

If the chicken livers are frozen, thaw them before using. Clean chicken livers and cut into 1-inch pieces. Cook in smoke oven at 300° until done. Use lots of wood smoke. Sauté onion in chicken fat. Cut livers into smaller pieces and add cut-up hard-boiled eggs. Mix with sautéed onion, chicken fat, salt and pepper. Run this through a meat grinder twice. If paste is dry, add a little more chicken fat. Put in small crock or jar and refrigerate. Serve cold on crackers or lettuce. Makes wonderful sandwiches.

LIVER BALLS

1 pound chicken livers
4 slices bacon
1 clove garlic, crushed

½ teaspoon salt
¼ teaspoon pepper
1 cup chopped parsley

Clean chicken livers and cut in half or smaller. Cook in oven at 300° with wood smoke. Cut up bacon and fry until crisp. Add crisp bacon, bacon fat, garlic, salt and pepper to chicken livers and run through a meat grinder or electric blender. Form meat mixture into small balls and roll in chopped parsley. Refrigerate for 2 or 3 hours. Serve on toothpicks.

MOLDED CHICKEN LIVER

1 pound chicken livers
1 cup chopped onion
1 clove garlic, crushed
¼ cup chicken fat
1 cup chopped celery

2 hard-boiled eggs
1 teaspoon salt
½ teaspoon black pepper
Finely chopped parsley

Cut chicken livers in half and smoke-cook at 300° until done. Sauté onion and crushed garlic in chicken fat. Add celery, hard-boiled eggs, salt and pepper to chicken livers. Grind through a meat grinder at least twice. Pack into a greased mold and refrigerate for several hours. To serve, turn out of mold and sprinkle with finely chopped parsley.

STUFFED EGGS

½ pound chicken livers
12 hard-boiled eggs
2 teaspoons chopped green
  onions

½ teaspoon salt
¼ teaspoon pepper
1 teaspoon bacon fat

Smoke chicken livers in a 300° oven until they are no longer red inside. Cut hard-boiled eggs in half and remove yolks. Mix egg yolks, cooked livers, green onions, salt, pepper and bacon fat. Run through a meat grinder or electric blender. Stuff the egg halves and chill.

SMOKED LIVER WITH BRANDY

1 pound liver
½ cup chopped onion
2 teaspoons butter
2 teaspoons bacon fat

¼ teaspoon marjoram
1 teaspoon salt
¼ teaspoon black pepper
2 tablespoons brandy

Cut up liver into 1-inch pieces and smoke-cook at 300° until done. We like lots of wood smoke with this. Sauté onion in butter and bacon fat. Mix sautéed onion, fat, cooked liver, marjoram, salt and pepper and run through a meat grinder or electric blender. Sprinkle with brandy and grind once more. Serve chilled on crackers, or place in small greased molds and refrigerate for a day before turning out to serve in thin slices.

SMOKED LIVER BALLS

¼ pound bacon, chopped
1 cup minced onion
1 pound liver
1 teaspoon salt

½ teaspoon black pepper
2 cloves garlic, crushed
1 tablespoon brandy

Sauté chopped bacon and onion for 3 or 4 minutes. Run liver through a food chopper with salt and pepper. Add crushed garlic, brandy, sautéed onion and bacon and run through the chopper again. Form into small ¾-inch balls and place in hot smoke oven until done—about 10 or 15 minutes at 325°. Serve hot on toothpicks right out of the oven.

MOLDED LIVER PATE

2 pounds chicken or calf's
    liver
¼ pound bacon
1 cup chopped onion
2 teaspoons salt

1 teaspoon black pepper
½ teaspoon ground ginger
1 cup heavy cream
2 eggs, slightly beaten
2 ounces brandy

Cut liver into 1-inch squares and smoke-cook at 300° until done.
(The reason for cutting up the meat is to have more surfaces that
can be smoked.) Chop bacon and sauté it with onion. Add salt,
pepper, ginger and cream. Stir but do not heat. Cut up liver squares,
add liver to cream-onion mixture and mix well. Put this mixture into
a bowl to cool a little, add the eggs and the brandy and mix with
your hands. Blend in an electric blender or run through a meat
grinder. Pack firmly into one or two molds. Place molds in a shallow
pan of water and place in a 300° smoke oven for 30 minutes. Chill
and turn out of mold. Garnish with parsley or water cress.

WINE-LIVER PATE

1 pound chicken livers
½ cup minced onion
½ cup butter
½ cup red wine

2 teaspoons capers
1 teaspoon salt
½ teaspoon black pepper

Cut chicken livers into 1-inch pieces and smoke-cook at 300° until
they are no longer red inside. Sauté the onions in the butter until
they are cooked but not brown. Add the wine and simmer until mixture is reduced by about one third. Put livers in a bowl with capers
and pour over them the wine, butter and onions. Add salt and
pepper and mix well. Run through a food grinder until smooth.
Pack paste in a bowl and chill in refrigerator. Serve on thin slices
of buttered French bread with a grind of fresh black pepper on the
top of each.

LEFTOVER POT ROAST PATE

1 pound ground pot roast
1 tablespoon prepared
    mustard
4 teaspoons butter

1 clove garlic, crushed
1 teaspoon salt
½ cup chopped parsley
½ cup chopped green onions

Grind up the leftover smoked pot roast (or any other meat) and mix well with mustard, butter, crushed garlic and salt. Add parsley and green onions and mix with your hands. If dry, add a little wine or consommé and mix to a smooth spreading consistency. Place in a bowl and refrigerate until well chilled.

BROCHETTES OF SWEETBREADS

1 pound sweetbreads	12 skewers
1 pound unsliced bacon or cooked ham	½ cup melted butter

Cut sweetbreads and bacon into ¾-inch squares and place in a saucepan. Cover with cold water and bring to a boil. Stir frequently but gently. Remove at first sign of boiling and chill with cold water. If cooked ham is used, parboil only the sweetbreads. Alternate pieces of bacon or ham with pieces of sweetbreads on a skewer, putting 2 of each on a skewer. Brush with melted butter and place on grill in a 300° smoke oven. Cook until bacon is done. Serve on a hot plate.

SUBRICS DE BOEUF

1½ cups smoked pot roast	Salt
2 eggs, beaten	Pepper
1 tablespoon flour	½ cup butter
½ cup grated cheese	½ cup cooking oil

Subrics are made from leftover meat of almost any kind—beef roast, pork roast, poultry, lamb or veal. They are similar to croquettes, only smaller. Subrics are not coated in egg and bread crumbs the way most croquettes are. The chopped meat mixture is combined with beaten egg, seasoned and sautéed in butter.

Cut leftover smoked pot roast into small dice. Add beaten eggs, flour and grated cheese. Salt and pepper to taste. Heat equal parts of butter and oil in a pan. Put spoonfuls of meat mixture in pan and brown both sides. Serve with a meat sauce; keep hot in a chafing dish or a dish over a candle warmer.

JELLIED LIVER PATE

1 pound chicken livers	½ teaspoon soy sauce
2 tablespoons gelatin	½ teaspoon salt
1½ cups condensed consommé	½ teaspoon black pepper

Smoke chicken livers at 300° and grind twice or blend well in an electric blender. Soften the gelatin in ½ cup cold condensed consommé. When this is well dissolved, add the rest of the consommé. Heat to a simmer. Add soy sauce, salt and pepper and stir well. Add ground chicken liver and stir until thoroughly mixed. Pour into a quart mold and chill until firm. Turn out of mold and garnish with parsley.

MOLDED PORK AND LIVER

¾ pound chicken livers	1 teaspoon salt
¾ pound lean pork	½ teaspoon thyme
1 cup minced onion	1 teaspoon monosodium
1 egg, well beaten	glutamate
½ teaspoon black pepper	

Grind livers and pork together with a meat grinder. Add onion, egg, pepper, salt, thyme and mono. Blend well with your hands and run through the grinder again. Butter 3 or 4 small molds or 1 large one. Fill molds with meat mixture and place them upside down on a mesh screen. Place screen over a broiling pan in a 300° oven. Meat should pull away from pan after 1 hour. Carefully remove mold and add green wood to fire. Smoke-cook for 1 more hour at 300°. Remove rack and let smoked pâté cool; chill well before serving. Cut in thin slices.

SMOKED KIBBI

1 cup cracked wheat	1 teaspoon pepper
2½ pounds lean lamb	½ pound butter, melted
2 medium onions	¼ cup shelled pine nuts
1 teaspoon salt	

Wash cracked wheat and soak for 1 hour in cold water. Divide lamb in half and put one half through a meat grinder with one of the onions. Drain wheat and mix with ground meat, salt and pepper.

Put wheat and meat mixture through the grinder. Cut the other half of the lamb into ½-inch cubes and smoke-cook for 10 minutes at 300°. Use plenty of smoke. Chop the other onion and sauté in butter until transparent. Butter a baking pan with melted butter and line the bottom with half of the meat paste. Press down firmly. Smooth with a spatula dipped in water. Spread smoked lamb over this layer and sprinkle with pine nuts and sautéed onions. Roll out a layer of paste with ground meat that is left. Roll it out the size of the pan on a piece of wax paper. Put your hand under the paper and turn it over, meat side down, on top of the cooked lamb; then remove the wax paper. (The kibbi can be refrigerated at this point and cooked later.) Cut the loaf into small squares and pour the rest of the butter on it. Bake indirectly (see Chapter 4) in a 350° oven for 45 minutes. Cut again on the score marks and serve hot.

STUFFED WINE-SOAKED PRUNES

A variety of appetizers can be made from prunes that have been soaked overnight in wine. Use a sweet red wine. They can be kept for days. When ready to use, open the prune with a knive and remove the pit. Stuff with a small dab of cooked meat or a piece of chicken liver. Wrap with a piece of bacon and pierce with a toothpick. Cook in a 300° smoke oven until bacon is done. Serve hot.

TURKEY BLEND

1 pound smoked turkey meat	¼ teaspoon ground cloves
1 teaspoon salt	2 dashes Tabasco
2 tablespoons sage	3 tablespoons mayonnaise
½ teaspoon savory	

Chop the meat and put about one third of it in a blender. Mix the dry ingredients together and add them to the blender. Put in a tablespoon of mayonnaise and turn on the machine. Add the rest of the meat and mayonnaise, about one third at a time so the machine can handle it, mixing it into a smooth texture. Let it stand 24 hours in a refrigerator. Serve it on crackers or small pieces of toast, or as a celery stuffing. If you do not have a blender, you can mix the ingredients by using a meat grinder, then working in the mayonnaise with a fork in a bowl.

CURED CHICKEN HEARTS

2 pounds chicken hearts
½ cup basic curing salt
(see Index)

½ teaspoon black pepper
1½ cups water

Put hearts in a bowl and cover with a brine made from salt, pepper and water. Let stand in refrigerator for 2 or 3 days. When ready to use, rinse hearts and allow to dry. Skewer 2 hearts to a toothpick and smoke-cook for 15 minutes in a 350° oven. Serve hot as they come from the oven or keep hot in a little chicken consommé in a chafing dish.

CHICKEN HEARTS WESTWOOD

½ pound chicken hearts
¼ cup soy sauce
¼ cup chopped green onions
⅛ cup dry vermouth
1 tablespoon sugar

¼ teaspoon aniseed
½ teaspoon ground ginger
Salt
Pepper

Combine all ingredients and let the hearts marinate overnight. Place them on a fine-meshed grill and smoke at 300° about 30 minutes. Remove to a warm plate and serve with toothpicks.

CHICKEN HEARTS ASPEN

1 pound chicken hearts
1 cup soy sauce
½ teaspoon ground ginger

½ cup sherry
½ teaspoon black pepper
1 clove garlic, crushed

Combine all ingredients and marinate hearts for 3 hours or longer. Skewer 2 on a toothpick and smoke-cook for 30 minutes in a 300° oven. Brush once with marinade during cooking. Serve hot on the toothpicks with an extra sprinkle of freshly ground black pepper.

SMOKY OYSTERS

2 dozen oysters
½ gallon water

12 ounces salt

Soak shelled oysters in the salted water for 10 minutes. Remove, rinse in fresh water, and drain the oysters. Steam them for 10 to 15 minutes until well swelled. Slice them into strips about ½ inch thick. Place them on a fine-meshed screen and put them in the smoker at low heat (under 100°). Smoke them 30 minutes at low heat. Raise temperature to 150° by adding more lighted coals, and smoke the oysters another 30 minutes. They will take on a desirable coloring in the last half hour.

CHICKEN LIVERS

1 pound chicken livers	1 medium onion, sliced
2 tablespoons dry vermouth	1 teaspoon salt
1 tablespoon soy sauce	½ teaspoon pepper
2 tablespoons salad oil	8 ounces mushrooms
2 cloves garlic, crushed	1 10-ounce can water chestnuts

Bring a pan of water to a boil, and put in the livers. When the water resumes boiling, take the pan off the heat, remove the livers and drain them. Cut the livers into pieces about 1 inch across. Place them in a bowl with the vermouth, soy sauce, salad oil, garlic, onion, salt and pepper. Marinate overnight. When ready to cook, alternate pieces of liver with mushrooms and water chestnuts on skewers. Place in a 325° smoke oven until done (about 20 minutes).

OYSTERS ON THE HALF SHELL

1 dozen medium oysters	2 tablespoons chopped onion
¼ cup melted butter	2 dashes Tabasco
2 tablespoons chopped green	Juice of ¼ lemon
pepper	½ cup bread crumbs
2 tablespoons pimiento	3 slices bacon

Leave oyster in half shell. Pour melted butter into blender and add the green pepper, pimientos, onion, Tabasco and the lemon juice. Blend well. Remove the mixture and combine with bread crumbs. Place 1 tablespoon of the mixture on each oyster. Cut each bacon slice into 4 pieces and place 1 piece atop each oyster. Place in a 300° smoker. Use moderately heavy smoke until the bacon is done (about 30 minutes).

SMOKY CLAMS

2 dozen clams   12 ounces salt
½ gallon water

Steam the clams until the shells open. Shuck the edible meat into the brine made with water and salt. Let the clams soak for 5 minutes, then rinse in fresh water and drain. Smoke them for 30 minutes with the temperature under 100°. Add more coals to raise the temperature to 150° and smoke another 30 minutes. If the clams are larger than bite-size, cut them into small portions.

SMOKY PICKLED FISH

5 pounds fish   ½ cup sliced onions
1 cup salt   1 tablespoon pepper
1 pint distilled vinegar   2 teaspoons dry mustard
1 pint water   1 teaspoon cloves
¼ cup olive oil   2 bay leaves

We prefer this with salmon, but it will work with any fish of firm flesh. Cut fish into small pieces about 1 inch square. Dredge in salt. After 30 minutes, rinse off the salt and place fish in a 150° oven. Use heavy smoke while the fish cooks. It will be done when it loses its translucence and a toothpick test shows it is about ready to flake.

While the fish is cooking, sauté the onions in olive oil until the color is golden. Add the other ingredients and simmer 45 minutes. Remove the fish from the smoker when it is done and let cool. Let sauce cool before pouring over the fish. Make sure all pieces are covered. Let stand at least 24 hours before serving.

SOLE SNACKS

2 pounds fillet of sole   2 cups tarragon wine vinegar
Salt

Cut the fish into bite-size pieces. Salt the fish heavily. After a few minutes, put the pieces into a bowl with the vinegar, making sure all pieces are covered. Marinate them 30 minutes; then smoke in a 300° oven about 20 minutes. Use moderate smoke. If sole is not available, mullet, snapper, swordfish or any of a dozen other fish will serve.

SAUSAGE AND LIVER PATE

1 pound calf's liver   2 teaspoons salt
1 pound pork sausage   ¼ teaspoon sage
½ cup chopped parsley   ⅓ cup white wine
½ cup chopped onion   2 eggs, beaten

Cut liver into small squares. Form sausage into small loose balls. Place sausage on wire screen and smoke-cook for 15 minutes at 300°. Add pieces of liver and continue to smoke-cook another 10 minutes. Sausage should be almost done. Grind liver and cooked pork in a meat grinder and mix with parsley, onion, salt, sage, wine and eggs. Pack into a greased loaf pan or mold. Set into a pan of water in the smoke oven and bake for 40 minutes at 300°. Cool, chill and remove from mold to serve. Cut into slices ½ inch thick.

ITALIAN-STYLE LIVER PATE

1 pound liver   1 teaspoon salt
3 anchovies, puréed   ½ teaspoon black pepper
½ cup dry white wine   ⅓ cup chopped parsley

Cut liver into small pieces, but large enough not to fall through a fine-mesh grill. Put anchovies, wine, salt, pepper into a bowl and blend well. Place small-mesh grill with livers over a small broiling pan, pour sauce over livers and let drip through into pan. Place pan and screen in indirect position in a 300° oven. Cook until livers are done. Remove small grill and dump livers on a cutting board. Chop fine with a knife and stir into hot wine and anchovy sauce until well mixed. Spread hot mixture on thin buttered pieces of bread cut about 2 inches square. Garnish with chopped parsley.

6

Ground Meats

There should be a rehabilitation movement for ground meat. It needs to be freed from stigmas, from the belief that it is somehow an inferior product. Most of all, it needs to be freed from unimaginative cooks.

"What did you have for dinner?" asks Mrs. Neighbor. "Oh, we just had hamburger," replies Mrs. Nextdoor, and immediately you suspect she has fried ground meat patties in a skillet and served this greasy concoction with little seasoning, sense or savor.

It does not need to be this way. Ground meat can be a superior product. Wine, spices, onion, milk or cheese can be mixed in before cooking. It can be served as a steak, a sandwich, meat balls, meat loaf or shish kababs. There are more flavors and more versatility to be found in ground meat than in any other form of meat. And perhaps nothing lends itself better to smoke cooking than ground meat. The smoke oven makes the hamburger a delicacy. The fried hamburger is trapped in its own grease, but the smoked hamburger lets excess fat drip away. Ground meat absorbs a smoky flavor readily, yet the amount of smoky taste can be controlled simply by placing the meat to one side of the coals. Thus the drippings are not converted into smoke, and the amount of smoke can be determined by the amount of wood chips placed on the coals.

Most of the recipes in this chapter deal with ground beef, although veal and pork are used too. Most markets offer three grades of ground beef. The highest-priced is ground round, which comes from lean beef round. It has the deepest red color and the least fat. Ground chuck is a little fattier and a little pinker. It is flavorful and a favorite of many for steak or sandwich use. The third grade is regular ground beef, which comes from lean meat and fat from a whole side of beef. It is speckled pink and white, with more fat than the other two grades. This means it will shrink more in cooking.

If a recipe calls for a mixture of ground beef and pork or veal, ask the butcher to grind it in the proportion you want. Some markets offer packaged ground meat mixes for meat or ham loaf. Or you can grind it yourself and be sure of the quality of meat in the mix.

Our recipes usually call for about a half pound of ground meat for each person. This may be too generous a serving for some. Cut the amount of meat in that case. The proportion of the other ingredients will be unchanged in most situations, as the amount of meat is not a critical factor—unless reduced drastically.

Patties

The recipes that follow immediately deal with patties—to be served as steaks or sandwiches. They can be delicious, but let us caution you that many ventures, started in prospect of pleasure, are ruined because of lack of attention to detail. Indulge us then, if we now go over ground already familiar to you.

The first danger point comes with the preparation of a patty. Ground meat varies in consistency. Some is moist and pliable, some dry and crumbling. It is frustrating to prepare a patty carefully, only to have it fall apart as you try to put it in the smoker.

So first, when you start to form a patty, note the consistency. If it seems too dry, add a little wine, milk or water to increase adhesion. If it is so moist that you fear it would sag between the wires of the grill, add cracker or bread crumbs or cornflake-type dry cereal.

The meat is easier to handle if it is at room temperature, but it does not matter if it is cold from the refrigerator. Don't let it sit around, though. Ground meat spoils quickly. Two to three days in the refrigerator is the limit. And it should never be outside the refrigerator unless you are preparing it or plan to cook it within an hour or two.

If you have two pounds of ground beef, score it in the middle, then score each half into two equal portions. You now have four portions of half a pound each. Separate them. Place one of the sections on a piece of aluminum foil, clear plastic wrap or meat paper, about eight inches square.

The less handling ground meat undergoes, the more tender and juicy it will be. Do not use your hands to knead and smash the meat flat. Instead take a fork and with the tines pat it down to uniform flatness, about one half to three quarters of an inch thick. The uniformity of thickness is important to ensure uniformity of doneness. It will also mean that all patties will be done at the same time. As you form the patties, the edges tend to separate and crumble. They can be pressed back into shape with the tines of the fork from the sides. When the patty is round and uniform in thickness, use the fork to prick through and aerate the meat in many places. This ensures a more tender result, and enables the smoke and seasoning to penetrate.

You do not prick with the fork, of course, if you intend the meat to be one layer of a stuffed patty. When you form the meat to be such a layer, it is usually thin enough—one quarter of an inch or so—not to need aeration. Besides, you want to form a seal on the edges that will keep the stuffing inside. When preparing a stuffed patty, spread the cheese, onion or other ingredients on the bottom layer of meat, place a top layer of meat over it and pinch the edges together to seal the stuffings inside. It is important to have the top and bottom layers the same size. When the meat is of uniform thickness, press a saucer or other small dish, upside down, onto the meat. That will outline a uniform size and you trim away the excess. A hamburger press also can be used if you can find one with the dimensions you want.

In recipes calling for a top and bottom layer of meat it is important to seal the edges tight; otherwise the juices will escape and be lost on the coals. If the meat is a little dry, it is sometimes difficult to get the edges to seal. It's best to test the meat before forming the patties. If it seems a little dry, add a few ounces of liquid—dry vermouth is always good, but any dry wine will blend into the meat and please the taste.

Grated cheese and other ingredients can be mixed into ground meat easily. You can flatten the meat somewhat with your hands, sprinkle on the ingredients and work them into the meat with your hands. Or you can form the patties, sprinkle the ingredients on top, and press them into the meat lightly with the tines of a fork. This latter way has several advantages: It keeps the handling of meat at a minimum. It enables you to see that the ingredients are distributed evenly, if that is what you want. If that is not what you want, it enables you to put more cheese on a selected patty, more onion on another, etc.

The sandwich and steak recipes that follow call for salt and pepper to be added just before the meat is placed in the smoker, rather than to be mixed into the meat at patty-forming time. This is because we feel it is difficult to distribute, for instance, a half teaspoon of pepper uniformly through two pounds of ground meat by mixing. It is far easier to sprinkle the amount you want on top. It also enables you to give one person little or no seasoning and another all the pepper he wants.

Ground meat takes on a smoke taste easily, so do not load the firebox with hardwood sawdust or chips. Two or three chips an inch or two long and half an inch thick are enough for four patties. Soak the chips in water in advance so they will produce the maximum amount of smoke. It's a good practice to keep a number of chips soaking in water near the smoker so there's a continuing supply.

The patties can be stacked one upon the other in one hand if each patty was left on the foil, plastic wrap or paper on which it was formed. Lift off the top patty, so that the foil or paper rests on the palm of your hand. With a rolling turn of the wrist, place the patty gently on the grill, upside down—that is, with the meat side down. Do not hold onto the foil or paper as you place the meat down. Peel it off after the patty is safely in place on the grill.

Many of the recipes call for the patties to be cooked for 10 minutes at 300°. This does not, however, mean 10 minutes from the time you put the oven top in place. Allow a minute or two for the oven to get up to 300°. And if your patty is thicker than usual, it will take longer than 10 minutes to cook. For those who like meat well done, it may take 15 minutes. Try it at 10 minutes the first time. After you have removed the patty from the grill, preferably with a pancake turner, you can open it with a fork to test for doneness. If it's too well done, there is nothing you can do about it this time. But if it's not quite done enough, put it back in the oven for a few more minutes.

Ground meat is excellent for experimentation. If you think a certain combination of herbs would make a roast taste wonderful, you don't have to risk a whole roast. Make a small ground meat patty and try your idea there first.

WESTWOOD STEAKS

2 pounds ground round or chuck	Salt
	Pepper
Worcestershire	

If you have never had smoky ground round or chuck, you will be unprepared for the tastiness of this simple dish.

Form the ground beef into four patties about ½ to ¾ inch thick. Spread the coals in the smoker so all steaks will be over the heat. Throw 4 or 5 wet or green pieces of hardword onto the coals. Place the patties on the grill and sprinkle each liberally with Worcestershire sauce. Salt and pepper to taste. If the oven temperature is about 300°, the meat will be done in 10 to 12 minutes. If anyone likes his meat well done, start it about 5 minutes before the others. You do not need to turn the meat on the grill. The heat is above as well as below and both sides will be done. Remove the meat carefully with a large pancake turner to preserve the juices atop each steak. If you like to see grill marks on the meat, turn the steaks upside down onto the serving plate. *Serves 4.*

SEAL BEACH SPECIAL

2 pounds ground beef	2 tablespoons chopped parsley
2 tablespoons finely chopped or grated green pepper	Paprika
	Salt
2 tablespoons finely chopped or grated green onion	Pepper

Mix all ingredients except paprika, salt and pepper. Form into 4 patties about ¾ inch thick. Place on grill of smoke oven. Sprinkle on a dash of paprika, salt and pepper to taste. Smoke over direct heat in 300° oven about 10 minutes. Pour the following sauce over each patty when serving:

3 tablespoons butter	1 tablespoon lemon juice
¼ cup chili sauce	1 teaspoon prepared mustard
¼ cup orange juice	6 drops Tabasco

Melt the butter, stir in the other ingredients, heat to the boiling point and spoon over meat patties. *Serves 4.*

SMOKY CHEESEBURGERS

¼ pound cheddar cheese, grated
½ teaspoon dry mustard
2 tablespoons mayonnaise
2 tablespoons Worcestershire

2 dashes Tabasco
2 pounds ground beef
Salt
Pepper

In a bowl, blend the cheese, mustard, mayonnaise, Worcestershire and Tabasco. Pat the meat into 8 uniform patties about ¼ inch thick. Place cheese mixture equally on 4 of the patties. Place the other 4 patties on each of the cheese-spread patties. Pinch edges together to seal in the cheese. Place on smoke-oven grill, salt and pepper to taste, and smoke 10 to 12 minutes over direct heat. *Serves 4.*

CHEHALEM PATTIES

1½ pounds ground beef
½ cup nuts, chopped (preferably filberts)
½ cup crunchy cereal flakes
1 cup grated cheddar cheese

½ cup dry wine
Worcestershire
Salt
Pepper

Mix the meat with all ingredients except Worcestershire, salt and pepper. Form into 4 patties. Place on smoke-oven grill. Sprinkle on Worcestershire, salt and pepper to taste. Smoke over direct heat in 300° oven for about 10 minutes. *Serves 4.*

TOMATO STEAKS

1½ pounds ground beef
2 cups cracker crumbs
2 cups tomato juice
2 eggs

1 large onion, chopped
Salt
Pepper

These ground-beef patties look like any other. Wait until you bite into one. You won't wait long for a second bite. Mix all the ingredients except the salt and pepper. Form into 4 patties about ¾ inch thick. Place on smoke-oven grill. Salt and pepper to taste. Smoke over direct heat in 300° oven about 10 minutes. *Serves 4.*

STEAKS BORDELAISE

4 green onions
2 tablespoons butter
½ cup dry red wine
1 cup beef gravy

Juice of ½ lemon
Salt
Pepper
2 pounds ground chuck

Chop the onions fine and sauté in butter. Add wine, gravy and the lemon juice. Simmer a few minutes. Salt and pepper to taste. Form 4 meat steaks about ¾ inch thick. Cook over direct heat about 10 minutes, using a moderate amount of wood chips or sawdust on the coals. Serve the sauce over the meat. If the sauce has simmered until it is too thick, add a little wine to it. *Serves 4.*

IRISH HAMBURGER

3 medium potatoes
1½ pounds ground chuck
1 medium onion

2 tablespoons chopped
   parsley
Salt
Pepper

Wash the raw potatoes, then slice them. Mix them with the meat by running both through a food grinder, skins and all. Chop the onion fine and mix it into the meat with the parsley. Add salt and pepper to taste. Smoke 10 to 15 minutes in a 300° oven. *Serves 4.*

SURPRISE STEAKS

2 pounds ground round or
   chuck
4 ounces blue cheese

Salt
Pepper

Shape the meat into 8 round patties about ¼ inch thick. Divide the cheese into 4 equal portions and spread it on 4 of the patties. Lift the remaining patties with a pancake turner and place on the patties which have the cheese spread. Squeeze the edges of the meat together all around (see p. 54) and smoke for 10 minutes over direct heat. *Serves 4.*

CHEDDAR BURGER

½ cup grated sharp cheddar
   cheese

2 tablespoons finely chopped
   onion

½ teaspoon celery salt   2 dashes Tabasco
½ teaspoon garlic salt   2 pounds ground chuck

Form the meat into 4 patties about ¾ inch thick and smoke over direct heat 10 to 15 minutes. Just before serving, melt the cheese in a saucepan over low heat and add the onion, salt and Tabasco sauce. When ready to serve, pour some of this sauce over each patty. *Serves 4.*

CHUCK SUPREME

1 small clove garlic   1 tablespoon Worcestershire
1 small can mushrooms   2 pounds ground chuck
12 olives   Salt
2 ounces dry vermouth   Pepper
1 raw egg

Chop the garlic fine. Chop the mushrooms and olives into small pieces and mix all the ingredients into the meat. Form into 4 patties about ¾ inch thick and smoke in a 300° oven 10 to 15 minutes. *Serves 4.*

BEANS AND BURGER

½ pound dry red beans   1 pint clear meat stock
1 ounce butter   Salt
1 medium chopped onion   Pepper
1 teaspoon ground cloves   ½ pint beer
1 pinch thyme   2 pounds ground chuck
1 teaspoon dried parsley

Cover the beans with water and soak overnight. Drain them and put into a saucepan with the butter, onion, cloves, thyme and parsley. Add enough stock to cover. Salt and pepper to taste. Several shakes of the Tabasco bottle may go well here. Simmer until the beans are tender but dry. Add the beer. When the beans have absorbed the beer, taste and correct seasoning. Heat and serve over 4 ground chuck patties, about ¾ inch thick, which have been smoked in a 300° oven for 10 to 15 minutes. This is quite unlike the usual baked-bean or chili-bean dishes. The cloves and the beer melt into the over-all flavor and make this a distinctive dish. And the combination with smoked chuck is unbeatable. *Serves 4.*

MUSHROOM BURGERS

1½ pounds ground beef
1 4-ounce can mushrooms,
   chopped
1 tablespoon soy sauce

Worcestershire
Salt
Pepper

Mix well the meat, chopped mushrooms and soy sauce. Form into 4 patties about ¾ inch thick. Place on smoke-oven grill. Sprinkle with Worcestershire, salt and pepper to taste. Smoke over direct heat in 300° oven about 10 minutes. *Serves 4.*

COFFEE PATTIES

2 tablespoons strong brewed
   coffee
Salt
Pepper

1 small onion, grated
1½ pounds ground beef
1 medium tomato, sliced
1 large dill pickle, sliced

Mix coffee, salt, pepper, onion and meat. Form into 8 patties about ¼ inch thick. Put tomato and pickle slices on 4 of the patties. Cover with the remaining 4 patties and crimp the edges together, being certain the seal is complete so the tomato and pickle juices will not ooze out during the cooking (see p. 54). Smoke over direct heat for about 10 minutes at 300°. Excellent when served as a sandwich. *Serves 4.*

LONG JOHNS

1 pound ground beef
1 teaspoon salt

¼ teaspoon pepper
4 frankfurter rolls

Mix the salt and pepper into the meat and form into 4 frankfurter-shaped rolls, about the length of the bread rolls. Smoke over direct heat for about 10 minutes at 300°. Serve on warm frankfurter rolls, spooning on the following sauce:

2 tablespoons dry mustard
¼ cup milk
2 tablespoons Worcestershire

1 tablespoon chili sauce
¼ pound cheddar cheese,
   grated

Blend the mustard with the milk, stir in Worcestershire and chili sauces, add the cheese and heat until the cheese melts and the sauce thickens. *Serves 4.*

PACIFIC PATTIES

2 pounds ground beef
2 tablespoons soy sauce
1 tablespoon grated lemon
   rind

½ teaspoon ground ginger
2 tablespoons lemon juice
Salt
Pepper

Mix well all ingredients except salt and pepper. Form into 4 patties about ¾ inch thick. Place on smoke-oven grill. Salt and pepper to taste. Smoke over direct heat in 300° oven for about 10 minutes. *Serves 4.*

SAUERKRAUT STEAK

2 pounds ground beef
½ teaspoon caraway seeds
1 teaspoon garlic salt

½ cup drained sauerkraut
Worcestershire
Pepper

Mix the beef with the caraway seeds and garlic salt. Form into 8 uniform patties about ¼ inch thick. Use a little wine vinegar or dry wine if the meat is not moist and pliable. Place equal portions of the sauerkraut on 4 patties. If sauerkraut is not spicy, sprinkle a little coarse-grain pepper on it. Cover with the 4 remaining patties and pinch the edges together, sealing so that no juices will escape. Place on smoke-oven grill. Sprinkle on Worcestershire and pepper to taste. Smoke over direct heat in 300° oven for about 10 minutes. *Serves 4.*

BACON BURGERS

4 slices bacon
1½ pounds ground beef
½ cup grated cheddar cheese
½ cup dry wine

Worcestershire
Salt
Pepper

Fry the bacon until crisp, then chop and mix into meat along with the cheese and wine, salt and pepper. Form into 4 patties about ¾ inch thick. Place on smoke-oven grill. Sprinkle on Worcestershire. Smoke over direct heat in 300° oven about 10 minutes. *Serves 4.*

SOUTH FORTY

1½ pounds ground beef
1 egg
¼ cup chopped spinach,
   cooked
¼ cup chopped fresh parsley

⅛ cup chopped onion
1 teaspoon paprika
Salt
Pepper

Mix all ingredients except salt and pepper. Form into 4 patties about
¾ inch thick. Place on smoke-oven grill. Salt and pepper to taste.
Smoke over direct heat in 300° oven for about 10 minutes. *Serves 4.*

GINGERBURGER

1 large onion, chopped fine
2 pounds ground beef
2 cloves garlic
1 cup soy sauce

1 teaspoon ground ginger
Salt
Pepper

Mix the chopped onion into the meat. Form 4 patties, about ¾ inch
thick. Place patties side by side in a bowl or dish deep enough for
marinating. Crush the garlic, combine with soy sauce and ginger and
heat to the boiling point. Pour the hot sauce over the steaks and let
marinate for 1 hour. Place patties on smoke-oven grill and add salt
and pepper to taste. Smoke over direct heat about 10 minutes at
300°. *Serves 4.*

TARRAGON TREAT

2 pounds ground beef
1 teaspoon tarragon

Salt
Pepper

Form meat into four patties about ¾ inch thick. Place patties on
smoke-oven grill and sprinkle on tarragon, salt and pepper. Smoke
over direct heat about 10 minutes at 300°. Meanwhile have this
sauce ready to spoon over steaks when done:

½ cup tarragon vinegar   4 green onions, chopped

Combine the tarragon vinegar and chopped onions and simmer
until reduced by one half. *Serves 4.*

PEACH PATTIES

1½ pounds ground beef
1 small onion, grated
¼ teaspoon ground cloves
1 4-ounce jar strained
    peaches (baby food)

1 tablespoon brown sugar
1 tablespoon wine vinegar
Salt
Pepper

Mix all ingredients except salt and pepper, making the effort to grate or extract the juice from the onion rather than chopping it. Form into 4 patties about ¾ inch thick. Place on smoke-oven grill. Salt and pepper to taste. Smoke over direct heat in 300° oven for about 10 minutes. *Serves 4.*

GREENGROCER

1½ pounds ground beef
2 carrots, grated
2 celery stalks, chopped
1 green pepper, chopped
1 medium onion, chopped

1 clove garlic, chopped
1 egg
2 tablespoons Worcestershire
Salt
Pepper

Mix meat with all ingredients except salt and pepper. Form 4 patties, about ¾ inch thick. Place on smoke-oven grill. Salt and pepper to taste. Smoke over direct heat in 300° oven about 10 minutes. *Serves 4.*

THYME ON MY HANDS

1 egg
2 pounds ground beef
1 teaspoon thyme

¼ cup chopped green onions
Salt
Pepper

Break the raw egg into the meat and mix with the other ingredients except salt and pepper. Form into 4 patties about 1 inch thick and place on smoke-oven grill. Salt and pepper to taste. Smoke over direct heat about 15 minutes at 300°. If a smokier taste is desired, cook patties in indirect heat 25 minutes or longer. Serve on a hot dish with a pat of butter on each patty. *Serves 4.*

PARSLEY PATTIES

2 pounds ground beef
½ cup finely chopped fresh
  parsley
2 cloves garlic, chopped fine

Worcestershire
Salt
Pepper

Blend parsley and garlic into meat. Form into 4 patties about 1 inch thick. Place patties on smoke-oven grill and sprinkle on salt, pepper and Worcestershire sauce to taste. Smoke over direct heat about 15 minutes at 300°. *Serves 4.*

STEAK PROVOLONE

2 pounds ground beef
4 thin slices provolone cheese

Salt
Pepper

Form 4 patties, about ¾ inch thick. Place on smoke-oven grill. Salt and pepper to taste. Smoke over direct heat about 10 minutes at 300°. A minute or two before meat is done, place a slice of cheese on each patty. Remove when cheese starts to melt. *Serves 4.*

MARINATED STEAKS

2 pounds ground beef
  Salt

Pepper

Form seasoned meat into 4 patties about ¾ inch thick. Place side by side in a flat baking dish. Pour over them the following marinade:

1 medium onion, chopped
2 cloves garlic, pressed
1 tablespoon chili powder

¼ cup olive or salad oil
8 ounces tomato juice

Combine all ingredients. Marinade should be simmered 10 minutes, then cooled, before pouring over the meat.

    Marinate meat at least 1 hour. Cook over direct heat, about 10 minutes at 300°. Baste once with marinade. *Serves 4.*

YOUR GROUND BEEF

1 pound good lean beef
1 clove garlic, crushed
1½ teaspoons cumin

Salt
Pepper

If you want to make ground round that has a different touch, try this: Cut the meat into thin strips. Sprinkle the garlic juice over the strips. Mix the other ingredients and spread over the meat. Run the strips through a meat grinder. Form the ground meat into patties about ¾ inch thick and smoke in a 300° oven for about 10 minutes. If the meat seems a bit dry and crumbly when forming the patties, add a little cooking oil or wine. This enables you to make a patty that will stick together, and—especially in the case of the wine—enhances the flavor. *Serves 2.*

THE OVEN CAPER

1 tablespoon capers	Worcestershire
¼ cup butter	Salt
2 pounds ground meat	Pepper

Mix the capers into the butter. Form into 4 equal patties about 2 inches square. Separate the patties with foil and freeze until firm. Make 8 meat patties, about ¼ inch thick. Place a frozen butter patty on four of them. Use the other 4 meat patties to cover these, pinching the edges together well so that the butter will not leak out as the meat cooks. Place the patties in the smoker and sprinkle on salt, pepper and Worcestershire sauce to taste. Cook about 10 minutes at 300°. *Serves 4.*

DEUTSCH DELIGHT

2 pounds ground beef	1 teaspoon grated lemon rind
2 eggs	¼ cup dry milk powder
1 teaspoon garlic salt	

All ingredients mix. Four patties about ¾ inch thick form. Over direct heat, about 10 minutes at 300°, smoke. With the following sauce serve:

2 cups brown gravy	4 tablespoons lemon juice
½ cup dry white wine	¼ teaspoon ginger
¼ cup brown sugar	3 whole cloves
1 tablespoon butter	

All is together mixed and simmered. When thickened slightly, serve. *Serves 4.*

NORTHERN STEAKS

¼ cup dry white wine   2 pounds ground beef
1 beef bouillon cube   Salt
2 tablespoons Worcestershire   Coarse-ground black pepper

Heat the dry wine to boiling point and dissolve the bouillon cube in
it. Add the Worcestershire sauce, then mix into the meat. Form into
4 patties about ¾ inch thick. Place on smoke-oven grill and sprinkle
with salt and pepper to taste. Smoke over direct heat for about 10
minutes at 300°. *Serves 4.*

HOT STEAKS

¼ cup chili sauce   6 drops Tabasco
1 tablespoon brown sugar   1½ pounds ground beef
1 tablespoon wine vinegar   Salt
1 tablespoon prepared
    mustard

Mix the chili sauce, sugar, vinegar, mustard and Tabasco, then work
it into the meat. Form 4 patties about ¾ inch thick. Smoke over direct
heat about 10 minutes at 300°, salting the patties at the start of the
cooking process. *Serves 4.*

BORDER BURGERS

2 pounds ground beef   2 cups grated cheddar cheese
1 1-pound can chili con carne   Salt
    with beans   Pepper
¼ cup dry red wine

Form 4 meat patties, about ¾ inch thick. Smoke over direct heat,
about 10 minutes at 300°. While the meat is cooking, stir together
the chili con carne, wine and cheese in a saucepan over low heat.
When the cheese melts and the contents of the saucepan are hot,
pour over the meat patties, which have been removed from the
smoke oven to serving plates. *Serves 4.*

SOUR CREAM STEAK

2 tablespoons finely chopped onion
2 tablespoons butter
2 pounds ground beef
Salt
Pepper
½ cup sour cream

Sauté the onion in the butter and mix into the meat. Form into 4 patties about ¾ inch thick. Place patties on smoke-oven grill and sprinkle on salt and pepper. Smoke over direct heat about 10 minutes at 300°. Put a generous soupspoon of cream on each steak a few minutes before meat is done. The sour cream will melt into the meat in the cooking process. *Serves 4.*

PEANUT PATTIES

1½ pounds ground beef
1 small onion, grated
¼ cup peanut butter
2 tablespoons Worcestershire
Salt
Pepper

Mix all ingredients well and form into 4 patties about ¾ inch thick. Place on smoke-oven grill and smoke over direct heat about 10 minutes at 300°. *Serves 4.*

NESTUCCA STEAK

1 medium onion, chopped fine
2 pounds ground round steak
1 teaspoon curry powder
4 tablespoons vermouth
1 egg
1 tablespoon Worcestershire
1 4-ounce can mushrooms, chopped
Salt
Pepper

Sauté the onion until golden, then mix it into the meat along with all other ingredients except the salt and pepper. Form into 4 patties about ¾ inch thick. Place on smoke-oven grill. Salt and pepper to taste. Smoke over direct heat in 300° oven about 10 minutes.

Ground round is leaner, therefore preferable to the other meat grades for this recipe. *Serves 4.*

Meat Balls

The smoke oven gives you two immediate advantages in making meat balls. The first, of course, is the smoky taste. The second is the fact that you don't have to stand by the stove rolling meat balls around in a hot pan, trying to brown them evenly in hot fat. Instead you put them on a grill, as many as you can get in a single layer, close the smoke oven and go about your business. When you take them out, they will be as brown as if you had watched each one individually.

If your favorite recipe calls for meat balls to be cooked in a sauce after they are browned, just dump the browned balls into an ovenproof dish, pour the sauce over them, and leave the dish in the smoke oven until they are done the way you like them.

MEAT BALLS STROGANOFF

2 small onions	Pepper
1 tablespoon butter	1 4-ounce can mushrooms,
1½ pounds ground beef	sliced
Salt	1 pint sour cream

Chop the onions and sauté in the butter until golden. Mix the sautéed onion with the meat and form into small balls. Brown the balls on a grill over a pan in the smoker. Use a light amount of wood for smoking. They will be browned in about 20 minutes if the balls are about 1 inch thick and the oven is about 300°. Dump the balls into the pan. Add the mushrooms and the sour cream. Stir until the balls are covered with the cream. Cook another 10 minutes, adding more cream if necessary to keep from becoming too thick. *Serves 4.*

PORK BALLS IN SOUP

3 slices bread	¼ teaspoon paprika
1½ pounds ground pork	Salt
¼ cup chopped onion	Pepper
1 egg, slightly beaten	1 10½-ounce can tomato soup

Slice the crust from the bread, soak bread in water, and squeeze dry. Mix with the ground pork, onion, egg, paprika, salt and pepper. Form into the size of golf balls and cook in a 300° oven for about 20 minutes if over direct heat, about 30 minutes if indirect. Before removing them from the oven, heat the soup to the boiling point. Drop the balls into the soup pan and simmer 10 minutes, then serve. *Serves 4.*

APPETIZER MEAT BALLS

1 pound ground beef
½ cup bread crumbs
1 medium onion, finely minced

¼ teaspoon Tabasco
Salt
Pepper

Mix all the ingredients together and form into small balls. Place on the grill with some green wood or sawdust on the coals. If the oven is at 300°, they should be done in 15 minutes, perhaps less if they are under 1 inch in diameter.

Serve with toothpicks. For variation you can roll them in toasted sesame seeds or in grated Parmesan cheese. *Makes about 40.*

SMOKE AND CREAM MEAT BALLS

1½ pounds ground chuck
½ pound ground lean pork
1 cup bread crumbs in 1 cup
   milk
½ teaspoon ginger
¼ teaspoon freshly ground
   pepper

1 small onion, minced
2 eggs, slightly beaten
½ teaspoon ground cloves
Salt
Pepper
2 cups cream

Reserve the cream. Mix everything else together and form into 1-inch meat balls. Place them on a broiling rack over a shallow pan. Use plenty of green wood chips or sawdust. Cook them for 10 minutes at 300°. They should be browning and about half done at that point. Dump them into the shallow pan, add the cream and simmer another 10 to 15 minutes. Serve with egg noodles. *Serves 4.*

SWEDISH MEAT BALLS

2 pounds ground beef
2 eggs, slightly beaten
1 cup minced onion
1 teaspoon nutmeg
2 teaspoons dill seed

1 cup chopped ripe olives
3 cups sour cream
1 cup beer
Salt
Pepper

Mix the meat with the eggs, onion, nutmeg, dill seed and olives. Form into 1-inch balls. Place the balls on a grill over a shallow pan in the smoker. Brown the meat about 10 minutes at 300°. Use a moderate amount of green wood chips or sawdust on the coals. Dump the meat into the shallow pan, and stir in the sour cream and the beer. Cook this over the coals with the oven lid off until the sauce has thickened to the consistency you like. *Serves 4.*

LEFTOVER MEAT BALLS

1 pound pork, beef, lamb or
    veal
2 eggs
2 slices bacon, chopped

1 tablespoon grated lemon
    rind
½ cup bread crumbs
Salt
Pepper

If you have about a pound of roast left over, try this. Grind the meat with the eggs, chopped bacon, grated lemon rind and bread crumbs. Form into 1-inch meat balls and cook in heavy smoke for about 15 minutes at 300° over direct heat. These can be dropped into a light soup. If you use them that way, let the soup and meat balls simmer a few minutes before serving. *Serves 2.*

DUTCH MEAT BALLS

½ pound ground pork
1 pound ground beef
1 medium onion, minced
1 egg, slightly beaten
½ cup bread crumbs

1 cup beef broth
1 pint sour cream
2 tablespoons tomato paste
Salt
Pepper

Mix the meat, minced onion, egg and bread crumbs together. Form into 1-inch meat balls. Put the beef broth in an ovenproof dish and place the balls on a grill over the dish. Put into smoke oven. When the balls have browned (about 25 minutes at 300°), place them in the broth, add the sour cream and tomato paste, stir carefully and let simmer for 10 minutes. *Serves 4.*

MEAT BALLS IN WINE

2 pounds ground beef
2 eggs, slightly beaten
1½ cups bread crumbs, soaked
    in ½ cup milk

3 cups dry red wine
2 tablespoons flour
Salt
Pepper

Mix the meat with the eggs, the milk-soaked bread crumbs and seasoning. Form into 1-inch balls and cook in moderate smoke for about 20 minutes at 300°, using a rack over a pan. The drippings will fall into the pan to be used later. After the 20 minutes, put the balls into the pan along with the wine and flour. Stir well and simmer for ½ hour. Add a little water if the sauce gets too thick. *Serves 4.*

ITALIAN MEAT BALLS

2 pounds ground beef
2 eggs, slightly beaten
1 cup bread crumbs
1 cup grated Parmesan cheese

2 cloves garlic, chopped fine
1 teaspoon orégano
Salt
Pepper

Mix all ingredients together well in a large bowl. Form into balls about the size of a golf ball. Place them on the grill over coals and a moderate amount of green wood chips or sawdust. They will be done in about 15 minutes at 300°. *Serves 4.*

DILLY MEAT BALLS

2 pounds ground beef
2 tablespoons dill seed
1 cup bread crumbs, soaked
    in ½ cup milk

Salt
Pepper

Mix all ingredients together well. Form into 1-inch balls. Put plenty of wood chips or sawdust on the coals, and smoke the balls about 20 minutes at 300°. These are good served with almost any kind of sauce. *Serves 4.*

SCANDINAVIAN MEAT BALLS

2 pounds ground beef
1 pound ground pork (very -
    lean) or ham
2 eggs, slightly beaten
1 cup minced onion
1 cup bread crumbs, soaked
    in 1½ cups milk

2 teaspoons nutmeg
1 teaspoon allspice
2 cups cream
2 tablespoons brown sugar
Salt
Pepper

Reserve the cream and brown sugar. Mix the other ingredients together and form into small balls. Brown these in the smoker, placing the balls on a rack over a shallow dish or pan to catch the drippings. They should be done in 20 minutes in a 300° oven. Then dump them into the dish, add the cream and sugar, stir well and let simmer 20 minutes. *Serves 6.*

GARLIC MEAT BALLS

2 pounds ground beef
½ pound ground pork
3 cloves garlic, pressed
½ cup chopped parsley
2 eggs, slightly beaten

1 cup bread crumbs,
    moistened with milk
Salt
Pepper

After mixing all ingredients together, form into 1-inch balls and place in the smoker. Because of the pork, these will take about ½ hour at 300°. They can be cooked with or without smoke, and can be enjoyed hot or cold. *Serves 6.*

GERMAN MEAT BALLS

2 slices bacon, chopped
2 slightly beaten eggs
2 slices bread (soaked in milk)
1 pound ground beef or veal

2 tablespoons parsley
Salt
Pepper

Fry the chopped bacon until it is crisp. Mix with the slightly beaten eggs. Add the bread, meat, parsley and seasoning. Mix well and form into small balls. Cook until done. About 15 to 20 minutes in a 300° smoker will do it. These are delicious with any rich meat sauce. *Serves 2.*

SAUERKRAUT BALLS

½ pound sliced bacon
2 eggs, slightly beaten
½ cup bread crumbs
1 tablespoon grated lemon
   rind
1 pound ground lean veal

Salt
Pepper
2 cups sauerkraut
2 medium onions, chopped
1 tablespoon caraway seed

Fry the bacon until crisp. Dry on a paper towel and chop fine. Mix the bacon, eggs, bread crumbs and lemon rind into the meat. When it has a smooth, even texture, form it into balls about 1 inch in diameter. Smoke until they brown, about 15 to 20 minutes at 300°. While they are smoking, mix the sauerkraut with the chopped onions and caraway seed. When the balls are brown, put them in an ovenproof dish and mix in the sauerkraut, covering the balls well. Cover the dish and put it back in the smoker (no smoke needed now) until the onions are done. *Serves 4.*

MEAT BALLS SAUERBRATEN

2 pounds ground beef
2 eggs, slightly beaten
1 cup minced onion
   Salt
   Pepper
2 cups dry white wine

1 sliced onion
1 bay leaf
2 teaspoons dry mustard
1 teaspoon thyme
½ pint sour cream

Mix the meat with the eggs and minced onion; add salt and pepper to taste. Form into small balls. In a nonmetallic container, make a marinade consisting of the wine, sliced onion, bay leaf, mustard and thyme. Place meat balls in marinade, and add more wine if necessary to cover the meat. Marinate for 2 days. Dry the meat balls and brown slightly in a smoker with the grill over a pan (about 15 minutes at 300°). When browned, put the balls in an ovenproof dish and pour the marinade over them. Cover the oven and cook for 30 minutes. Strain the sauce, thicken if necessary, add the cream and reheat. Pour it over the balls. Good with egg noodles. *Serves 4.*

RUSSIAN MEAT BALLS

3 slices bread
½ cup milk
1½ pounds ground beef or veal
2 eggs, slightly beaten

1 medium onion, minced
Salt
Pepper
1 pint sour cream

Reserve the sour cream. Soak the bread in the milk. Mix with the other ingredients. Form into meat balls about 1 inch thick. Smoke until barely brown. This will take about 10 minutes in a 300° oven. Place in an ovenproof pan, pour the sour cream over the balls and put back in the oven for another 20 minutes. Add a little white wine if the cream gets too thick. *Serves 4.*

HERB MEAT BALLS

2 pounds ground beef, veal or
    lamb
1 teaspoon ginger
2 eggs, slightly beaten
1 small onion, minced

¼ tablespoon curry powder
2 cloves garlic, pressed
Salt
Pepper
2 cups beef broth

Reserve the broth. Mix all other ingredients together. Form into small balls. Cook in the smoke oven, using little smoke. If the balls are about 1 inch thick, they will be done in about 15 minutes in a 300° oven. Dump them into an ovenproof dish, pour the beef broth over them and let them simmer for 10 minutes. Serve with rice. *Serves 4.*

PINE NUTS AND CHICKEN

1 chicken, cut into pieces and
    fried
½ cup chopped bacon
1 egg, slightly beaten

½ pound pine nuts
Salt
Pepper

Cut the cooked chicken from the bones with a small, sharp knife and run it through a meat grinder with the chopped bacon, slightly beaten egg and the pine nuts. Run it through a second time if needed to distribute the bacon and pine nuts equally. Form walnut-sized balls and cook at 300° in moderate smoke for about 20 minutes. *Serves 4.*

Meat Loaf

A handy meat-loaf pan for the smoker can be made by cutting the bottom from an inexpensive pan. Place it on an old cookie sheet, which will act as a bottom for your pan. Put the prepared meat into the pan, and place it all in the smoker. After 20 minutes of cooking, when the meat has shrunk a little, turn the pan over and push the meat onto the grill, removing the pan and cookie sheet. This way all sides can be browned.

If the fire is hot, and you are willing to turn the meat every 20 minutes or so, you can achieve a brown smoky crust on all sides of the loaf—a specialty no one can make in a regular oven.

If you don't want to keep turning the loaf, however, use a shallow broiling pan with a rack under the meat. The rack and pan method will keep the underside from becoming overcooked.

A regular loaf pan can be used without altering the bottom. After the loaf has been in the oven for a half hour, slide a knife around the edges and slip the loaf out of the pan and onto the rack. A two-pound meat loaf will take about 1½ hours at 300°. A meat thermometer will help you tell when the loaf is ready.

Meat loaf makes an excellent sandwich filling, so when you make a loaf, make it big enough to have some left over after dinner.

LEFTOVER MEAT LOAF

2 pounds ground meat
½ cup green pepper, chopped
1 teaspoon ground mustard
1 onion, chopped
1 clove garlic, crushed
2 teaspoons horse-radish

2 eggs, slightly beaten
1 cup bread crumbs, soaked
   in milk and squeezed dry
Salt
Pepper

When you have meat left over from a meal—pot roast, pork roast, a turkey or whatever—use it this way. If you do not have 2 pounds of meat, add some ground beef. It will blend in well with whatever you have. Mix all the ingredients together and form into a compact loaf. Put it on a roasting rack over a broiling pan. Baste a few times with butter and water or butter and vermouth. Use green wood chips or sawdust for smoke. A 300° oven should cook this loaf in about 1 hour. *Serves 4.*

MUSTARD LOAF

2 pounds ground beef
1 medium onion, chopped fine
2 teaspoons dry mustard
2 eggs, slightly beaten
1 tablespoon Worcestershire

1 cup bread crumbs, soaked in
  milk
Salt
Pepper

Mix all ingredients together and place in a pan. Bake in smoke oven for 30 minutes, to make the loaf firm. Remove from the pan, place on the grill and cook in the smoke until crusty brown. This will take about 1½ hours at 300°. *Serves 4.*

ITALIAN MEAT LOAF NO. 1

3 slices bread, soaked in milk
2 pounds ground beef or veal
1 large onion, chopped
1 teaspoon rosemary
2 cloves garlic, pressed

1 teaspoon basil
2 eggs, slightly beaten
Salt
Pepper

Squeeze the bread and mix with the other ingredients until well blended. Grease a baking dish and fill with the mixture. After 30 minutes at about 300°, the meat may be removed and placed on the grill for another hour or 1½ hours, until brown and done. *Serves 4.*

ORIENTAL LOAF

1 pound fresh pork sausage

2 pounds ground fresh chicken
  or beef

SAUCE

½ cup soy sauce
2 tablespoons brown sugar
1 clove garlic, crushed
½ teaspoon ground ginger

½ teaspoon Worcestershire
¼ teaspoon freshly ground
  black pepper
2 eggs

FRUIT FILLING

1 cup canned pineapple pieces
1 cup apricot halves
1 4-ounce jar maraschino
  cherries

½ cup pineapple juice
1 teaspoon ginger
Cornstarch

TOPPING

¼ cup toasted sesame seeds

Make thin patties, about ¼ inch thick, of the ground meats, and cook in a 300° smoker until done. That will take 5 to 8 minutes. Use an abundance of green wood for smoke. Remove the patties and allow them to cool enough to run through a meat grinder, or chop fine.

Take half the sauce, combine it with the 2 eggs and then mix it with the ground meats. Fill a 2½-pint ring mold with this mixture. Place the mold in a 300° smoker with a handful of green wood on the coals. After 20 minutes, slide a knife around the meat in the mold. Turn the mold over onto a broiling rack so the meat comes out on the rack over a shallow pan. Return to the smoker and continue to cook for about 1 hour, basting frequently with the other half of the sauce.

Mix the fruit filling together, using the cornstarch to thicken the pineapple juice. Heat this mixture, but do not cook it.

When the meat is done, place it on a hot platter. Baste it again and sprinkle it with toasted sesame seeds. Fill the center of the meat ring with the hot, gingered fruit. *Serves 6.*

FANCY MEAT LOAF

⅔ pound ground beef
⅔ pound ground pork
⅔ pound ground chicken
3 eggs, slightly beaten
1 cup fresh bread crumbs
3 slices bacon

1 onion, finely chopped
1 cup grated sharp cheddar
  cheese
Salt
Pepper

Mix each meat separately with salt and pepper to taste, 1 egg and ⅓ cup of crumbs. Chop the bacon into small pieces and sauté it slowly with the chopped onion. Spread the seasoned ground beef over the bottom of the pan. Spread a layer of cheese and half of the onion-bacon mixture. Add a layer of seasoned ground chicken and then a layer consisting of the rest of the cheese, onion and bacon. The layer of seasoned ground pork goes last. Cook in a 300° smoker, using hardwood chips or sawdust, for 40 minutes. Turn the pan carefully and slip the loaf onto a broiling rack over a shallow pan. Add more green wood and cook another 40 minutes. Allow to cool 10 minutes before slicing. *Serves 4.*

ITALIAN MEAT LOAF NO. 2

2 pounds ground beef
2 eggs, slightly beaten
1 small onion, chopped fine
1 teaspoon orégano

½ cup bread crumbs
½ cup grated cheese
Salt
Pepper

SAUCE

1 large onion, minced
1 tablespoon olive oil
1 6-ounce can tomato paste
½ teaspoon rosemary

½ teaspoon orégano
1 cup red wine
Salt
Pepper

Mix the meat with the eggs, chopped onion, orégano, bread crumbs and cheese. The mixture will need no pan. Shape the loaf to make nice slices. Place on a rack over a broiling pan, add wood chips or sawdust to the coals and cover the oven. Baste with the sauce about every 20 minutes. To prepare the sauce, sauté the onion in olive oil until golden, then stir in the tomato paste, seasonings and wine. Let it simmer until time for the first basting. It also may be served when the meat is sliced. *Serves 4.*

PARSLEY LOAF

1 onion, minced
2 cloves garlic, crushed
1 tablespoon butter
2 eggs
½ cup finely chopped parsley

Salt
Pepper
1 pound ground beef
½ pound ground pork
½ cup bread crumbs

Sauté the onion and garlic in butter until golden. Stir into a bowl with the eggs and beat slightly with a fork. Add the parsley, and salt and pepper to taste. Mix this well with the meat and bread crumbs. Form into a compact loaf. Place on the grill over a broiling pan in a 300° smoke oven. Put a handful of wood chips on the coals. This should take about 1½ hours. *Serves 4.*

STUFFED MEAT LOAF

1 pound ground beef
½ pound cooked ground ham
2 eggs, slightly beaten
1 cup bread crumbs
  Salt

Pepper
½ cup drained, chopped
  pineapple
½ cup cottage cheese

Mix the meat with the eggs, bread crumbs and the seasoning. Divide into 2 equal portions. Mix the drained pineaple chunks with the dry cottage cheese. Place a layer of meat in the bottom of the pan. Press on the meat to form a slight depression and to force the meat up higher on the sides of the pan. Place the cottage cheese and pineapple in the depression. Place the other layer on top and close the sides to keep the cheese-pineapple mixture sealed. Put in a 300° oven with a little smoke. You can use pineapple juice and melted butter for a baste. If the loaf can be slipped out of the pan without breaking it after about 45 minutes, you can brown it on all sides, cooking it another 30 to 45 minutes. *Serves 4.*

SPICE MEAT LOAF

2 pounds ground beef
2 eggs, slightly beaten
1 small onion, grated
2 tablespoons parsley flakes
1 cup bread crumbs, soaked
  in milk

3 cloves garlic, chopped fine
½ teaspoon rosemary
½ teaspoon orégano
  Salt
  Pepper

Mix the ingredients carefully. Add the seasoning a little at a time to ensure even distribution. Squeeze through your fingers until the mixture has a fine, even texture. This will fill to the top a pan that measures 8 × 4¾ × 2¾ inches. Grease the inside of the pan, fill with the mixture and cook in a smoke oven for 30 minutes at 300° to 350°. Use wood chips or sawdust for smoke. After 30 minutes, remove the meat from the pan, put the loaf on the grill, add more wood chips or sawdust and cover the oven. This may take about 1½ hours, but check it after 1 hour. *Serves 4.*

COMBINATION LOAF

1½ pounds ground beef   1 medium onion, chopped
½ cup finely chopped celery   fine
1 cup grated raw potato   Salt
2 eggs, slightly beaten   Pepper

Mix all the ingredients and form into a loaf. Roast at 300°. If you
have it on a rack over a pan, the heat can be increased to 350° to
cut down the cooking time. If you use the rack-and-pan method,
you will get no smoke flavor unless you add green wood chips or
sawdust to the coals. The cooking time will depend on the thickness
of your loaf. A meat thermometer in the center of the loaf will tell
you when it is done. *Serves 4.*

7

Beef

There is a doctor in our town who insists the only way to cook a beef roast is for twenty-four hours at 125°. He believes any other way drives out the natural juices, the flavor and the nutrition.

He should discover smoke ovens. When we first did, it took us a while to recognize the remarkable things a smoke oven accomplishes.

In a stove oven the only moisture comes from the roast itself. By the time the meat is done, much of its moisture has been cooked out of it. In the smoker, however, there is a continual supply of air moving through the oven. Whatever humidity is in the air goes into the oven. This means the roast is cooked amid greater humidity than in a stove oven. There is markedly less drying out. Even cuts of meat that are not particularly enhanced by smoke flavor go into our smokers. We cook them by the indirect method—that is, not directly over the coals. We do not use wood chips or sawdust in this case. So there is no smoke flavor, but there is a taste difference. The meat is juicier, has better flavor and is usually more tender.

Perhaps more important is the difference in aroma. Meat cooked in a smoker, especially if wood chips or sawdust have been used to produce smoke, has greater aroma than meat cooked in a conventional oven. The Food and Container Institute's research concludes that the aroma of cooked meat is more important than the flavor. Nothing can compete with a smoke oven when it comes to creating a mouth-watering aroma.

The most popular meat in this country is beef. The number of beef cuts available far exceeds the choice available in any other kind of meat. There are rib roasts, rump roasts, chuck roasts, pot roasts, sirloin, rolled roasts, porterhouse steaks, T-bone steaks, club steaks, flank steaks—to name a few and not include the array of variety meats and ground meats.

After you have tried the standard beef cuts and have received the plaudits of family and guests, you will be willing to try anything in your smoke oven. We got carried away once and even tried beef shanks—those dark red slices of beef that look so good and are priced so low. We learned that even a smoke oven is not up to reducing their toughness into anything palatable. Even four days in a marinade of red wine and oil made no difference. Shanks are for soup, and that's where they landed—in the pot, smoky aroma and all. The soup was delicious.

Meat in interstate commerce must have government inspection. You probably will not find prime grade in your market. It is the most expensive and goes to restaurants and hotels that can afford to charge top prices.

You will, however, find choice and good grades. Choice has white fat and flecks of fat—called marbling—in the lean part of the meat. It is excellent in the smoker. Good grades have fat that is more yellow. The lean meat is darker and seldom has marbling. It also is good in the smoker. Commercial grade usually has yellow fat and no marbling in the steer beef. If you see some marbling in a commercial grade of beef, it's probably meat from a cow. We recommend that you do not purchase meat below these grades. Utility or canner and cutter grades are tough and go into hot dogs, sausage and cured beef.

Look for a market that specializes in good meat and a butcher who will try to please you. Tell him of your smoke oven and how well the roast turned out, and you will have a friend with a cleaver who can help you more than all the government stamps and meat guidebooks you care to read. Learn as much as you can about recognizing the grades, because butchers, like all other friends, may move away. Ask him questions. Meat is expensive and you have as much right to discuss the merits of a six-dollar roast as you have in the purchase of a shirt or a handsaw.

PACIFIC STEAK

4 steaks, 6 to 8 ounces each   Pepper
Salt

MARINADE

½ cup water
½ cup soy sauce
2 jiggers whisky
½ teaspoon chopped garlic

¼ teaspoon ground ginger
2 tablespoons Worcestershire
1 tablespoon brown sugar

Combine marinade ingredients and marinate the steaks at least 4 hours, preferably longer, in the refrigerator. The marinade not only flavors the meat; it makes it more tender. Remove meat from refrigerator 2 hours before cooking to allow it to reach room temperature. Leave it in marinade until time to cook. Place steaks on smoke-oven grill. Salt and pepper to taste. Throw a few chips of hardwood or a handful of dampened hardwood sawdust on the coals. Cook over direct heat in a 300° to 350° oven. Cook to desired doneness— if the steaks are about 1 inch thick they will be medium rare in about 20 minutes. *Serves 4.*

TART STEAK

4 steaks   Pepper
Salt

MARINADE PASTE

3 lemons
½ cup salt
⅛ cup black pepper
4 cloves garlic, crushed

½ teaspoon orégano
¼ teaspoon thyme
½ cup olive oil

Squeeze juice from lemons and combine with other marinade paste ingredients. Smear a coating on both sides of the first steak, put it on a plate, then coat the top of the other steaks and stack them one on top of the other above the bottom steak. Let them stand about 8 hours in the refrigerator. Remove meat from refrigerator to allow it to reach room temperature. Scrape off most of the coating. Place on smoke-oven grill and cook to desired doneness in a 300° to 350° oven. *Serves 4.*

MIL'S FLANK STEAK

1 2½- to 3-pound flank steak,   Salt
    scored by the butcher   Pepper
½ teaspoon meat tenderizer
    per pound of meat

MARINADE

¼ cup soy sauce   1½ teaspoons powdered ginger
2 tablespoons honey   ¾ cup salad oil
1 teaspoon garlic salt   1 medium onion, chopped

Sprinkle meat with tenderizer.

Combine marinade ingredients, stir well and marinate flank steak in it for 24 hours in refrigerator, turning occasionally. Remove meat from refrigerator 2 hours before cooking to allow it to reach room temperature. Leave it in the marinade until time to cook. Scrape off any onion clinging to meat, as it will char in smoke oven if left on. Build a brisk fire big enough so entire steak will be over coals. Coals may be spread if necessary to achieve this. Throw on a few chips of hardwood. Place steak on grill and put cover on smoker. This is one of the few times we recommend that meat be turned over in a smoke oven. After about 3 minutes cooking on one side use tongs and spatula or pancake turner (because meat is so tender) to turn the steak. Cook 3 to 5 minutes on second side with smoke-oven top on. Remove to cutting board and slice thin slices diagonally across grain.

A flank steak weighing 2½ to 3 pounds seems far too much for four people, but this combination of flavors is so delicious seconds are almost always called for—and if not, what's left makes fine nibbling food the next day. *Serves 4.*

MUSTARD ROAST

1 4- to 6-pound high quality   Pepper
    beef roast   Prepared mustard
Salt

Rub the roast with salt and pepper and place in a 300° smoke oven for 10 minutes amid heavy smoke. Put on plenty of wet chips or sawdust to impart all the smoke flavor possible at this stage of the cooking process. After the 10 minutes open the oven and slather as much mustard over the meat as it will take. The mustard will eventually dry and crack off before serving, but not until it has imparted its taste to mingle with the smoke flavor. Cook to desired doneness, using a meat thermometer or your own guide of minutes per pound. *Serves 4.*

STEAK WITH ROQUEFORT SAUCE

2 pounds good-quality sirloin steak, 1½ inches thick

Salt
Pepper

ROQUEFORT SAUCE

1 teaspoon Worcestershire
2 teaspoons cream

2 ounces Roquefort cheese

Place steak on smoke-oven grill. Salt and pepper to taste. Throw a few chips of dampened hardwood or a handful of dampened hardwood sawdust on the coals. Cook over direct heat in a 300° to 350° oven. Cook to desired doneness—if the meat is 1½ inches thick it will be cooked rare to medium rare in about 25 to 30 minutes. While meat is cooking blend the Worcestershire sauce, cream and cheese. Shortly before removing meat from the oven, spread the cheese sauce on it and let it melt. *Serves 4.*

ITALIAN STEAK

2 cloves garlic, crushed
¾ cup olive oil
4 steaks, top quality and tender

6 tablespoons grated Parmesan cheese
1½ cups bread crumbs
Salt
Pepper

Crush the garlic in a bowl. Pour in the oil and blend well. Dip the steaks in the oil. Mix the cheese and crumbs together, and place the steaks on this mixture, making sure each gets an even coating of crumbs and cheese. Salt and pepper to taste when steaks are placed on the smoke-oven grill. Can be cooked with or without smoke; we prefer light smoking. Cook over direct heat at about 300°. If this browns the crumbs too quickly or too much, use indirect heat area of grill. If the steaks are about ¾ inch thick, they will be done in 12 to 15 minutes. *Serves 4.*

SMOKY BEEF STROGANOFF

2 pounds top-quality round
    steak
3 tablespoons prepared
    mustard
3 tablespoons shortening
1 large onion, sliced into rings
2 tablespoons Worcestershire

2 tablespoons paprika
1 teaspoon salt
1 cup canned mushrooms with
    liquor, or ½ pound fresh
    mushrooms with ½ cup dry
    vermouth
1 pint thick sour cream

Trim fat and gristle from meat. Pound thoroughly. Cut into strips 1½ × 1 inch. Cold-smoke for 30 to 45 minutes on small-screen rack placed on smoke-oven grill. There should be an abundance of smoke but little heat in the oven. Use a few coals, the temperature no higher than 85° to 90°, and heavy smoke from hardwood sawdust or chips on the coals. The aim is flavor without cooking.

After cold-smoking the meat, place it in a bowl. Mix mustard into meat strips, thoroughly covering each piece. Cover bowl and let stand overnight in refrigerator until ready for preparing the Stroganoff. This marinating gives superb flavor to the dish.

Heat shortening in a large skillet. Add onion and cook until tender. Remove. Add meat and brown on all sides. Try not to add any more fat. Fry a little at a time, transferring as it cooks into a heavy pan or Dutch oven. To the browned meat add Worcestershire sauce, paprika, salt and mushrooms. Cover and simmer for about 35 minutes. In the last 5 minutes of cooking add the onions and sour cream. Heat but do not boil after the cream has been added. Serve with fluffy boiled rice.

This dish tastes better on the second day than the first, so cook it 24 hours ahead and, if your will power is up to it, wait. *Serves 6.*

SIRLOIN AND SAUCE

1 4- to 5-pound sirloin tip roast

MARINADE

3 cloves garlic, chopped
3 tablespoons Worcestershire
1 onion, chopped

½ bottle catsup
1 cup dry red wine

¼ cup sherry   Pepper
Salt

Mix garlic, Worcestershire, onion, catsup and red wine in a deep
bowl. Add meat and place in refrigerator to marinate for 24 hours,
turning occasionally. Remove from refrigerator in time to bring
meat to room temperature before roasting. Pour the marinade into
a shallow pan and put it on the smoke-oven grill. Place the meat
on a roasting rack and place that over the pan. Pour about half the
sherry over the meat, close oven cover, and start roasting at 300°.
Use plenty of wood chips for smoke.

Baste the meat after about 10 minutes, adding ½ cup of water or
wine to the pan to keep ingredients from browning. Baste roast
with pan ingredients every 20 to 30 minutes until meat is done to
your liking. Add water or wine as necessary to keep the pan drippings liquid. Salt and pepper to taste.

About 5 minutes before removing the roast from the smoke oven,
pour the rest of the sherry over the meat. After the meat is removed,
add a little water or wine if necessary to the drippings to make a
sauce to serve with the meat. Carve the roast across the grain.
Serves 8.

OLIVE ROAST

1 4- to 5-pound boneless beef   Pepper
  roast   Olive oil
10 to 15 stuffed green olives   Dry red wine
Salt   Liquid from the olives

Cut 10 to 15 slits in the roast. Force olives into the slits and close
with skewers or toothpicks. Place on rack over baking pan (to catch
the juices) and place on smoke-oven grill. Salt and pepper to taste.
Cook in 300° oven until meat is done to your liking. Baste occasionally with equal parts of olive oil, red wine and the liquid from
the jar of olives. This roast is good either hot or cold. Try baking
peeled potatoes in the drippings pan—an extra taste treat. *Serves 8.*

BEER STEAK

4 steaks (cook's choice of size)   Pepper
Salt

MARINADE

8 ounces beer   3 dashes Tabasco per steak
PASTE

2 tablespoons chopped parsley   ¼ cup soft butter
2 tablespoons chopped onion

Some meat shops carry less tender and less expensive steaks than the well-known but usually high-priced cuts. These are identified by a myriad of names in the various sections of the country. This is the recipe to use if you know the steaks that fall into this category or you suspect the meat might be tough, no matter what the cut.

Marinate the steaks in the beer-Tabasco combination in the refrigerator for 12 to 24 hours. Remove from refrigerator in time to bring to room temperature before cooking. Mix the parsley, onion and butter into a paste and just before cooking smear the steak tops with a coating of the paste. Salt and pepper to taste. Cook at 300° for 15 to 20 minutes, renewing the butter spread every 5 minutes. *Serves 4.*

The following sauce is excellent served on the steaks:

1 teaspoon chopped garlic   2 tablespoons butter
2 tablespoons chopped parsley   ½ cup dry red wine

Lightly sauté the garlic and parsley in the butter, add the wine, bring to a boil and simmer gently. Pour it over the steaks after they have been served.

MARINATED RIB ROAST

1 5-pound beef rib roast   Pepper
Salt
MARINADE

2 cups red wine   1 large onion, chopped
½ cup cooking oil   ½ green pepper, chopped
2 garlic cloves, minced   1 tablespoon orégano

Mix marinade well and pour over roast in a deep bowl or container. Keep in refrigerator at least 24 hours, turning the meat occasionally. Remove from refrigerator in time to bring roast to room temperature before cooking. Place roast on rack over baking pan (to catch the juices) and put on smoke-oven grill. Salt and pepper to taste. Cook in 275° to 300° smoke oven until meat is done to your liking. *Serves 8.*

MARINATED ROLLED ROAST WITH SAUCE POIVRADE

1 4-pound rolled beef roast	Pepper
Salt	

MARINADE

2 cups dry red wine	¼ teaspoon thyme
1 cup tarragon wine vinegar	¼ teaspoon cloves
1 onion, sliced	¼ teaspoon ground bay leaves

Mix marinade well and pour over roast in a bowl. Cover and refrigerate 3 days. Turn meat twice a day at least, preferably 4 or 5 times. Remove roast from refrigerator in time to bring it to room temperature before cooking. Salt and pepper to taste. Place on rack over broiling pan and roast indirectly at 300° to desired doneness. Use green hardwood or sawdust for smoke. Baste frequently with marinade. While roast is cooking, prepare:

SAUCE POIVRADE

½ cup diced carrots	2 tablespoons butter
½ cup chopped onions	8 ounces brown sauce or beef
¼ cup chopped celery	gravy
¼ teaspoon thyme	6 peppercorns, crushed
½ bay leaf	

Cook vegetables and seasonings in butter until vegetables are soft. Stir frequently. Add ¾ cup of the roast marinade and boil to reduce by ⅓. Stir while boiling. Add 1 cup brown sauce or beef gravy (may be canned) and simmer for 30 minutes. Five minutes before straining, add crushed peppercorns. Strain the sauce. Press as much as possible through the mesh. Heat again and serve with sliced marinated roast. *Serves 4 to 6.*

POT ROAST TIP

A good wine has flavor which conceals the fact that there is acid present. That's why wine makes such an excellent marinade. While it adds a subtle flavor to the meat, it also tenderizes it; acid turns tough meat fiber tender. Some cuts also call for commercial meat tenderizer to be used with the marinade.

When you marinate a pot roast or one of the tougher cuts, let it stand at least 24 hours. The longer it stands, the more tender it will be. We marinate a 2½-inch-thick pot roast for 24 hours and cook it in the smoke oven for about 1 hour at 325° and it emerges as tender and juicy as steak. We eat it like steak too, cutting thin slices at an angle across the grain.

ALCOHOLIC POT ROAST

1 3- to 4-pound best-grade pot   Pepper
    roast, 1½ to 2 inches thick   ½ teaspoon meat tenderizer
Salt   per pound of meat

WINE MARINADE

2 to 3 cups dry red wine   ¼ cup salad oil
2 cloves garlic, quartered

ALE MARINADE

1 pint ale   ½ cup salad oil
1 onion, chopped

Where but in a smoke oven can you get steak for the price of pot roast? That is what you achieve if you get the best grade of pot roast at the market. Sprinkle with tenderizer, using the tines of a fork to work the tenderizer into the meat. Marinate the meat in the wine or ale mixture from 6 to 24 hours, keeping it under refrigeration. Marinating it in wine or ale helps tenderize it too, and adds tantalizing flavor. Turn the meat in the marinade occasionally.

Remove meat from refrigerator in time to allow it to reach room temperature before cooking. Place the roast on the smoke oven grill directly over the coals at about 300°. Salt and pepper to taste. If the meat is less than 2 inches thick, it will probably be medium rare in 45 to 60 minutes. When cooked to desired doneness, remove from smoker and cut meat into serving portions. Each person then cuts his own slices on his plate, thereby preserving juices and saving carving time.

For a taste variation and to make the roast seem richer, put strips of bacon or salt pork on top of the roast while it is cooking. *Serves 4 to 6.*

PRIME RIB OR SIRLOIN ROAST

There is nothing tricky about cooking a big roast of beef in a smoke oven. It is less trouble than preparing 4 hamburger patties.

If a prime rib is to be roasted, select a two- or three-rib standing roast. A smaller cut than this is not a satisfactory roast. Prime rib should be roasted with the curved or fat side up, making it self-basting. If sirloin is to be roasted and it does not have a layer of outside fat, tie or skewer a layer of beef suet to the top side, making it self-basting. Rub the meat with salt and pepper, insert a meat thermometer, place on a roasting rack over a broiling pan, put in 300° smoke oven away from the coals and close the oven. Remove the roast when the thermometer registers the degree of doneness you desire. For a rare roast take the meat from the oven when the thermometer reads 140°; for medium, 160°; for well done, 180°. If you have no thermometer, allow 18 to 20 minutes per pound for rare, 22 to 25 minutes for medium and 27 to 30 minutes for well done. Remove roast from smoke oven to a serving platter and let stand 15 minutes before carving—to "set" the juices.

Remove most of the fat in the broiling pan. Add a little consommé or stock and stir with roast drippings and brown bits. Add the red juice that has collected in the platter from the roast, plus a dab of butter, salt and pepper to taste. Serve hot with the sliced meat.

SMOKED TONGUE

1 2½ to 3-pound beef tongue   1 garlic clove, halved
⅛ cup sugar   1 tablespoon vinegar
½ cup salt   Water to cover
1 teaspoon black pepper

Combine the ingredients and simmer the tongue until tender. Cool, then peel the skin from the tongue.

Prepare smoke oven for cold smoking: a few coals, the temperature no higher than 85° to 90°, and heavy smoke created by the use of hardwood sawdust or chips on the coals.

Place tongue on a rack and put the rack on the grill of the smoke oven in an area removed from the coals. Watch the heat closely. If it climbs the tongue will dry out. Smoke the tongue at least an hour, longer if possible provided the meat is not drying.

Tongue is delicious hot or cold. It can be heated in some of the liquor in which it was originally boiled. Horse-radish complements tongue, either alone or mixed with mayonnaise or mayonnaise and whipped cream. *Serves 3.*

FILET DE BOEUF

The beef fillet, which weighs from 2 to 3 pounds, is the undercut of the sirloin and is most often made into steaks. It is an expensive roast, but makes a dramatic entrée.

The fillet is so lean you may want to have the butcher lard it with a few pieces of suet or pork fat back. Whether you have done this or not, rub the meat generously with butter or olive oil after trimming it of any skin or sinews.

Have the smoke oven adjusted to 350° with an even bed of coals. Place the meat on the smoke oven grill over the coals, salt and pepper to taste, add damp wood chips, cover and roast for 15 minutes. Turn meat over,* baste with butter or olive oil, add more wood chips or sawdust and roast for another 15 to 20 minutes. The fillet, of all cuts of meat, should be rare. Slice thin and serve plain or with your favorite sauce or with butter. Any size fillet should cook between 25 and 35 minutes only. *Serves 4 to 6.*

* This is one of the few recipes in which we recommend that meat be turned—it just isn't necessary in smoke cooking. In this case, however, the meat is so lean it needs to be oiled on both sides during the roasting process.

STUFFED ROAST OF VEAL

1 4-pound veal roast   Pepper
  Salt

STUFFING

2 cups cooked spinach	1 teaspoon orégano
1 small carrot	1 chicken bouillon cube
1 small onion	1 tablespoon water
1 celery stalk	1 cup bread crumbs
1 clove garlic	1 egg
¼ cup olive oil	Salt
2 tablespoons catsup	Pepper

Cut a slit in the veal so that a moist vegetable stuffing can be inserted. Chop the spinach, carrot, onion, celery and garlic. Heat the olive oil and sauté the vegetables about 3 minutes. Add the catsup, orégano and the bouillon cube after it has been dissolved in the tablespoon of water. Cover and simmer until the vegetables are tender but not limp. Salt and pepper to taste. Stir in bread crumbs if needed to give the mixture enough body for stuffing into the meat. Do not use all the crumbs if they are not needed. A moist stuffing is preferable. Sew or skewer the slit shut after the stuffing is completed. Roast on grill of smoker at 300° for 2 to 2½ hours, basting with oil if surface appears too dry. Use light smoke. *Serves 6.*

STEAK MARCHAND DE VIN

4 steaks (cook's choice)   Pepper
  Salt

SAUCE

⅛ cup chopped onion   2 tablespoons brown sauce or
4 tablespoons butter   canned gravy
1 cup dry red wine   1 teaspoon chopped parsley
1 tablespoon cream   1 teaspoon lemon juice

Sauté onions in 2 tablespoons of butter. Add the wine and simmer until reduced to about one half. While the wine is simmering, place the steaks on the grill of a 300° smoke oven; salt and pepper to taste; put damp wood or sawdust on coals; close cover and cook for 15 minutes, if the steaks are ¾ inch thick and are to be rare. Alter cooking time if necessary. Remove the steaks to pre-heated plates. Stir cream into wine sauce. Add 2 tablespoons butter, the gravy, chopped parsley and lemon juice. Blend well, season to taste with salt and pepper and pour boiling hot over the steaks. *Serves 4.*

8

Lamb and Pork

Charles Lamb, who liked to spoof the world, once wrote this version of how roast pork was discovered: A Chinese peasant's son accidently set the family home afire. It was destroyed. Worse, so were the family's pigs. The boy accidentally put his hand to a still hot pig carcass. The hot fat burned his hand. He put it to his mouth to ease the burn, and surprise came to his face as the taste registered. His father discovered the loss and began beating the boy, but the blows failed to stop the child from moving his hands from porker to mouth. Curious, the father tried it—and never went back to beating the boy. Roast pork became very popular among the Chinese. After a while they even quit burning houses and invented other ways to get roast pork.

There are some who have accepted the story as fact, even though it was sheer invention. They accept it because the elements of truth are there: The Chinese love roast pork. The Chinese roast it splendidly. So can anyone who cooks it in the original way of roasting—with a free flow of air available. Smoke flavor helps too.

Pork was made for roasting. It has flavor, eye appeal and aroma, and it is so fat it is virtually self-basting. One thing, though. It must be cooked thoroughly; otherwise the fat makes it indigestible. Slow roasting is the way. Use a meat thermometer, not only to make sure it is digestible, but also to prevent trichinosis. This disease can be passed from hog to man if the meat is not cooked to a high enough temperature. The nematode that causes trichinosis is killed at 137°. You want the center of your roast to get well beyond that point, not only to make the meat safe, but also to

95

make it palatable. Remember that pork is fat and to be digestible it should be cooked to around 180°.

Beef is the overwhelming favorite in the United States, but around the world sheep provide the meat for the common man. A sheep can be readied in dry country that will not support cattle. Sheep also reach maturity more quickly. Furthermore, lamb is the meat most free from contamination, an important consideration in the areas without refrigeration. Even in this country, where refrigeration helps protect meat, it is lamb that is the least likely to be rejected in government inspection.

Garlic has been so universally used in cooking lamb that there are those in this country who don't know that lamb can taste otherwise. They mistake the flavor of garlic for that of lamb. In truth, however, lamb can be mistaken for beef if cooked without garlic, especially if done rare. Some people insist rare cooking is the only way with lamb. They want it to be pink and juicy, never gray as a lamb roast tends to become when well done.

Lamb or pork can be cooked directly on the grill but, unless you want grill marks on the meat or want to brown the sides heavily, we recommend putting the meat on a rack over or in a pan. It is a little slower, for the direct heat does not get at the meat, but it keeps the drippings from going into the coals or collecting on the bottom of the smoke oven. Also it is easier to baste the meat. The baste and drippings go into the pan, where they can be drawn by a baster and squirted back over the meat from time to time. The collected drippings also can go into a gravy or sauce.

Cooking time will depend on the thickness of the cut, the number of coals, how well done you want the meat, the distance from the fire and other factors. A meat thermometer is the best guide for roasts. Let it get up to 140° for medium rare in lamb. Pork should be well done, so it must stay in longer. For safety let the thermometer climb to at least 180°.

SHERRY LAMB CHOPS

8 lamb chops   Pepper
Salt

MARINADE

1 onion, chopped
1 clove garlic, chopped
1½ teaspoons dry mustard

1½ teaspoons melted butter
1½ cups sherry

Mix marinade ingredients and pour over lamb chops in a shallow marinating dish. Marinate at least 4 hours, basting or turning the chops several times. Place the chops on the grill of a 300° to 325° smoke oven, salt and pepper to taste and cook over direct heat until done. Strain the marinade and use it to baste the chops as they cook. *Serves 4.*

LAMB CHOPS VERMOUTH

8 lamb chops   Salt

MARINADE

1 cup dry vermouth
½ cup salad oil
1 tablespoon lemon juice
1 small onion, chopped

1 clove garlic, chopped
1 teaspoon tarragon
8 peppercorns, crushed

Combine marinade ingredients and pour over lamb chops in a shallow marinating dish. Let stand at least 4 hours, basting or turning the chops several times. Place the chops on the grill of a 300° to 325° smoke oven, salt to taste and cook over direct heat until done. Baste with the marinade after it has been strained. *Serves 4.*

HERB ROAST LAMB

1 5-pound leg of lamb
1 onion
1 clove garlic
¼ teaspoon marjoram

½ teaspoon rosemary
1 cup dry red wine
Salt
Pepper

Cut 6 to 8 slits in the lamb. Grind together—with either a blender or a mortar and pestle—the onion, garlic, marjoram and rosemary. Rub this mixture into the slits. Salt and pepper the roast and cook in a 325° smoke oven about 25 minutes per pound or until meat thermometer reaches desired temperature. Use the wine to baste the roast about every 20 minutes. *Serves 6 to 8.*

BACON-TOPPED ROAST LAMB

1 5-pound leg of lamb Rosemary
1 onion, sliced 6 bacon slices
2 cloves garlic, chopped Salt
2 bay leaves Pepper
2 cups dry red wine

Marinate the lamb at least 4 hours in the mixture of onion, garlic, bay leaves and wine. Remove meat from marinade, dry it, cut slits in the roast and insert pieces of garlic and bits of rosemary. Salt and pepper to taste, then pin strips of bacon over the roast with toothpicks. Cook in a 325° smoke oven about 2½ hours or until meat thermometer registers desired temperature. Throw a few hardwood chips on coals occasionally. *Serves 6 to 8.*

GENTLE LAMB ROAST

1 5-pound leg of lamb 10 cloves garlic
2 tablespoons butter 1 bottle white wine
Salt 1 cup water
Pepper

That looks like a lot of garlic, but do not fear. It adds only a subtle taste to the meat because the garlic does not come in contact with it. Remove any skin from the lamb, then rub it with the butter and sprinkle with salt and pepper to taste. Put the roast on a rack and pierce it repeatedly with the tines of a carving fork. Peel the garlic and drop it in a pan. Pour in half the wine. Place the racked meat over the pan and put it in a 325° smoke oven. Throw a handful of hardwood chips on the coals. The lamb must be basted frequently with the wine and meat juices that drip into the pan. Pierce the meat again each time it is basted, also adding a few more wood chips to the coals at that time. More wine will be needed to keep the pan from becoming dry. This may be stretched by adding a little water with the wine. The garlic will cook in the juices before adding its flavor to the meat. You will be surprised at how this tames the garlic flavor. The roast will be done medium rare in about 2½ hours. Strain the garlic from the juice and use the sauce on an accompanying dish, preferably rice or sautéed mushrooms. *Serves 6 to 8.*

INDONESIAN LAMB

1 5-pound leg of lamb, boned
Juice of 1 lemon
1 tablespoon grated onion
1 clove garlic, crushed or
  chopped
1 tablespoon melted butter
2 tablespoons chopped parsley
½ teaspoon ground ginger

1 teaspoon curry powder
1 cup pineapple chunks and
  juice
1 tablespoon brown sugar
1 cup sherry
1 cup shredded coconut
Salt
Pepper

Place the lamb flat in a marinating dish. Squeeze the juice of the lemon over the meat and rub the flesh with the rind. Except for the salt and pepper, mix the ingredients and pour over the lamb. Marinate at least 4 hours. Remove the meat from marinade and scrape off any pieces of marinade. Salt and pepper to taste. Cook in a 300° smoke oven until medium rare. Cooking time will depend on the thickness of the meat. Throw a handful of hardwood chips on the coals at the beginning of cooking. While the meat is cooking, put the marinade in a saucepan and simmer. Use as a sauce with the meat. *Serves 6 to 8.*

KAREN'S KABABS

1 5-pound leg of lamb
1 cup salad oil
3 cloves garlic, crushed
¼ cup chopped parsley
1 teaspoon thyme
1 cup dry red wine

Salt
Pepper
2 1-pound cans small whole
  onions
1 pound mushrooms

Have the butcher remove the leg bone and cut the meat into cubes about 1 to 1½ inches square. If you do it yourself, remove the white connective tissue as you work, but leave a little of the fat. Marinate it overnight in the mixture of oil, garlic, parsley, thyme, wine, salt and pepper, stirring several times. When meat is ready to cook, slide it onto skewers, alternating with onions and mushrooms. Make the meat the first and last pieces on the skewer, with 4 or 5 pieces of meat on each skewer. Cook about 20 minutes in a 350° smoke oven. *Serves 8.*

ASTORIA LAMB

1 large onion, sliced
1 5-pound leg of lamb, boned
2 cloves garlic, chopped
1 tablespoon salt
1 teaspoon pepper

¼ teaspoon cayenne
2 teaspoons orégano
½ cup dry red wine or vinegar
½ cup olive or salad oil

Place the sliced onion on the bottom of a shallow marinating dish. Spread the lamb on the onion, skin side down. Sprinkle over it half the garlic, salt, pepper, cayenne and orégano. Turn and season the other side. Pour in the wine or vinegar and oil and marinate overnight in refrigerator. If you use vinegar instead of wine, the meat will have a slightly more tart taste. Both the wine and vinegar act as tenderizing agents. While the meat is marinating, turn it or baste it a few times. When meat is ready to cook, remove it to a cutting board, slice pockets in the flesh and insert pieces of the garlic. Roll the meat to resemble its shape before the bone was removed. Tie it and place in a 325° smoke oven. Cook to desired doneness. Throw a handful of hardwood chips on the coals at the outset of roasting and add more at 45-minute intervals. *Serves 6 to 8.*

SOUTH SEAS LAMB

4 lamb shanks
4 cloves garlic
    Salt
    Pepper
1 cup dry vermouth
1½ cups rice
1 small onion, chopped

½ green pepper, chopped
3 celery stalks, chopped
3 ounces shredded coconut
1 teaspoon nutmeg
    Salt
    Pepper
2 cups water

Rub lamb shanks with garlic and sprinkle them with salt and pepper. Put on a rack over a pan and cook for an hour at 325° in moderate smoke. Baste every 15 minutes with the vermouth. Remove pan from smoke oven and skim as much of the fat from the drippings as possible. Add the rice and other ingredients and return to smoke oven for another 30 minutes. At the end of that time the rice should have cooked and become fluffy dry. The coconut is the taste surprise here. *Serves 4.*

LAMB SLICES

1 bunch green onions
3 tablespoons butter
3 tablespoons flour
1 tablespoon lemon juice
1 strip of lemon rind
¼ teaspoon cayenne

1 cup stock or bouillon
1 cup dry red wine
2 pounds smoke-cooked lamb
Salt
Pepper

Try this if you have part of a smoked lamb roast left over. Slice the onions and sauté in butter. Add flour. After cooking a moment, add the other ingredients. Simmer for 5 minutes, then add the lamb slices. Allow the meat to warm, but do not cook or it will toughen. Remove the lemon rind before serving. Serve with rice. *Serves 4.*

STUFFED SPRING LAMB

1 5-pound leg or shoulder of
   lamb
¼ pound ham
¼ pound fresh veal
¼ pound fresh pork
½ teaspoon marjoram
¼ teaspoon nutmeg

¼ cup bread crumbs
1 egg
1 clove garlic, chopped
Salt
Pepper
½ pound mushrooms
2 tablespoons butter

Whether you use a leg or shoulder cut, have the butcher cut the meat to remove the bone. This will leave a cavity for stuffing. Grind together the ham, veal and pork. Mix well with marjoram, nutmeg, bread crumbs, egg, garlic, salt and pepper. Chop mushrooms and sauté them in butter. Add them to the mixture. Stuff the mixture into the lamb cavity and sew the opening shut. Bacon can be tooth-picked to any opening that cannot be sewn shut. Rub the roast with butter, season with salt and pepper and place on a rack over a roasting pan. Roast it in a 325° smoke oven until done. If you prefer basted roasts, use red wine over the roast every 30 minutes. Garlic, thyme and savory salt can be mixed with the wine for added flavor. And don't forget the hardwood chips on the coals throughout the roasting period. They may be added when roast is basted, or about every 30 minutes. *Serves 6 to 8.*

ORANGE LAMB

1 5-pound leg of lamb
½ cup orange juice
¼ cup chili sauce
1 cup dry red wine
1 tablespoon salad oil
1 tablespoon chili powder

1 medium onion, chopped
2 cloves garlic, chopped
1 teaspoon crushed cumin
1 tablespoon brown sugar
Salt
Pepper

Put the meat in a marinating dish. Combine the other ingredients and pour over the meat. Marinate 24 hours in the refrigerator, turning or basting the roast occasionally. Before roasting, bring meat to room temperature. When ready to cook, place the roast on a rack over a pan and put in a 325° smoke oven. Use the marinade liberally to baste the meat. Add water if necessary to keep pan from becoming dry. Place a few hardwood chips on coals of smoke oven each time roast is basted. Juices left in the pan can be used as a sauce after the fat is skimmed off. The roast will cook to medium rare in about 2½ hours, or a meat thermometer can be used to determine desired doneness. *Serves 6 to 8.*

NIPPY KABABS

2 pounds uncooked lamb
1 large onion
½ cup salad oil
1 bay leaf
1 teaspoon thyme

4 crushed peppercorns
6 dashes Tabasco
½ cup dry red wine
Vegetables, chef's choice

Cut the lamb into 1-inch squares and place in a marinade dish. Cut the onion into chunks and make a pulp of it in a blender, a food grinder or with a mortar and pestle. Add the oil, bay leaf, thyme, peppercorns, Tabasco sauce and wine. Pour over the meat and let it stand 24 hours in a refrigerator. When ready to cook, slide the meat onto skewers, alternating with the chef's choice of vegetables. The meat should be the first and the last pieces on the skewer. Cook about 20 minutes in 350° smoke oven, using moderate smoke. The long marinating with the peppercorns and the Tabasco adds a' fiery nip but does not destroy the taste of the lamb. *Serves 4.*

FLAMING LAMB

1 5-pound leg of lamb
3 tablespoons lemon juice
2 cloves garlic, crushed or
    chopped
½ teaspoon ground ginger
½ teaspoon dry mustard

½ teaspoon curry powder
Salt
Pepper
4 tablespoons jelly
½ cup dry red wine
¼ cup brandy

Rub the meat with the lemon juice and garlic. Combine the ginger, mustard, curry, salt and pepper and sprinkle over the meat. Leave it on a platter in the refrigerator for 24 hours. Before cooking, bring meat to room temperature. When ready to cook, place meat on a rack over a pan and put into smoke oven. Cook meat about 30 minutes per pound at 325° for medium rare, using hardwood chips on coals to produce smoke. While the roast is cooking, use heat to mix the jelly and wine together. About ½ hour before the lamb is done, remove it from the oven and brush the jelly-wine mixture over it 4 or 5 times to glaze the lamb. When the lamb is done, place it on a warm platter, pour warmed brandy over it and set aflame at the table before carving. *Serves 6 to 8.*

LAMB FROM A CROCK

5 cloves garlic, crushed
¼ cup salt
1 5-pound lamb roast
3 large onions, sliced

3 lemons, sliced
1 tablespoon paprika
Pepper

Crush garlic into the salt and rub it over the lamb. Place a layer of sliced onions in the bottom of a crock or large earthenware bowl. Put in the meat and pile slices of onion and lemon on the sides and top. Cover and let stand in a cool place at least 24 hours. Before cooking, scrape off the lemon and onion slices and sprinkle the meat with paprika and pepper to taste. Put the roast on a rack over a pan and place in a 325° smoke oven. Throw a handful of hardwood chips on coals at the start of the roasting period and add a few more at 30-minute intervals. Cook roast until done, about 30 minutes to the pound for medium rare. Lamb chops also can be crocked and cooked this way. *Serves 6 to 8.*

THREE-DAY LAMB

1 5-pound leg of lamb   Pepper
Salt

MARINADE

1 cup sherry   ¼ pound sautéed mushrooms
1 cup tomato sauce   1 2-ounce jar pimientos,
1 10½-ounce can consommé   chopped
2 tablespoons tarragon wine   1 lemon, sliced
   vinegar   2 bay leaves
2 onions, chopped   1 teaspoon thyme
1 green pepper, chopped

Sprinkle the lamb with salt and pepper. Combine marinade ingredients in a roasting pan. Marinate the lamb in the mixture in the refrigerator for 3 days, turning occasionally. Before roasting, bring meat to room temperature. When ready to roast, put the meat on a rack over a pan and place in a 325° smoke oven. Cook about 30 minutes per pound, using moderate smoke and basting with marinade every 30 minutes. Spoon the grease off the marinade. Strain the marinade and serve it as a sauce with the meat. *Serves 6 to 8.*

PACIFIC LAMB

2 pounds lamb   ¼ teaspoon salt
2 medium onions, chopped   ¼ teaspoon red pepper
2 cloves garlic, chopped   ¼ cup soy sauce
¼ cup smooth peanut butter   3 tablespoons lemon juice
2 tablespoons brown sugar

Cut the lamb into 1-inch squares. Combine the other ingredients in a blender, or mix well in a bowl after chopping the onion and garlic. Put in the lamb and stir until all pieces are coated with the thick marinade. Leave in refrigerator 24 hours. Skewer the lamb and cook in a 325° smoke oven about 20 minutes. The coating will not be quite dry and the meat will be pinkish on the inside but done. If you aren't accustomed to East Asian food, you may be dubious of the peanut butter, but it turns out to be the ingredient that makes this a delectable treat. *Serves 4.*

LAMB CHOPS OCHOCO

8 lamb chops
4 small carrots, chopped
4 small celery stalks, chopped
1 green pepper, chopped
  Salt
  Pepper

1 medium onion, chopped
2 tablespoons butter
3 tablespoons flour
½ cup orange juice
½ cup dry red wine
1 teaspoon rosemary

This recipe combines smoke-oven and casserole cooking. Place the chops (preferably thick ones) in a 150° smoke oven. Put in plenty of hardwood chips or sawdust and smoke for 20 minutes. Remove the chops to a casserole, in which the chopped carrots, celery and green pepper and salt and pepper have been placed. Sauté the onion in the butter. When it is translucent, add the flour, orange juice, wine and rosemary. Let simmer a few minutes, then pour over chops. Put on casserole cover. The cooking can be finished in smoke oven or stove oven, at 300°. Start testing for doneness after an hour. *Serves 4.*

MEXICAN LAMB

4 lamb shanks
  Salt
  Pepper
2 cloves garlic
2 cups chicken broth
1½ cups uncooked rice

1 onion, chopped
½ green pepper, chopped
3 celery stalks, chopped
2 tablespoons chili powder
¼ teaspoon ground cloves
1 cup water

Sprinkle lamb shanks with salt and pepper. Place meat, garlic cloves and broth in a baking dish or pan and put on grill of smoke oven over direct heat. Simmer until tender—plan on about 1½ hours at 325° or longer if temperature is lower. Use moderate to heavy smoke. Turn shanks several times during cooking period, basting with broth and juices each time. More broth or water may have to be added to keep meat from drying out. When meat is tender, remove pan from smoke oven, remove garlic cloves, skim off fat drippings, add other ingredients to the meat in the pan and return to smoke oven until rice has cooked. *Serves 4.*

KUFTE

2 pounds uncooked ground
   lamb
1 cup bread crumbs
2 medium onions, grated
2 egg yolks
¼ cup milk

½ teaspoon allspice
½ teaspoon cayenne
½ teaspoon cumin
Salt
Pepper

Mix all the ingredients together, shape into patties about ¾ inch thick and place over a 300° fire in the smoke oven. This adaptation from an old Armenian recipe should be ready in about 15 minutes. *Serves 5 or 6.*

'RIBS 'N' 'KRAUT

6 pounds pork spareribs
2 tablespoons sage
1 cup flour
1 teaspoon garlic salt
1 teaspoon pepper
1 teaspoon savory salt
½ cup salad oil

½ cup wine vinegar
½ cup dry wine
1 quart sauerkraut
1 apple, peeled and grated
½ teaspoon caraway seeds
   (optional)

If you prefer to cook spareribs entirely on the grill, try this: Rub the ribs with a mixture of the sage and flour. Place on the grill of the smoke oven with the heat at 250° to 275°.

Combine the other ingredients to make a basting sauce. Turn the ribs occasionally so that all parts can be basted. The time of cooking will depend on the thickness of the ribs, the amount of bone and the heat, but plan on about 1½ hours.

Ribs are wondeful with sauerkraut. For variety, remove the ribs from the grill about 20 minutes before they are to be served. Put them in a baking dish atop sauerkraut. Sprinkle with apple and caraway seed. Put this back in the smoke oven. The ribs will finish cooking while the sauerkraut warms. In the last 5 minutes spoon some of the sauerkraut over the ribs for an exchange of flavors.

A dish like this is even better-tasting if prepared ahead of time. Do it if you can resist temptation. Then serve hot when ready. *Serves 6.*

TENDER SPARERIBS

6 pounds lean spareribs

SAUCE

3 tablespoons salad oil	⅛ teaspoon orégano
6 large tomatoes	⅛ teaspoon rosemary
2 large onions, chopped	Salt
1 green pepper, chopped	Pepper
1 celery stalk, chopped	¼ cup wine vinegar
⅛ teaspoon sage	½ cup water
⅛ teaspoon thyme	

Place spareribs in a 250° smoke oven and smoke-cook moderately while preparing this sauce:

Sauté the onions in the oil until translucent. Peel and quarter the tomatoes and combine with the onions, green pepper, celery, herbs, salt and pepper. Simmer until tomatoes are soft. Add wine vinegar and water.

When the spareribs turn light brown, put them in a roasting pan and pour the sauce over them. Put the pan in the smoke oven and let the ribs simmer until done, about an hour. If the oven heat subsides, take off the top to revive the coals. Replace the top when the coals glow again. Be careful that the sauce does not get too thick. If it does, add more water, wine or both.

The spareribs can be cooked entirely over the grill and the sauce served separately at the table, but we have found they are juicier and more tender when simmered in the pan. *Serves 6.*

APPLE PORK

4 pork chops	Salt
Apple juice	Pepper

Place the pork chops in a shallow dish suitable for marinating. Pour commercial apple juice over chops, enough to completely cover them. Marinate 1 hour, then place in a 300° smoke oven. Salt and pepper to taste. Place them on a part of the grill that's not over the coals, so the pork drippings won't get onto the coals and be converted to smoke. Use pure wood smoke only. What kind of wood? Apple wood, of course. *Serves 2.*

SWEET AND SOUR SPARERIBS

3 pounds spareribs
½ teaspoon Tabasco
¼ cup soy sauce
¼ cup vinegar
½ cup dry white wine
½ cup pineapple juice

3 tablespoons honey
1 tablespoon prepared
  mustard
1 teaspoon salt
½ teaspoon pepper
1½ cups pineapple chunks

Put the spareribs in a smoke oven with plenty of hardwood sawdust or wood chips. The temperature should be low—about 125°—
for the object is not to cook the spareribs at this time, but to
impart a smoky taste. After 20 minutes of heavy smoking, remove
the spareribs to a roasting pan and add the other ingredients, except the pineapple. Add coals to heat the oven to 300°. Simmer
the ribs, basting frequently, until they are tender, about 1 to 1½
hours. Add the pineapple near the end of the cooking period.
Serves 3.

PEIPING ROAST

1 5-pound pork roast
3 cloves garlic, slivered
1 teaspoon dry mustard
  Salt
  Pepper

1 cup tarragon wine vinegar
¼ cup salad oil
2 cups strong coffee
1 teaspoon dry mustard

Cut small slits in the roast and insert the garlic in the slits. Rub
roast with salt, pepper and mustard. Place the meat in a marinade
dish and pour the vinegar and oil over it, making sure the vinegar
gets into the slits. Marinate the roast in the refrigerator 2 days,
basting and turning it occasionally. Place on a rack over a pan and
cook in a 300° smoke oven until thermometer, placed in the thick
part of the meat, gets to 180°. Baste frequently with the coffee.
Add more coffee if it evaporates. *Serves 6 to 8.*

LEG OF PORK WITH FENNEL

1 5-pound leg of pork
1 bunch green fennel, chopped
3 cloves garlic, slivered
  Salt

  Pepper
1 teaspoon dry mustard
2 cups dry white wine

Cut slits in pork and fill with a mixture of fennel and garlic. Rub roast with salt, pepper and mustard. Put in a 325° smoke oven on a rack over a pan. Baste occasionally with the wine or with wine and water. Cook until thermometer inserted in the thick part of the meat gets to 180°. Pork is safe when heated above 137°, but it is best to have some leeway in case the thermometer is not accurate. *Serves 6 to 8.*

RED AND WHITE

4 large pork chops	1 teaspoon chopped parsley
Salt	⅛ teaspoon basil
Pepper	⅛ teaspoon thyme
1 medium onion, chopped	1 cup dry red wine

This is another recipe combining smoke-oven and casserole techniques. Place the chops in the smoke oven at 150°, season with salt and pepper to taste, and subject them to heavy smoke for 10 minutes. Remove the chops. Add briquets to smoke oven—briquets already started outside the smoker—until the temperature goes to 350°. Put the chops in a casserole or baking pan and add onion and other ingredients. Put casserole in oven. A half hour's cooking will make the chops succulent. *Serves 2.*

LAMB ARMEN

2 pounds lamb	Salt
2 teaspoons cumin	Pepper
½ teaspoon allspice	1 8-ounce can tomato sauce
6 dashes Tabasco	3 medium onions, chopped

Cut the lamb into 1-inch cubes. Mix the herbs and spices with the tomato paste. Combine with onions. Put meat cubes in a bowl with the other ingredients and mix until the meat is thoroughly coated with the mixture. Leave in refrigerator 24 hours. When ready to cook, skewer the lamb and place in a 325° smoke oven. Use moderate smoke for the 20 minutes it will take the lamb to cook. The cumin is a distinctive touch in this recipe. If you don't like a peppery taste, you may want to cut the amount of Tabasco sauce. Personally we prefer at least this much Tabasco and a generous measure of cayenne for this dish. *Serves 4.*

TOMATO RIBS

1 tablespoon chili powder
1 tablespoon celery seed
3 tablespoons brown sugar
1 teaspoon paprika
Salt

Pepper
4 pounds spareribs
1 10½-ounce can tomato soup
1 cup dry red wine

Combine chili powder, celery seed, brown sugar, paprika, salt and pepper. Rub this over the spareribs. Place the ribs in a 150° smoke oven and subject to heavy smoke for 15 minutes. Remove the ribs to a roasting pan and pour in the undiluted soup and the wine. Add to smoke oven briquets which have already been started outside the smoker, to bring the temperature to 350°. Put casserole in oven and cook until done, about 1½ hours. Baste occasionally. Add water to baste if necessary to keep the consistency correct. *Serves 4.*

CHINESE PORK STRIPS

1½ pounds lean pork
2 cloves garlic, halved
1 tablespoon salt
1 teaspoon paprika
1 tablespoon catsup

5 tablespoons honey
½ cup white wine
½ teaspoon monosodium
glutamate

Cut the pork into thin strips about 1 inch wide, several inches long and ¼ to ⅛ inch thick. Let these marinate 24 hours in the remainder of the ingredients, mixed in a glass or porcelain bowl and placed in the refrigerator. When ready to cook, build a low fire. The temperature should be about 200°. Place the meat strips on a rack and put the rack in the smoker so it cooks by indirect heat (place to the side, not directly above fire). Use a moderate amount of hardwood sawdust or chips. The slow heat will keep the strips from shrinking too much. They will glisten with marinade and fat when they begin to cook, will turn red from the smoke and will be done in about 30 to 40 minutes. If the heat is higher, watch the meat closely. It will be done sooner and there is a danger of charring. The cooked meat is delicious as an appetizer (served with hot mustard and sesame seeds), with Chinese vegetables or chow mein. *Serves 4.*

SWEET AND SOUR PORK WITH GRAPES

1½ pounds pork
2 tablespoons butter
2 tablespoons cornstarch
5 tablespoons brown sugar
5 tablespoons vinegar

5 tablespoons soy sauce
½ cup water
1 carrot, chopped
1 green pepper, chopped
1 can white grapes

Cut the meat into 1-inch cubes, string on skewers and cook over the coals in 325° smoke oven until done, about 25 minutes. They may have to be turned to keep them from browning too much on one side.

In a skillet combine the butter, cornstarch, brown sugar, vinegar, soy sauce and water. Heat and stir until the mixture clears. Add the carrot, pepper and grapes and cook until the carrot is barely tender. Transfer the meat to the skillet and heat 2 or 3 minutes, then serve. *Serves 3.*

9

Fish

Not everyone likes raw fish. The Scandinavians and the Japanese sometimes eat it, athough they brine it first. Your first bite of raw fish will demonstrate why it never caught on. No only is the taste different—raw salmon does not taste like cooked salmon—but it has a surprising resilience. In fact, it is as rubbery as an old galosh.

Yet it takes very little to convert that tough flesh to the most tender meat known. Heat is one way. Soaking in vinegar or citrus juice is another. South Sea Islanders soak fish in papaya juice until it loses its translucence, becomes tender and to all appearances has been cooked. Yet little use has been made in this country of the varied ways to prepare fish.

Millions of people, due to religion or habit, eat fish once a week and once a week only. They fry it. Some fish can be tastefully fried, but monotony will set in. Even peacocks' tongues get monotonous if they are prepared and served the same way every week.

There is a probability that at least some of this will change. As it stands now, only about one sixth of the world is fed adequately. Meanwhile the population increases. The demand for food increases too, especially the demand for animal protein. The amount of protein that can be produced on land is limited. But the riches of the sea are relatively untouched. Pound for pound, fish has about as much protein as the flesh of land animals. Yet there are so many more fish. An estimated 90 percent of the world's animal protein is in the ocean. It seems inevitable that fish will become increasingly important to man's diet.

As fish appears at the table more often, it will be important to have alternatives to the frying pan, and here the smoke cooker can help. If you insist, you can even fry fish in a smoker, but you can also smoke, bake, poach, steam or use a combination of some of these methods. And in any one of them you can catch the added flavor of smoke.

Fish of course have a long association with the smokehouse. For centuries they have been cold-smoked for preservation. This can still be done, using temperatures of 90° or less. See Chapter 16 for that kind of smoking.

Hot-smoking, which prepares fish for immediate serving, is the topic here.

The first thing to learn about hot-smoking is that the fire does not have to be very hot. Or if it is, the cooking period should be short. Fish requires only a short cooking period to make it tender, and if anyone manages to make fish tough, or serves it dry and tasteless, it was achieved by overcooking.

The second point with fish is to get it fresh—the fresher the better. Fish spoils rapidly. A fish that lies in a boat all day before being cooked is far less tasty than one cooked within an hour of the time it was caught. If the fish is being sold as fresh, poke it. If the flesh springs back, it is fresh. If a dent remains, it is stale.

Commercial fishermen have attempted to overcome the rapid deterioration of fish by freezing it. Most of the fish marketed these days is frozen.

Many people thaw frozen fish to room temperature before cooking it, but this isn't necessary. However, if you put frozen fish directly into the smoke oven, you'll have to allow longer cooking time than is given in the directions here, which assume the fish to be at room temperature.

If you have to clean the fish, cover your fingers with salt; the fish is easier to handle that way. Unless the fish is in brine, don't leave it in water. It becomes flabby and loses flavor.

When it's time to cook the fish, put it on oiled foil or a special grill. Use foil whenever possible. It keeps the fish from tainting your grill and keeps drippings from leaving an odor in the smoker. The smoke gets at only one side of the fish, but this is enough. Smoke penetrates fish easily. If you don't use foil, go to the trouble of getting a special grill and use that for fish so that your regular meat grill won't have a fish flavor. Grease the grill first, so that the fish won't stick to it. If you like to see grill marks on the fish, put the grill in the oven before the fish so that it will be hot and will brand the flesh. If the fish is fat, put the grill over a pan or over foil to catch the drippings.

If you are sprinkling dressings or a baste on the fish, crimp up the edges of the foil to keep the liquid from dripping onto the coals.

If you have a large piece of fish on the foil, it may be difficult to remove from the smoke oven. Sometimes the foil will break. The whole can be lifted easily, however, if a cookie sheet is used under the foil.

If you have a large fish, and want to make sure it's done in the middle, stick a meat thermometer into the fleshiest part. It will be edible when the thermometer reaches 140°. Do not leave the fish in the smoke oven any longer. At 150° the juices and flavor escape.

If it is a smaller piece of fish, such as a fillet, stick a toothpick or the tines of a fork into the thickest part of the flesh. The fish will be done when it is no longer translucent and when the toothpick or fork easily penetrates the flesh, but the fish is just short of flaking.

With the smoke oven placed outside the house there will be no cooking odor inside the house, of course. One acquaintance of ours objects to this. She likes the smell of food cooking. We have advised her to leave her door open. Maybe the odor will drift in.

WHOLE FISH

If your smoker is large enough any fish can be cooked whole. It needs to be cleaned, of course, and even if too large for the smoker, it can be cut in half or even smaller pieces. Some fish, such as salmon or bonita, can be split open and placed skin side down on a rack. The time of cooking varies with the size of the fish and the heat in the smoker. Use less heat than for beef—250° is about right—and use plenty of hardwood chips or sawdust. Test the fish from time to time with a fork. When it flakes easily it is done.

SMOKED SALMON

This recipe can be used for any large fish. Split a small salmon (6 to 8 pounds) or a large piece almost all the way through so it will lay flat, skin side down. Rub the flesh side with two parts of salt to one of sugar and let stand overnight in the refrigerator. Scrape off the salt mix and sprinkle with coarsely ground pepper. Smoke-cook at 250° or less until the fish flakes. If you are in a hurry, salmon fillets or steaks (and other fish) can be smoke-cooked without any preparation other than cleaning. Do this once and you probably will never fry fish again.

FISH IN BEER SAUCE

1½ to 2 pounds smoked fish

SAUCE

1 pint beer	1 bay leaf
1 large onion, chopped	Salt
½ teaspoon caraway seeds	Pepper
3 tablespoons chopped	4 tablespoons flour
parsley	4 tablespoons butter

The smoked fish can be fresh from a hot smoke oven, or it can be from the refrigerator, freezer or can. In any case, it must have been cooked.

Make this sauce for it: Pour beer into a saucepan. Add onion, caraway seeds, parsley, bay leaf and a pinch each of salt and pepper. Simmer 15 minutes. The sauce may be strained at this point if a smooth texture is desired. We prefer to remove just the bay leaf, leaving the other ingredients in the sauce. Put ½ cup of the liquid aside to cool. The remainder goes into the top of a double boiler or chafing dish—either must be over water and heat. Blend flour in the ½ cup of cooled liquid. When smooth, pour into the rest of the mixture, stirring constantly. Adjust seasoning and the salt and pepper. Add butter. Stir over heat until sauce thickens. Flake the fish and add to the sauce. Serve when all ingredients are hot. May be served on rice or toast or just as is. *Serves 4.*

HALIBUT NEWPORT

¼ cup butter   Worcestershire
4 halibut steaks   Salt
  Juice of 1 lemon   Pepper

SAUCE

¼ pound cheddar cheese   1 teaspoon lemon juice
2 tablespoons butter   Salt
1 cup beer   Pepper
½ cup shrimp   2 eggs, beaten
1 teaspoon Worcestershire

Melt butter in foil which has been crimped at the edges to keep juices from dripping into the smoke oven and leaving a fishy odor. Place the halibut steaks on the melted butter, then turn them over, making sure fish is coated with butter on both sides. Squeeze lemon juice on steaks. Place foil with fish on an old pie pan or cookie sheet to stabilize it in smoke oven, and cook at 300°, using moderate smoke. After fish has been in the smoker a few minutes, lift the cover and sprinkle the Worcestershire sauce, salt and pepper on the fish steaks. Test the fish with a fork in about 15 minutes. When the fork slides in easily and the flesh flakes, it is done.

To make the sauce, grate the cheese and put it into a saucepan with the butter and beer. Heat gently while stirring. Add shrimp and continue stirring for 2 minutes. Add Worcestershire sauce, lemon juice, salt and pepper. Heat to the boiling point. Remove from stove and stir in beaten eggs until sauce is thick. Serve on the halibut steaks. *Serves 4.*

STUFFED MACKEREL

3 mackerel, about 1 pound each after boning and cleaning

STUFFING

3 tablespoons butter   ¼ cup grated Romano cheese
1 large onion, chopped   Salt
¼ cup chopped mushrooms   Pepper
1 tablespoon chopped parsley   1 lemon, wedged
1 cup bread crumbs

Clean and bone the fish. In a frying pan, melt the butter and sauté the onions, mushrooms and parsley until tender. Mix the bread crumbs, cheese, salt and pepper, and add to the frying pan mixture. Mix well; then stuff the fish cavities with it. Skewer the edges together and place fish on grill of 250° smoke oven. Cook with moderate smoke about 20 to 30 minutes. Serve with lemon wedges. *Serves 6.*

SKEWERED OYSTERS

1 dozen oysters	1 teaspoon chopped parsley
¼ pound salt pork	Salt
½ cup butter	Pepper
Juice of 1 lemon	

Great as an appetizer, this can also be the entrée. Slip the oysters onto a skewer, alternating with slices or cubes of salt pork. Each piece should be tight against the other. Place on a rack in the smoke oven and leave it from 10 to 15 minutes at 250°. Meanwhile, make a sauce of the melted butter, the lemon juice, the chopped parsley, salt and pepper. Remove skewers from the smoker and discard the salt pork. Its juices will have seeped into the oysters and flavored them. Spoon sauce over oysters or put the sauce in the center of the table and let each person dip oysters into it.

OYSTERS YAQUINA

1 pint oysters	1 tablespoon chopped parsley
½ cup white wine	4 dashes Tabasco
4 tablespoons chopped green pepper	1 cup cocktail sauce
3 tablespoons chopped pimiento	Salt
	Pepper

Smoke the oysters in a 250° oven for 10 to 15 minutes. Meanwhile, put the wine and green pepper in a saucepan and simmer 5 minutes. Add pimiento, parsley, Tabasco sauce, cocktail sauce and salt and pepper to taste. Combine the smoked oysters and the sauce on toast. *Serves 3 to 4.*

DILLET FILLETS

2 pounds fish fillets   Melted butter to coat fish
  Dill pickle juice

When the last dill pickle in the jar has been used, do not throw
away the juice. Instead, decide to have fish that night. Get
flounder, sole or whatever fillets you prefer, for this recipe works
well with all fish. Marinate the fillets an hour in pickle juice. Pat dry
with a paper towel. Brush both sides of the fillets with melted
butter. Place fish on a rack over a broiling pan, place on smoke
oven grill and cook in 250° oven for 10 to 20 minutes, depending
on the thickness of the fillet, or until fish will flake easily when
tested with a fork. At the first taste, you will know you will never
again discard dill pickle juice. *Serves 4.*

PICKLED FISH ROMAN STYLE

10 pounds firm-fleshed fish   1 quart water
 ¼ cup salt

PICKLING MIX

3 ounces olive oil   2 teaspoons cumin
1 onion, sliced   2 teaspoons marjoram
2 cloves garlic, minced   3 bay leaves
1 tablespoon black pepper   1 quart distilled vinegar
1 tablespoon red pepper

The pickling of fish was popular among the Romans. This recipe
is an adaptation of one that comes down to us from them. This
makes an excellent main course for dinner or lunch on a hot
summer day. It can also be used for appetizers or snacks.

Cut the fish into small portions and place in a brine made by
dissolving the salt in the water. Let the fish soak 30 minutes, then
remove, wipe dry and place in a 250° smoke oven. Use moderate
smoke. While the fish is being smoke-cooked, pour the olive oil
into a frying pan and add the onions and garlic. Sauté until
golden, then add the remaining ingredients. Simmer 20 minutes,
then cool. When fish is done, remove it from the smoker to
cool. Put the cooled fish in a large ceramic bowl or crock and

pour pickling mix over it. Make sure all pieces are covered. Keep fish covered in refrigerator. It will be ready to eat in 24 hours, but will be even better if you wait a day or two longer. It will keep for several weeks under refrigeration. *Serves 10 to 20.*

FILLET OF SOLE

Melted butter to coat fish   Salt
4 sole fillets   Pepper
Juice of ½ lemon   1 small onion, sliced

Melt butter in foil which has been crimped at the edges to confine juices. Place fish on melted butter, then turn over, making sure fish is coated with butter on both sides. Squeeze lemon juice on the fillets; then sprinkle with salt and pepper. Sprinkle onion slices over fish and uncovered foil. Fish absorbs smoke readily, so only a medium smoke is needed. Place foil on smoke oven grill, close cover and cook 10 to 20 minutes at 250° to 275°, or until fish flakes easily when tested with a fork. *Serves 2.*

SMOKED FISH ITALIANO

1½ pounds fish   ½ cup halved mushrooms,
4 tablespoons butter   fresh or canned
4 tablespoons flour   2 tablespoons chopped
1½ cups milk   pimiento
½ cup grated Parmesan   ½ cup dry white wine
   cheese   Salt
                                    Pepper

The fish may be leftover smoked fish, but if not, lightly salt and pepper the fresh fish, place it in a 250° smoke oven and cook until done. Time depends on the texture and thickness of the fish. If done, it will flake when fork-tested.

While fish is cooking, melt the butter, and blend in flour in a double boiler or chafing dish, either of which must be over gently simmering water. Add the milk. When the sauce thickens, add Parmesan cheese, the mushrooms, pimiento, wine, fish and salt and pepper to taste. Heat ingredients thoroughly—10 to 15 minutes. Serve on buttered toast or rice, in patty shells or just as is. *Serves 4.*

FAVORITE FISH FILLETS

Italian dressing to coat fillets
2 pounds fish fillets (cook's
   choice)

Juice of 1 lemon
Salt
Pepper

This is one of the best ways devised by man to cook fish; it's also the simplest and quickest. Build the smoke oven fire to 250° to 275°. Take a piece of aluminum foil large enough to hold the fish, and crimp the edges to confine the juices. Pour Italian dressing, which can be bought in a bottle at the grocery store, onto the foil. Place the fillets in the Italian dressing, then turn them over, making sure fish is generously coated with dressing. Sprinkle lemon juice on each fillet, then salt and pepper to taste. Use moderate smoke. Place fillets on foil on smoke oven grill and cover. The fish will take on the smoke flavor, along with that of the zesty Italian dressing and tart lemon juice. The fillets will be done in about 10 to 15 minutes, depending on the thickness of the fish, or when they flake easily when fork-tested. *Serves 4.*

SCALLOPS

½ cup salad oil
¼ cup lemon juice
   Salt

Pepper
2 pounds scallops
½ pound sliced bacon

Combine oil, lemon juice, salt and pepper and pour over scallops, which are in a bowl. Marinate 1 hour. Prepare bacon by cutting each piece in half lengthwise, then crosswise. Remove scallops from the marinade and wrap a piece of bacon around each one, securing with a toothpick or skewer. Place the wrapped scallops on a rack and put the rack on the grill of a 300° smoke oven over direct heat. Cook about 15 minutes, until bacon is done. *Serves 4.*

CARP

1 4-pound carp
   Salt

Pepper
1 tablespoon paprika

SAUCE

2 tablespoons butter

1 tablespoon chopped onion

½ teaspoon salt
2 tablespoons flour
1 cup milk
2 hard-boiled eggs, chopped

⅛ teaspoon black pepper
Parsley
1 egg, well beaten

Carp has never found popularity in the United States, probably because Americans prefer to fry fish. They like to drop a fish into a skillet, usually with too much hot cooking oil, and take it out a few minutes later, ready to serve with no fuss. Carp does not do well under those conditions. Carp needs a complementary sauce.

Fillet the carp and cut each fillet in half, so that there will be 4 pieces of fish. Sprinkle with salt, pepper and paprika and cook in a 250° smoke oven until done. Use moderate smoke.

To prepare the sauce, melt the butter in a frying pan. Add onion and sauté until golden. Blend in the flour, making sure the mixture does not brown. Add the milk, salt and pepper and stir over low heat until it bubbles and thickens. Adjust milk if necessary. Add hard-boiled eggs and parsley, and heat until mixture returns to the bubbling point. Remove from heat and stir in beaten egg. Do not return it to the heat or the mixture will separate. Pour sauce over the smoke-cooked fish. *Serves 4.*

PERCH FILLETS

2 pounds perch fillets   1 teaspoon paprika

MARINADE

½ cup salad oil
¼ cup lemon juice
¼ cup chopped onion
2 tablespoons catsup
1 tablespoon salt

2 teaspoons sugar
2 tablespoons Worcestershire
2 bay leaves, crushed
2 cloves garlic, chopped
½ teaspoon pepper

Thaw the fish if it has been frozen, and place in the bottom of a shallow dish suitable for marinating. The fish should be in a single layer. Combine marinade ingredients and pour over the fillets. Let marinade 1 hour, turning the fish to make sure it is exposed well to the marinade sauce. Place the fish in the smoker on a rack over a broiling pan, sprinkle with paprika, close the cover and cook in moderate smoke at 250° to 275° until done. *Serves 4.*

STUFFED FISH

1 3-pound cleaned white-fleshed fish

STUFFING

¼ cup butter
¼ cup chopped onion
½ cup chopped celery

2 tablespoons minced parsley
½ teaspoon salt
2 cups shredded bread

SAUCE

¼ cup chopped onion
¼ cup chopped celery
½ teaspoon salt
½ teaspoon sugar
1 cup water

1½ tablespoons cornstarch
1 teaspoon lemon juice
½ cup halved and seeded
    green grapes

Make the stuffing by melting the butter in a small frying pan and adding the onion, celery, parsely and salt. Sauté until tender. Add the bread and brown it slightly. Stuff the fish and close the opening with skewers. Place on oiled foil with edges crimped to confine the juices. Smoke-cook until done—about 1 hour at 250° to 300°. Remove to serving platter, remove skin, and serve with sauce.

Sauce: Simmer the onion, celery, salt and sugar in water until the vegetables are cooked, then add the cornstarch to thicken it. Add the lemon juice and halved grapes, heating just long enough to warm them adequately. *Serves 4.*

DELECTABLE SHRIMP

2 pounds large shrimp
½ cup salad oil
½ cup chopped onion
¼ cup chopped parsley
2 tablespoons lemon juice

2 cloves garlic, chopped
1 teaspoon dried basil
1 teaspoon dry mustard
Salt
Pepper

Peel and devein the raw shrimp. Put them in a bowl. Combine the other ingredients and pour over the shrimp, adding more oil if it seems necessary. Let stand 1 hour or more, mixing occasionally. Remove from marinade and place on a fine-meshed rack in smoker. Cook over direct heat in moderate smoke at 300° to 325° for 25 minutes or until tender. It is necessary to test one to determine whether it is tender. *Serves 3.*

SAND ISLAND FISH

8 small trout, bass, mackerel or other small fish

BRINE

1 quart water
1½ cups salt
¾ cup sugar

1 teaspoon pepper
3 bay leaves, crushed

This recipe works well with all fish. If it is bass, carp, mackerel or any fish that needs skinning, dip it in hot water and skin before placing in the brine. Trout does not need to be skinned.

Make a brine. Soak the fish in the brine about 5 hours. Larger fish can be done this way, but they should be soaked longer. When the fish are removed from the brine, let the moisture drip from them, then finish drying them by blotting with paper towels. Place the fish in the smoke oven with a very low fire. Keep the temperature under 100° for the first hour, using damp sawdust or small hardwood chips to produce smoke. After the first hour, start some coals outside the smoker, enough so that when they are placed inside the smoker they will increase the temperature. Cook the fish until done. This will depend on the size of the fish and the temperature of the oven. Poke a toothpick or fork tines in the thick part of the flesh. If it flakes easily it is done. Small trout are usually done in 20 to 30 minutes at 250°. *Serves 4.*

SNAPPER WITH CHEESE AND MUSHROOMS

½ teaspoon salt
½ cup milk
4 red snapper fillets, 6 to 8
    ounces each

1 cup bread crumbs
¼ pound cheddar cheese,
    grated
¼ pound mushrooms, chopped

Any white-fleshed fish will do—we like red snapper prepared this way. Dissolve the salt in the milk and dip fillets in it. Roll the fish in the bread crumbs and place on oiled foil, with edges crimped to confine juices. Place on smoke oven grill away from the coals. Sprinkle the cheese and mushrooms on fish. Have the smoke oven at 250° to 275°. Use sawdust or wood chips to produce smoke. Cook fish 10 to 20 minutes, depending on the thickness of the fillet, or until fish flakes easily when tested with a fork. Garnish with chopped parsley or chives when serving. *Serves 4.*

MRS. KEEFAUVER'S CLAMS

1 dozen small steamer clams,   13 pieces salt pork, each about
    such as butter, cockles or   ½ inch thick
    littlenecks

SAUCE

¼ cup melted butter   Juice of ½ lemon
1 teaspoon chopped parsley   Pepper

On a skewer, alternate the uncooked clams and the salt pork, beginning and ending with salt pork. The pork and clams should butt together tightly. Place on rack and put into 300° smoke oven over direct heat. The heat melts the salt pork and its juices seep into the clams. Use moderate smoke. The clams need little cooking, but leave them in the smoker until they are hot throughout and the salt pork has given some of its flavor to them. Remove from oven and strip the clams and salt pork from the skewer. Discard the salt pork—it has done its job. Serve the clams with the melted butter, into which the parsley, lemon juice and a bit of pepper have been mixed. *Serves 2.*

STUFFED SALMON

1 4- to 6-pound salmon (or the   Dry white wine
    favorite fish of your region)   Salt

STUFFING

1 small onion, chopped   ¼ teaspoon thyme
1 stalk celery, chopped   ¼ teaspoon tarragon
4 mushrooms, chopped   ¼ teaspoon rosemary
3 tablespoons melted butter   Salt
2 cups bread crumbs   Pepper

SAUCE

4 tablespoons melted butter   ¼ cup dry white wine
2 teaspoons lemon juice   Dash Tabasco

The fish should be cleaned, slit wide open for stuffing, the inside sloshed with white wine, then salted.

Sauté the onion, celery and mushrooms in butter. When the

onion turns translucent, combine the mixture with the crumbs and seasonings. Add a little water or white wine if stuffing seems too dry. Place the stuffing in the fish and close with skewers. Place fish on oiled foil with crimped edges to confine the juices and cook in 250° to 275° smoke oven about 1 hour or until fish skin is loose.

Remove to platter, peel off the skin and pour the sauce over the fish. *Serves 4–6.*

SMOKED FISH LEFTOVERS
GARDEN PLATE

2 smoked fish fillets, cold	Hard-boiled eggs
Lettuce	Green onions
Celery stalks	Mayonnaise, salad dressing
Olives	or vinegar and oil
Lemon wedges	

Arrange lettuce on 2 salad plates. Put fish fillets in center and surround with celery, olives, lemon wedges, halved eggs and onions. Serve with your choice of salad dressing. *Serves 2.*

DELISH FISH

2 smoked fish fillets	2 hard-boiled eggs, diced
4 tablespoons dry white wine	4 tablespoons chopped ripe
4 tablespoons melted butter	olives
1 teaspoon chopped parsley	

Place the fish in the wine and heat thoroughly either in a chafing dish over warm water or over low heat on the stove. Put the fillets on warm plates and pour the hot butter with parsley over it. Sprinkle eggs and olives over fillets.

DILL FISH

2 smoked fish fillets	2 teaspoons dill seed
2 ounces vermouth	Hollandaise sauce

Place the fish in the vermouth with dill and heat thoroughly either in a chafing dish over warm water or on low heat of stove. Remove to warm plates and serve with Hollandaise sauce. *Serves 2.*

CAPPED FISH STEAKS

4 tablespoons melted butter
3 tablespoons lemon juice
4 onion rings, ¼ inch thick
4 slices fish, 6 to 8 ounces each
Salt

Pepper
4 mushroom caps
2 cups sliced mushrooms
4 tablespoons butter
3 tablespoons vermouth

In the Northwest we use salmon for this dish, but any firm-fleshed, tasty fish does well. Melt the butter and mix with lemon juice on a piece of foil large enough to hold the steaks, edges crimped to confine the juices. Dip onion rings in butter-lemon combination and set to one side. Place fish in butter-lemon combination, then turn over, coating fish thoroughly on both sides. Salt and pepper to taste. Place fish on foil in smoke oven away from the coals. Place an onion ring atop each steak. Smoke at 250° until done. Fork-test for doneness. While fish is cooking sauté the mushroom caps in butter and set to one side. Then sauté the mushrooms in the same butter. Add vermouth and mix thoroughly. When fish is served, arrange mushroom slices around fish steaks and place mushroom cap in the center of each onion ring. Garnish with parsley. *Serves 4.*

BACON-WRAPPED STUFFED TROUT

4 medium-sized trout

STUFFING

1 celery stalk
1 clove garlic
1 small white onion, chopped
½ green pepper
2 tablespoons salad oil

½ to 1 cup cracker crumbs
1 egg, beaten
½ teaspoon salt
¼ teaspoon pepper

8 bacon strips

Chop the celery, garlic, onion and pepper. Sauté in oil about 5 minutes. Add crumbs, egg, salt and pepper. Parboil the bacon while preparing fish for stuffing. Stuff the fish. Remove bacon from water before it cooks completely and wrap fish with bacon, securing with toothpicks or small skewers. Place fish on a rack over

direct heat in the smoke oven at a temperature of 250°. Smoke
until done. Parboiling the bacon partially cooks it so that when it
goes into the smoker it will be done at the same time as the fish.
Turn fish once to brown bacon on both sides of the fish. *Serves 4.*

SWEET AND SOUR FILLETS

2 perch, about 2 pounds each   Pepper
  Salt

SAUCE

1 cup chicken broth   1 green pepper, chunked
¼ cup brown sugar   2 tablespoons chopped
3 tablespoons white vinegar   pimiento
3 tablespoons cornstarch   1 grapefruit, cut into sections
¼ cup water   1 tablespoon soy sauce

Either sea or fresh-water perch is good in this recipe. Fillet the
fish, season it with salt and pepper and place in a 250° smoke
oven. Because the flesh of perch is delicate and falls apart easily,
it is best to place it on a grate of fine wire mesh or on buttered
foil. Cook until the flesh flakes easily when a toothpick is inserted
into the thickest portion.

While the fish is cooking, combine the broth, sugar and vinegar
and bring to a boil. Mix the cornstarch with ¼ cup water and stir
until smooth. Add it slowly to the broth, then put in the pepper,
pimiento, the peeled and cut-up grapefruit sections and the soy
sauce. Simmer a few minutes. Serve over the fish fillets. *Serves 4.*

SMOKE SCRAMBLE

4 tablespoons butter   1 teaspoon chopped parsley
4 eggs, slightly beaten   1 cup smoked fish
2 tablespoons chopped onion

Sauté the onions in a frying pan in which the butter has been
melted. Add eggs and parsley. When the eggs begin to change
from their liquid state, break pieces of the smoked fish into the
mixture. Mix gently until eggs are cooked and fish heated. Season
to taste. *Serves 2.*

FRED'S FISH FILLETS

2 pounds fish fillets   Pepper
  Salt

½ pound mushrooms, chopped   3 tablespoons butter

SAUCE

4 tablespoons butter   ½ cup dry white wine
3 tablespoons flour   1 tablespoon Worcestershire
½ teaspoon dry mustard   1 teaspoon lemon juice
1½ cups cream   Salt
2 hard-boiled eggs, chopped   Pepper

Salt and pepper the fish. Place on a rack over a broiling pan in a 250° to 275° smoke oven. Use moderate smoke. While the fish cooks, sauté mushrooms in butter.

In another pan melt the 4 tablespoons of butter and gradually stir in the flour and mustard. When smooth, add the cream. Stir until the sauce thickens. Then add the eggs, wine, Worcestershire sauce, lemon juice, mushrooms, salt and pepper. Heat thoroughly and serve over Fred's Fish Fillets. *Serves 4.*

STURGEON

1½ pounds sturgeon   ½ cup sugar
1 cup salt

Cut sturgeon into 1-inch-thick slices. Mix the salt and sugar together. Dairy-fine salt, the kind known as three-quarters-ground, is preferable to the coarse-ground or rock salt. Spread the mixture over the sturgeon and let it stand overnight in the refrigerator. Scrape off the mixture the next day and smoke the fish in a 250° oven for about 30 minutes. Use moderate smoke. When cool cut into bite-sized pieces.

SHAD

1 4-pound shad, cleaned   Salt

Shad, which once was found in the United States only on the East Coast, now thrives on both coasts. It was introduced in a California river around the turn of the century and spread northward. Its eating qualities are recognized more on the East Coast, where it has long been a favorite. Western anglers like the shad for its fighting nature, but despise its bones—there are thousands of them. Western anglers therefore concentrate on salmon and trout, whose bones are easier to manage.

There is a trick they should know for shad. It doesn't always work, but a smoke oven increases the chance that it will. There are two kinds of meat in the shad—dark meat at the bottom, and white meat above. It's the white meat we want to eat. The bones originate in the dark meat. So put the shad on the grill with the bottom down, closest to the coals. Sprinkle fish with salt. Cover the top of the fish with buttered paper for the first 5 minutes. Cook the fish at 300°. It will be done in about 40 to 45 minutes. Remove the whole fish from the grill, using pancake turners to get it off intact.

In the kitchen, lift the white meat off the bones. The white meat tends to slip away from the bones, while the dark meat holds on. If the white meat cannot be lifted from the bones, cut through the fish from top to bottom in 3-inch-wide cross-sections. This will expose the bones protruding from the bottom and they can be pulled with tweezers or pliers. *Serves 4.*

SARA'S SAVORY SWORDFISH

4 swordfish steaks, 1 inch thick   Salt
  Olive oil   Pepper

SAUCE

½ cup melted butter   ½ teaspoon chopped parsley
¼ cup dry white wine   ½ teaspoon finely chopped
¼ teaspoon paprika   green onion

Rub fish steaks with olive oil, then salt and pepper lightly. Place on rack, then place rack on grill, over coals, of 300° smoke oven. Smoke until done, about 15 to 20 minutes or until they fork-test for doneness. Have sauce warm and ready to serve over swordfish when fish is ready to be served. *Serves 4.*

SMOKE CURRY

4 tablespoons butter   4 hard-boiled eggs, diced
1 teaspoon curry powder   1 teaspoon chopped parsley
½ teaspoon pepper   2 cups cooked rice
½ cup milk   1½ pounds smoked, flaked fish

In the top of a chafing dish over water or the top of a double
boiler over water, melt the butter. Add curry and pepper. When
blended, add milk, eggs, parsley and rice. Stir lightly. Add the fish.
Mix gently. When steaming, serve on warm plates. *Serves 6.*

SMOKY BREAKFAST

2 smoked fish fillets   2 tablespoons butter
3 eggs, beaten   2 tablespoons grated cheddar
  Flour   cheese

Dip the fillets in the beaten eggs, then in flour. Sauté in butter on
each side until golden, sprinkling on the cheese after turning once.
Scramble remaining beaten egg in the same pan as the fish. Serve
fish with egg on toast. *Serves 2.*

10

Fowl

In many ways Americans have complicated their lives needlessly. In roasting turkey, for example. Some cooks insist the bird must be wrapped in foil. This is not easy. The bird is not a square, tidy package. He has odd proportions and protrusions, not meant for easy wrapping. And just as the cook surmounts the problem of turning the tail corner, she bumps into a drumstick and the foil splits. She has to start over, and this time one sheet does not overlap enough and a gap appears. In trying to move it down she splits the foil again. But eventually the bird gets covered, as she knows it must be; otherwise the turkey would cook dry.

Others get a huge brown paper bag and spend considerable time spreading shortening thoroughly over the inside of the bag. Invariably they succeed in spreading it over the upper part of themselves too. The turkey goes into the bag, which is stapled shut, and goes into the oven. And that too is the only way a turkey can be cooked until done and still be juicy.

The charcoal oven may not be the only way to arrive at a well-done but still juicy turkey, but at least you don't have to wrap or bag it. You just put it in a 300° to 325° smoke oven, and, if the bird weighs about 14 pounds, take it out 4½ hours later, well done and juicier than you might think possible. The temperature should be checked once in a while to make sure it doesn't slide too far below 300°. It doesn't matter much if the temperature dips. It just means you leave the bird in the smoke oven longer. And if you want a smoky flavor in the meat, add a few wood chips to the coals each time the temperature is checked, and baste occasionally. The charcoal oven is so easy, and the results so excellent, that we cook fowl there even when we don't want to add smoke flavor.

Smoked turkey, however, is a delicacy and we usually use wood chips when cooking this bird. For the price of a little charcoal an ordinary turkey can be converted to this smoked meat. Price smoked turkey in a delicatessen to see what a bargain the home-smoked variety is. The delicatessen turkey will have been prepared in a slightly different way from yours. It will have been cured, then smoked and cooked at the same time. Its keeping qualities will be better than yours. Chapter 16 explains the curing method. Meanwhile, the home-smoked turkey is just like any other home-cooked turkey; it keeps several days before spoiling. Cooked poultry can be frozen. Eat what you want, then strip the rest of the meat from the bones, wrap it securely and put it in the freezer. Put it in small packages—that way you can take out just what is needed. If more guests turn up than expected, take out several packages of turkey meat, which is delicious for cold snacks, sandwiches, or for a meal, when reheated.

Do not throw away the carcass. Put the bones and skin in a kettle with water and simmer for several hours. The broth can be used as is or as an excellent soup base. It too will keep for several days in the refrigerator, or it can be put in containers and frozen for later use in making soup or in cooking rice or vegetables.

Americans, despite the fact they eat less food than they did two decades ago, eat more poultry than they did then. This is because of the revolution in poultry raising. The key event was the isolation of vitamin D, the sunshine vitamin. Poultry cannot live without sunshine. Prior to the isolation of vitamin D it was necessary to let the poultry roam in the sunshine of the farm yard, where they scratched, screeched, got into fights and chases and in general developed muscles and tendons.

Once vitamin D was separated, it was possible to keep chickens inside a cage in a building constructed specifically for poultry raising. Feed and water come automatically to the cages. Some buildings are air-conditioned. Selective breeding and better feed induce rapid growth. While costs have gone down, because of the mass-production system, the chickens have become more tender, plumper and cheaper. Chicken was once the meal that could be afforded only for Sunday dinner or special occasions. It's different now. In 1945, the annual per-capita consumption of poultry in the United States was about 26 pounds. In 1965, it had risen to 40 pounds. During that 20-year period, the annual per-capita consumption of food dropped 220 pounds.

Another contribution to the increased popularity of fowl is the reduction in size of turkeys. The turkey once was a 40-pound bird, and the size alone argued against popularity. It created an unending series of turkey meals. And how many persons had an oven big enough to handle such a fowl? Now, selective breeding produces turkeys weighing from 7 to 20 pounds. They have proportionately less bone and more meat; and what's more, most of it is white meat.

It's possible to buy any size fowl you want. If a 10-pound turkey is more than you want, get what are marketed as chicken squabs, which weigh about one pound. Do not confuse them with the traditional squab, which is a young pigeon.

Broilers and fryers are older, usually 2½ to 3½ pounds in size and 13 to 18 weeks in age. Roasters run 3 to 5 pounds and are usually a little older than broilers and fryers. Still older and bigger are hens or stewing chickens. They're fine for the pot, but don't chance them in the oven, where they're too likely to be tough.

One other chicken which merits special attention is the capon, which is usually 7 to 19 months old and weighs from 3 to 5 pounds. You will find no finer bird for the smoke oven. The capon is tender and has fat in the lean tissue intead of in the pockets as in other fowl.

The capon comes to us from the days of the ancient Romans, invented because of a Roman law against pleasure. This was at the time the Roman Empire was flourishing. There were wealthy Romans and others who planned to win positions of influence and thus become wealthy. Both the rich and those who intended to be rich were lavish hosts. They had guests by the score at banquets, and the menus were staggering, not only in amount but in cost. Nothing was too exotic for the Romans—giraffe steak, flamingo tongue, shark liver, Spanish hind, German stag. The Roman Senate decided to curb this extravagance and put a ceiling on the cost of any feast. The law restricted the number of guests to three on an ordinary day and to five on special occasions. No roosters could be eaten and no hen could be especially fattened.

This outraged the populace and it wasn't long before hens found they didn't have to scratch around for food as they once did, and they all grew plump as if by accident. It still rankled, though, not to be able to eat roosters too. A doctor solved the problem. He perfected an operation that transformed the rooster to the sexless capon, at once creating a bird that was bigger, more tender and better-tasting than the hen, that grew plump of its own accord and yet did not violate the law against fattening chickens.

The Romans also enjoyed duck, but we owe our marketed duck to the Chinese, not the Romans. The Chinese specialized in breeding ducks for the table. They came up with superior strains and nearly all of our ducks descend from Peking, the original imports being made in the 1870s. A duckling at the market usually weighs from 3 to 4 pounds and is about 2 months old. Full-grown ducks weigh 5 or 6 pounds and usually are marketed at about 3 months.

Wild ducks are smaller. Often a wild duck seems too small for two persons and too large for one. Rather too much than too little, though, so plan on a wild duck for each person. There are those who insist a wild duck should be cooked rare. They use a hot oven and remove the duck as soon as the blood will not run when the duck is pierced by a fork. We have had better success, however, at slower, longer cooking. We prefer a 325° oven. If the duck is small, about 1 pound, allow 45 to 60 minutes, basting it regularly with red wine to make sure it does not get too dry. A bigger bird takes longer, but not as long per pound. A 3-pound mallard, for example, takes about 1½ to 2 hours.

The gamy taste of wild duck—and other wildfowl as well—can be reduced by soaking the bird a few hours in a brine solution: About 1 cup salt to ½ gallon water. Stuffing the bird also helps; use a stuffing of an onion and a few carrots, or quartered apples, oranges and a few raisins. Discard any stuffing when the roasting is completed.

When you buy fowl, generally allow about 1 pound of dressed weight per person—a 4-pound chicken for 4 persons, for example. If the fowl is to be stuffed, leave room for expansion of the stuffing. Sew or skewer the openings to close them. A stuffed bird will take longer to cook.

A turkey turns reddish rather than brown when cooked in a smoke oven. Some of the white meat will be quite reddish. Do not think the bird is underdone. It's usual for any meat to take on a red tone when cooked in smoke.

You can tell when the bird is done by several tests. The flesh will have retreated slightly from the skin. The thick part of the breast and thigh will feel tender. Use a folded paper towel to protect your fingers and grab the leg bone. The leg will move easily in its socket when done. A meat thermometer can be used on large birds.

BASQUE CAPON

1 large capon, cut in pieces
2 tablespoons vinegar
1 cup dry red wine
2 teaspoons sugar
1 teaspoon salt
⅛ teaspoon red pepper
1 teaspoon black pepper

2 teaspoons dry mustard
1 teaspoon chili powder
5 dashes Tabasco
1 tablespoon Worcestershire
1 tablespoon chopped onion
1 clove garlic, chopped

Put the capon pieces on a rack over a pan in a 300° smoke oven. Place pan in an indirect heat section of the oven. Use moderate smoke. Combine the other ingredients in a saucepan and simmer 5 minutes. Use this succulent sauce to baste the capon every 10 or 15 minutes. It will be done in 60 to 75 minutes; however, test for doneness. *Serves 3-4.*

SESAME CAPON

1 large capon, cut in pieces
½ cup beer
½ cup sesame seeds
½ cup prepared mustard

1 clove garlic, chopped
½ teaspoon paprika
Salt
Pepper

Roll the chicken pieces in a paste made by combining the beer, half of the sesame seeds, mustard, garlic, salt and pepper. Place the chicken pieces on buttered foil on a cookie sheet or a comparable substantial base. Then place in an indirect heat position in the smoke oven. Sprinkle the other half of the sesame seeds on the meat. Add the paprika. Cook for 60 to 75 minutes in a 300° oven, using moderately heavy smoke. *Serves 3-4.*

WALLOWA CAPON

1 4-pound capon, cut in pieces	2 green onions
Salt	1 teaspoon olive oil
Pepper	1 cup water
1 stalk celery	1 cup dry vermouth

Place the pieces of seasoned capon in a 325° smoke oven and smoke for 45 minutes in the area of indirect heat. Use heavy smoke. Meanwhile, take the neck and giblets of the capon and place in a saucepan along with the celery, onions and oil. Cover with about a cup of water and simmer until the capon comes out of the smoke oven. When it is removed, place it in a casserole and pour over it the liquid from the saucepan. Pour in the vermouth and put it back in the oven to cook another 45 minutes. *Serves 4.*

JORDAN VALLEY CAPON

1 large capon	Juice of 1 lemon
1 cup chopped ham	Juice of 1 orange
Salt	½ cup salad oil
Pepper	

SAUCE

1 8-ounce can tomato sauce	1 teaspoon chopped parsley
1 cup robust ale	Salt
12 stuffed green olives, sliced	Pepper

Put the ham into the cavity of the capon. There should be as much fat as lean in the ham. Rub the bird with salt and pepper, then place it on a rack over a pan and put it in a 325° smoke oven in an area of indirect heat. Mix the juices of the lemon and orange with the oil to use as a baste while the capon is roasting about 2 hours. Use light smoke. When the capon goes into the smoke oven, mix the sauce ingredients, heat to simmer, then remove from heat, allowing a mixing of flavors while the capon is roasting. When capon is ready to serve, skim as much fat as possible from the drippings and add remaining juices to sauce. Adjust salt and pepper and serve hot with capon. *Serves 4.*

SMOKE-BROILED CHICKEN WITH MUSTARD SAUCE

1 large broiling chicken   Pepper
Salt

SAUCE

½ cup butter   1 small can mushrooms,
4 tablespoons flour   chopped
3 tablespoons dry mustard   1 teaspoon chopped parsley
3 tablespoons vinegar   Salt
2 cups chicken broth or stock   Pepper

Have the butcher cut the chicken in half lengthwise. Wipe with a
damp cloth, then salt and pepper to taste. Place the chicken on
the smoke oven grill or on buttered foil, skin side down. Roast
chicken until done—about an hour in a 325° smoke oven, using
light smoke.

Meanwhile, prepare mustard sauce this way: Melt the butter and
mix in the flour and mustard. Add vinegar and broth. Stir sauce
over a low heat until it thickens. Add mushrooms and parsley.
Adjust seasonings and pour over the chicken. Rice goes well with
this combination. *Serves 2.*

SMOTHERED CHICKEN

1 broiling chicken, cut in pieces   ½ teaspoon salt
1 cup sour cream   ½ teaspoon pepper
2 tablespoons lemon juice   ¼ teaspoon celery salt
1 tablespoon Worcestershire   ½ teaspoon paprika
1 clove garlic, chopped fine

Put the chicken in a bowl. Mix the other ingredients and pour over
the chicken, making sure each piece is coated. Cover the bowl
and let stand in a refrigerator overnight. Place the chicken pieces
on buttered foil which is on a cookie sheet or a similar substantial
base. Then place in an indirect heat position in the smoke oven
and cook at 325° until done. Use moderate smoke. Ten minutes
before removing from smoke oven, put the sour cream marinade
(if there is any left) around chicken pieces and heat to use as a
sauce. *Serves 3.*

CHICKEN PAPRIKA

1 large capon, cut in pieces
1 cup chicken stock
1 cup dry white wine
1 clove garlic, chopped

2 tablespoons paprika
Salt
Pepper

Place the chicken pieces in a marinade of stock, wine, garlic and paprika. Leave in the mixture at least 4 hours. Remove and salt and pepper the pieces. Place on a rack over a pan in an area of indirect heat in the smoke oven at 325°. Baste with the marinade frequently while cooking in moderate smoke until done—test for doneness after 1 hour. *Serves 4.*

MEL'S CHICKEN

4 pounds of chicken pieces
1 can frozen orange
    concentrate, thawed
1 cup water
1 cup mayonnaise
1 tablespoon chili sauce

1 tablespoon chopped dill
    pickles
1 tablespoon chopped green
    pepper
¼ teaspoon sugar
Salt
Pepper

Place the chicken pieces in a marinade of all the ingredients except the salt and pepper. Leave overnight. Before cooking, remove and salt and pepper the chicken pieces and put them on a rack over a pan in a 325° smoke oven. Cook until done, using moderate smoke. The marinade liquid may be used as a baste if desired. *Serves 4.*

CHICKEN KILCHES

3 to 4 pounds chicken pieces
    (breasts, legs, thighs)

Salt
Pepper

SAUCE

1 cup orange juice
1½ cups sliced peaches
2 tablespoons brown sugar
2 tablespoons white vinegar

1 teaspoon nutmeg
1 teaspoon basil
1 clove garlic, chopped

Smoke-cook the seasoned chicken pieces for 40 minutes on a rack over a pan in a 325° smoke oven, using moderate smoke. While chicken is cooking, combine the other ingredients in a saucepan. Bring to a simmer a few minutes before adding the chicken. After the chicken is in the sauce, simmer another 20 minutes; then serve. *Serves 4.*

BRAD'S CHICKEN

1 large capon, cut in pieces
¼ teaspoon garlic powder
½ teaspoon paprika
2 tablespoons Worcestershire

4 tablespoons lemon juice
4 tablespoons salad oil
Salt
Pepper

Place the chicken pieces in a marinating dish. Combine the other ingredients, except salt and pepper, and pour over the chicken. Make sure each piece is coated. Leave overnight in refrigerator. Place chicken pieces on a rack over a pan in a 325° smoke oven in an indirect heat area. Cook using moderate smoke. *Serves 4.*

CHICKEN WITH SOUR CREAM AND CARAWAY

1½ tablespoons flour
1 cup stock or bouillon
½ cup caraway seeds
3 to 4 pounds chicken thighs
and breasts

Salt
Pepper
2 cups sour cream

Mix flour with stock or bouillon and thicken over low heat. Add caraway seeds, which have been ground fine in a mortar with pestle, or combine thickened mixture with seeds in a blender and blend until seeds are fine. Strain after either process. Dip the chicken pieces in the mixture and season with salt and pepper. Place on a rack over a pan in a 325° smoke oven in an area of indirect heat. Use moderate smoke for 45 to 60 minutes. Remove chicken pieces from rack to pan and smear the sour cream over the chicken pieces. Cook another 30 minutes without added smoke. Use drippings as a sauce, adding white wine for liquid if necessary. The caraway flavor is much more pungent if this dish is made hours before serving and then reheated. *Serves 4.*

CHICKEN BENDER

8 to 10 chicken pieces (thighs,
    breasts and/or legs)
2 cups beer
1 clove garlic, chopped fine
10 dashes Tabasco

2 medium onions, chopped
2 tablespoons chili powder
2 cups dry white wine
2 small chili peppers
Salt

Wait for a good buy in chicken pieces, and then plan this zesty dish. Marinate the chicken pieces in the beer, to which the garlic and Tabasco sauce have been added. After 4 hours, place in a 300° smoke oven and use heavy smoke for 30 minutes. Meanwhile, combine the other ingredients and simmer in a saucepan for 20 minutes. Take the chicken pieces off the grill and place in a baking dish. Pour the sauce over the chicken and cook without smoke for another hour. *Serves 4.*

McBEE'S CHICKEN WITH DRAMBUIE

1 4 to 5-pound roasting chicken
  Salt

Pepper

BASTE

1 cup Drambuie
¼ cup lemon juice
  Grated rind of 1 lemon

4 tablespoons melted butter
2 tablespoons soy sauce

Wash and dry the chicken; then rub it inside and outside with salt and pepper. It may be stuffed if the chef so desires. Put the chicken on a rack over a pan and place it in a 325° smoke oven until done, about 2½ hours. Combine the Drambuie—the liqueur that is based on Scotch whiskey—with the other ingredients and baste the chicken, spilling not a drop. *Serves 4.*

CHICKEN TILLAMOOK

1 3½- to 4-pound broiling
    chicken
  Wine or lemon juice
  Salt
  Pepper
2 cups bread crumbs

½ pint small oysters, quartered
½ cup grated sharp cheddar
    cheese
½ teaspoon thyme
¼ stick butter
1 small onion, chopped

3 celery stalks, chopped   ¼ cup cooking oil
½ green pepper, chopped   1 cup dry white wine

Rub the exterior and the body cavity of the clean, dry chicken with wine or lemon juice, then salt and pepper. Make a dressing of crumbs, oysters, cheese, thyme and the vegetables, which have been sautéed in the butter. Salt and pepper to taste, adding more crumbs if necessary. Stuff, but do not pack dressing into chicken cavity. Skewer shut. Place on a rack over a pan in a 325° smoke oven in an area of indirect heat. Use moderate smoke. Roast until done (start testing at 2 hours or use a meat thermometer), basting frequently with wine and oil mixture. *Serves 4.*

DOVES WITH GRAPES

4 doves   ½ cup dry white wine
4 slices onion, ½ inch thick   1 cup chicken stock or bouillon
2 cups seedless grapes   Salt
½ cup melted butter   Pepper

Into the neck cavity of each bird place an onion slice. Salt the body cavity of each dove; then stuff ½ cup grapes into each cavity. Close the openings with skewers. Salt and pepper the birds on the outside. Mix the butter, wine and stock for use as a baste. Place the birds on a rack over a pan and roast in a smoke oven about 1½ hours at 325°. Use light smoke. Baste frequently. *Serves 4.*

CHARLO SHERRY DUCK

4 wild ducks   4 small apples
  Salt   2 carrots
  Pepper   2 cups sherry

Slosh the duck cavities with a little wine, then salt and pepper the ducks, inside and out. Peel, core and quarter the apples and put one apple in each duck. Peel and halve the carrots and put a half in each duck. Skewer the cavities shut. Place ducks on a rack over a pan and cook in 325° smoke oven until done, about 45 to 60 minutes, depending on the size of the birds. Baste frequently with the sherry. *Serves 4.*

MOTT STREET DUCKLING

1 5- to 6-pound Long Island
    duckling
2 cloves garlic, chopped fine
    Salt
3 tablespoons honey
3 tablespoons sugar
3 tablespoons soy sauce
2 tablespoons cornstarch

2 tablespoons water
½ cup pineapple juice
1 green pepper, chopped
1 tablespoon soy sauce
1 cup pineapple chunks
1 10-ounce can water chest-
    nuts, sliced

Domestic duck has a thick layer of fat under the skin, which a wild duck does not. Slash the skin of a domestic duck at intervals so the fat can run off during the roasting period. Sprinkle duck cavity with chopped garlic and salt. Skewer shut.

Combine honey, sugar and soy sauce. Brush the duck with it and let stand about 45 minutes. Place the duck breast side up on a rack over a pan and cook in a 325° smoke oven in area of indirect heat for 2½ to 3 hours. Skim the fat off the juices as it accumulates in the pan, and use juices and any leftover honey-soy sauce to baste duck periodically.

When duck is done, combine pan juices (as little fat as possible) with cornstarch, water and pineapple juice. Stir while mixture heats and thickens, adjusting as necessary. Add green pepper, soy sauce, pineapple and water chestnuts. Serve with duck and fluffy rice. *Serves 4.*

OAK ISLAND DUCK

4 wild ducks
    Juice of 1 lemon
1½ cups dry white wine
    Salt

Pepper
4 apples
8 juniper berries (optional)

SAUCE

1 cup drippings
2 tablespoons flour
2 teaspoons brown sugar

1 tablespoon vinegar
    Juice of 1 orange
1 teaspoon grated orange rind

Most wild ducks are small and the servings not large enough if the birds are divided, so plan on a whole duck per person. This should be revised, of course, if the ducks are large. There are those who favor cooking wildfowl fast and hot and serving it rare, but we prefer slower cooking.

The day before roasting, marinate ducks in a mixture of the lemon juice and wine, turning occasionally. Refrigerate until an hour before roasting.

An hour before cooking, salt and pepper duck cavities. Insert quartered apples and juniper berries into cavities, then skewer shut. Salt and pepper the exteriors of the ducks, place on a rack over a pan and put into 350° smoke oven. Cook until tender, about 30 minutes per pound. Place pan in indirect heat position so the drippings will not burn. Use lemon-wine marinade to baste ducks. Near the conclusion of the roasting period remove a cup of drippings to a saucepan and blend in flour. Add remaining ingredients and stir until thick over low heat. Correct seasonings. Serve with duck. *Serves 4.*

SAUVIE ISLAND DUCK

4 wild ducks	2 cloves
Juice of 1 lemon	1 onion, sliced
1 bay leaf	Dry red wine

SAUCE

1 cup dry red wine	½ teaspoon lemon juice
1 teaspoon chopped onion	1½ tablespoons flour
¼ teaspoon thyme	½ cup beef stock or bouillon
Juice of 2 oranges	

Place the ducks in a marinade made by combining the juice of the lemon, the bay leaf, the cloves, onion and enough red wine to cover the ducks in an enameled pot or large bowl. Marinate 24 hours. Remove from marinade, salt and pepper to taste, then roast in a 325° smoke oven, using moderately heavy smoke, about 30 minutes to the pound. Baste occasionally with the marinade. Serve with sauce, which has been made at the chef's convenience prior to serving but which has been brought to simmering just before serving. Sauce may be made thicker if desired. *Serves 4.*

HERB DUCKLING

1 6-pound duckling
Salt
Pepper
Paprika
½ teaspoon ground ginger

½ teaspoon ground rosemary
½ teaspoon thyme
2 1-inch-long cinnamon sticks
½ cup bouillon or giblet broth

With a sharp knife and kitchen shears, cut off the legs and wings and separate the breast from the back piece. Cut the back and the breast in two. Sprinkle salt, pepper and paprika on the pieces and place on a rack over a pan in a 325° smoke oven in an area of indirect heat. Smoke heavily for 45 minutes. Remove to a skillet, sprinkle each piece with the combined ginger, rosemary and thyme, add cinnamon sticks and broth, cover and simmer until tender. *Serves 4.*

ROAST DUCKLING BURGUNDY

1 5- to 6-pound Long Island
    duckling
1 cup burgundy
Salt
Pepper

3 celery top leaves
2 onion slices
1 orange, cut in quarters
¼ teaspoon thyme

Wash and dry duckling exterior and cavity and rub each with a little of the burgundy, then with salt and pepper. Prick fatty surface of the duck with a fork. Mix other ingredients and put them in the body cavity. Skewer shut and place the duck on a rack over a pan in a 325° to 350° smoke oven in an area of indirect heat. Roast for 2½ to 3 hours, using moderate smoke. Baste with remainder of burgundy and more if necessary. Discard cavity ingredients before serving. *Serves 4.*

GUINEA HEN

1 2½- to 3-pound guinea hen
Salt
Pepper
1 apple
½ bay leaf

1 parsley sprig
1 clove
Juice of 1 lemon
1 cup dry white wine
¼ cup olive oil

Wipe the bird with a damp cloth and rub with salt and pepper, inside and out. Pare, core and quarter the apple and place inside the bird. Add bay leaf, parsley and clove. Sew or skewer the cavity shut. Place hen on a rack over a pan and put into 325° smoke oven. Baste frequently with wine-oil-lemon mixture, using more wine if necessary. Roast about 1½ hours. *Serves 2.*

SMOKED HOLIDAY GOOSE

1 young domestic goose, about	Pepper
10 pounds	¾ cup honey, warmed
Salt	2 teaspoons cinnamon

Wash and dry the goose outside and inside. Rub salt and pepper on and in the bird. Prick fatty surface of the goose with a fork, particularly around the legs and wings. Place on a rack over a pan and put into a 325° smoke oven. Use moderate smoke for the approximately 5 hours it will take to roast the goose. The pan is to keep the goose fat from dripping into the smoke oven. Drain the fat from the roasting pan as it accumulates, which will be in abundance, leaving the juices to use as basting, and basting must be done frequently. About 30 minutes before the cooking is completed, brush the skin with the honey and sprinkle with cinnamon. *Serves 6 to 8.*

WILD GOOSE

1 wild goose, about 6 pounds	1 onion, chopped
1 cup salt	2 stalks celery, chopped
½ gallon water	2 tablespoons sugar
Salt	2 cups bread crumbs
Pepper	½ teaspoon sage
6 slices bacon	¼ teaspoon thyme
3 cups diced apples	

Place the wild goose in a brine made by mixing the salt in the water. Leave overnight. Dry and rub inside and outside with salt and pepper. Sauté bacon slices until crisp. Remove from pan and crumble. To the fat add the apples, onion, celery and sugar. Sauté until apples are partly done. Add bacon, crumbs, sage and thyme. Blend well, adjust seasonings and stuff the goose. Cook the bird on a rack over a pan in a 325° smoke oven, basting occasionally. Allow about 30 minutes per pound. *Serves 6.*

SMOKED STUFFED NORTHWESTERN TURKEY

(For a 12- to 16-pound turkey)

Readying a turkey for the smoke oven is child's play—it is the preparation of the stuffing that consumes time and requires tender loving care.

Select a top-grade turkey. Wash the cavities thoroughly under cold running water, then the outside of the bird. Drain, dry, slosh a little wine around the inside of the cavities, drain, then salt and pepper. Remove the oil sac above the tail. The bird is ready for stuffing and roasting. Most cooks have favorite stuffing recipes; we will limit our recommendations to two.

SAUSAGE AND CORNBREAD STUFFING

3 cups cornbread crumbs
3 cups soft white bread
    crumbs
5 slices bacon, diced
1¼ pounds bulk sausage
¼ cup chopped celery
¼ cup chopped onion
1 clove garlic, chopped
1 small can mushrooms,
    chopped

2 tablespoons chopped parsley
½ tablespoon rosemary
½ tablespoon sage
½ tablespoon sweet basil
½ teaspoon thyme
¾ teaspoon salt
½ teaspoon pepper
⅛ pound butter

Put cornbread and bread crumbs in a large bowl. Fry bacon until crisp. Add to crumbs. Fry sausage until crumbly and brown. Add to crumbs. Sauté other ingredients in the bacon and sausage drippings, then add the butter. (If dressing is baked in a casserole rather than in a turkey, cut down on the sausage drippings.) Pour over crumbs. Mix well but lightly. Add water, milk or wine if moisture is needed. Stuff but do not pack the dressing into the bird cavities. Skewer cavities shut. Place turkey on a rack over a pan and put in a 325° smoke oven. Baste occasionally once juices start to drip into the pan. Use moderate smoke. Cook until tender or until meat thermometer reaches desired temperature.

GIBLET AND RICE DRESSING

2 cups finely chopped celery
2 onions, finely chopped
1 cup butter
6 cups cooked rice
4 eggs, well beaten
2 cups turkey or chicken broth

Turkey giblets, cooked and
  chopped
2 tablespoons Worcestershire
Salt
Pepper
Pinch saffron

Prepare the turkey for stuffing. Sauté celery and onion in butter and add to rice. Add the remaining ingredients. Stuff loosely into turkey cavities. Skewer cavities shut. Place turkey on a rack over a pan and put in a 325° smoke oven. Baste occasionally once juices start to drip into the pan. Use moderate smoke. Cook until tender or until meat thermometer reaches desired temperature.

If dressing is baked in a casserole rather than a turkey, bake at 325° for 30 to 45 minutes.

WOODWAY QUAIL

2 quail
Salt
Pepper
1 stalk celery, halved
2 slices onion

2 slices bacon
1 cup dry white wine
1 teaspoon prepared mustard
Juice of ½ lemon

Allow at least 1 quail per person. If the birds are small or the appetites large, increase to 3 birds for 2, or 2 per person.

Salt and pepper bird cavities then insert in each cavity ½ stalk celery and 1 slice onion. Skewer shut. Place quail on a rack over a pan. Bacon may be placed on the birds or in the pan—the object is to get the bacon grease and flavor mixed with the basting combination of wine, mustard and lemon. Cook until tender in 325° smoke oven, using moderate smoke. Baste frequently. *Serves 2.*

SMOKED SHANIKO SQUABS

2 1-pound squabs
Salt
Pepper
2 tablespoons butter
2 squab livers (substitute 1
    chicken liver if squab is
    sold without liver)

3 green onions, chopped
½ cup dry red wine
¼ cup chicken stock
½ cup chopped mushrooms
1 teaspoon chopped parsley
1 teaspoon Worcestershire

Season the squabs and place on a rack over a pan in a 325° oven. They may be stuffed if desired. Smoke them until they are tender, about 1½ hours. Melt the butter in a saucepan and add the chopped liver and green onions. Sauté a few minutes, then add the wine, broth, mushrooms and parsley. Remove from heat and add Worcestershire sauce. When squabs are done, add pan drippings to the sauce and bring to simmer before serving. *Serves 2.*

ORANGE PHEASANT

1 large pheasant, cleaned and prepared

STUFFING

2 tablespoons butter
¼ cup chopped onion
½ cup mixed nuts, slightly
    chopped
1 tablespoon sugar

¼ teaspoon marjoram
1 teaspoon grated orange rind
½ cup cooked rice
Salt
Pepper

BASTE

1 cup orange juice
2 teaspoons grated orange rind

¼ cup honey
2 tablespoons salad oil

Prepare stuffing by sautéing the onion and nuts in the butter until the onion turns translucent. Add other ingredients and mix well. Adjust seasonings and add more rice if it appears that the bird will hold additional stuffing. Stuff but do not pack the stuffing into the cavity; skewer shut. Place the pheasant on a rack over a pan and put into a 325° smoke oven in the area of indirect heat. Cook until done, about 1½ to 2 hours, and use moderate smoke. Baste frequently with mixture of orange juice and rind, honey and oil. *Serves 2.*

11

Skewer Cooking

Turning small chunks of meat over a bed of coals is an age-old way of cooking. It is a method that belongs to no time or place. A tribesman hunched over a small bed of coals is doing the same thing as the French chef in the air-conditioned kitchen at the Ritz. Meat eaters have always cooked on skewers. Metal rods, knives, swords, bamboo and green branches have all served to hold meat cubes over a fire.

The French call meat cooked in this manner *brochettes*, while *shish kabab* comes to us from the Near East. The Turks and Russians eat *sheshlick, kenjeh kahab* is eaten in Iran, and Indonesians eat their highly seasoned *sates.*

Most instructions caution the cook to turn skewers several times or "keep turning." Because this is a chore, assorted mechanical gadgets have been manufactured to turn several skewers at one time.

Not for us! The smoke oven does away with the need for any devices and the bother of constant turning. Just place the meat-filled skewer on the smoke-oven grill and close the cover. The closed smoke-oven heat cooks the meat on all sides. If you want more crusty meat or want to use a flavoring baste, the skewers can be turned, of course. Try cooking some recipes, such as pork or chicken, in the indirect heat area of the smoker. Put the skewers on a rack over a shallow pan. This method permits longer cooking with less danger of burning. Skewer cooking is simple this way and the results are delicious.

At times skewered meat is cooked in combination with vegetables and mushrooms. Although some women's magazines would have us believe that a shish kabab should be a colorful combination vegetable salad with a few pieces of meat, we feel that the meat should get first consideration and that the vegetables are secondary. Without careful attention to them, the vegetables are either over-cooked or almost raw and contribute little or nothing to the meat.

If you must use potatoes, parboil them for 10 to 15 minutes in salted water, then cut them into 1½-inch chunks. Mushrooms and tomatoes take about 10 minutes to cook, while green pepper pieces, parboiled potatoes, small or canned onions and zucchini need about 20 minutes. Pineapple chunks, pieces of apple, stuffed olives and soaked prunes also need about 20 minutes of smoke-oven heat to be at their tastiest. There are no strict rules. You will need to ex-periment if you feel inclined to assemble elaborate skewer foods. There is no question that they will bring oohs and ahs from guests. We don't mean to disparage the creativity of adding these oddments to your meat; just plan it so they all finish cooking at the same time. Try cooking vegetables on a separate skewer. This way they can be put into the smoke oven before or after the meat and reach doneness at the same time as the meat. If you want to bother, partially cook the meat, remove it from the skewers and replace in combination with the faster-cooking vegetables.

Skewer cooking in a closed smoke oven is easy if a few simple rules are observed. Cut the meat cubes the same size. If they vary, arrange the same-sized pieces on each skewer. Plan far enough in advance so the meat can be effectively marinated. A few marinades need no longer than two hours on the meat; others need several hours. All skewered meats do not have to be marinated. Tender cuts of beef, pork, chicken and lamb can be deliciously roasted on skewers with no marinating. They are good with sauces such as Diable, Bordelaise or Maître d'Hôtel butter.

Don't crowd the pieces of meat on the skewer—leave a little space between the cubes so the heat will reach all sides. Place a few pieces of test meat on the grill beside the loaded skewers. When you wonder if the meat is done, try one of the test pieces. This is easier than removing an entire shish kabab and pulling it apart to test the meat. If the test piece is not cooked, try a second test piece later.

Beef and lamb are best when cooked quickly and are a little rare inside. Pork, of course, must be thoroughly cooked, and this is achieved over a slower fire than for beef and lamb. Twenty minutes over a good bed of coals with the cover on should cook beef and lamb cubes 1½ to 2 inches square to a medium well done. Beef tenderloin will cook to rare in about 10 minutes. Don't, as one cookbook has suggested, cook the meat 50 minutes over a bed of 50 charcoal briquets.

Although lamb is the traditional shish kabab choice, almost any kind of meat can be cooked on a skewer. You can use beef, pork, veal, beef heart, beef liver, chicken livers and cubes of poultry. Tough cuts will need tenderizing and marinating for a longer time than the more tender meats.

Flat metal skewers are more satisfactory than round ones because the meat will not slip on them. Some skewers consist of two small rods—both are pushed through the meat cubes to prevent slipping.

In addition to the recipes in this chapter, you will find marinades and skewer cooking ideas in the Chapters 15 (The Oriental Touch) and 9 (Fish). Many meat ball recipes in Chapter 6 (Ground Meat) can be cooked on skewers. Spicy meat balls are delicious when cooked on a skewer with mushrooms, onions and tomatoes.

Most of the recipes in this chapter call for a generous half pound of meat per serving. This can, of course, be varied according to appetite. It is probably psychological, but two pounds of meat cut into cubes looks like more and seems to serve more than two one-pound steaks or one two-pound roast.

When cooking meat on skewers in a closed smoke oven, you have the choice of using wood smoke or not, for flavor. Some meats taste better cooked in smoke. For others, smoke doesn't do a thing to enhance the flavor. Everything cooked in a smoke oven does not necessarily have to be smoke-cooked. Experiment as you go along. We feel that pork and lamb taste better cooked with smoke than does beef or chicken. The rich flavor of a piece of beef tenderloin brushed with butter would suffer if cooked in heavy smoke. So try varying amounts of smoke, or none at all, when cooking skewered meats. You will soon learn what pleases you most.

The only constant in smoke-oven cooking is the cover. Always keep it on during the cooking process.

CALF LIVER EN BROCHETTE

2 pounds calf liver   ½ cup melted butter
½ pound bacon   1 cup dry bread crumbs

Cut liver and bacon into 1-inch pieces. Fry the bacon a couple of
minutes before alternating with liver on skewers. Brush with
melted butter and roll in bread crumbs. Cook in 325° smoke oven
until test pieces show meats are cooked. Serve with Bordelaise
sauce (see Index). *Serves 4.*

GINGER BEEF KABABS

3 pounds tender beef

MARINADE

½ cup minced onion   ½ cup dry white wine
1 teaspoon chili powder   1 teaspoon salt
3 slices fresh ginger, chopped,
    or 1 teaspoon powdered
    ginger

Cut meat into 1½-inch cubes and marinate 2 to 3 hours. Place
on skewers, leaving space between pieces of meat. Place on a hot
grill of the smoke oven and cover. Cook 5 minutes, turn and
baste with marinade. Cook another 5 minutes; then test. If meat is
not done, baste and turn again, cooking until desired doneness is
reached. Use a 350° smoke oven. *Serves 6.*

BEEF SHISH KABABS

2 pounds sirloin of beef   1 can small cooked onions

MARINADE

½ cup olive or salad oil   1 teaspoon salt
¼ cup wine vinegar   2 tablespoons Worcestershire
½ teaspoon black pepper

Cut beef into 1½-inch cubes. Mix marinade ingredients in a bowl
and marinate the meat for about 4 hours. Place cubes on skewers,
alternating with onions. Check for doneness after 10 minutes.
Smoke-cook at 350°. *Serves 4.*

BAY LEAF LAMB

2 pounds leg of lamb

MARINADE

1 cup dry red wine
¼ cup salad oil
1 teaspoon thyme

1 teaspoon garlic powder
2 bay leaves, crushed

Cut meat into 1½-inch cubes. Mix marinade ingredients in a bowl and marinate the lamb in it in a refrigerator overnight. Skewer the cubes and allow the meat to dry before placing on the grill of a 350° smoke oven. Cover and cook for 20 minutes or until desired doneness is reached. *Serves 4.*

LAMB 'N' LIVERS

2 pounds leg of lamb

MARINADE

1 large onion, chopped fine
1 teaspoon orégano
1 cup dry red wine
½ cup salad oil

1 clove garlic, chopped fine
1 teaspoon salt
½ teaspoon pepper

½ pound bacon, sliced
8 chicken livers in bite-sized
   pieces

1 can small cooked onions
12 large mushroom caps

Cut the meat into 1½-inch cubes. Prepare the marinade in a bowl, add meat, and marinate 2 to 3 hours.

Cut the bacon into pieces long enough to wrap around the chicken livers. Fill skewers with lamb cubes, onions, mushrooms and wrapped chicken livers, alternating as desired. Place skewers on a 325° to 350° smoke oven grill, add wood chips and cover. Cook 15 to 20 minutes or until bacon is crisp and lamb is cooked to desired doneness. During the cooking period, turn once and baste with the marinade. *Serves 4.*

LAMB ITALIAN

2 pounds leg of lamb   1 jar stuffed olives
1 can small cooked onions

BASTE

¼ cup dry red wine   ½ teaspoon monosodium
¼ cup olive oil   glutamate
½ teaspoon rosemary

Salt   Pepper

Put 1½-inch cubes of meat on skewers with olives and onions.
Brush with basting sauce, salt and pepper to taste, then place on
350° smoke oven grill and cover. Baste 2 or 3 times during cooking
period, which should be about 20 minutes. *Serves 4.*

BEEF OR LAMB KABABS

2 pounds tender meat

MARINADE

½ cup olive oil   1 teaspoon garlic salt
½ cup chopped onions   ½ teaspoon black pepper
1 teaspoon dry mustard

Cut meat into 1½-inch cubes. Prepare marinade in a bowl, add
meat and mix well so that each piece of meat is well coated. Allow
to marinate 3 to 4 hours. Skewer the meat, place on a 350° smoke
oven grill and cover. Cook 15 to 20 minutes. During cooking
period turn and baste once with leftover marinade, wine or a
combination of both. *Serves 4.*

SKEWERED LAMB

3 pounds lamb, leg or shoulder

MARINADE

1 cup dry red wine   ½ teaspoon thyme
1 onion, chopped   1 tablespoon Worcestershire
1 teaspoon salt   2 cloves garlic, crushed or
¼ teaspoon black pepper   chopped fine

If shoulder of lamb is used, it should be marinated overnight, whereas leg of lamb will be ready for smoke cooking in 4 to 6 hours. Cut meat into 1½- to 2-inch cubes and place in bowl with marinade. Mix well to expose meat thoroughly to marinade ingredients. When ready for cooking, skewer the meat, place it on a 350° smoke oven grill and cover. Cook 10 minutes, turn skewers, baste with marinade, cover and cook 10 minutes more or until desired doneness is reached. *Serves 6.*

TASTY VEAL KABABS

3 pound boneless veal roast
Salt
Pepper
2 cloves garlic, chopped fine

1 cup olive oil or melted
   butter
½ pound sliced bacon

Cut the meat into 1-inch cubes. Season well with salt and pepper. Mix thoroughly in a bowl with garlic and half the oil or melted butter. Cut the bacon into 1-inch pieces. Alternate the veal cubes and pieces of bacon on the skewers. Cook on the grill of a covered 325° smoke oven until bacon is crisp and veal is done. Before serving, brush with the remaining butter or olive oil. *Serves 6.*

TBILISI LAMB

2 pounds leg of lamb

MARINADE

½ cup wine vinegar
¼ cup olive or salad oil
1 tablespoon honey

1 large green pepper

1 teaspoon sweet basil
1 teaspoon black pepper
1 teaspoon salt

12 cherry tomatoes

Cut meat into 1-inch cubes. Prepare marinade and pour over meat cubes in a bowl. Mix well and marinate for several hours. Stir occasionally to expose meat thoroughly to marinade ingredients. Cut green peppers into 1-inch pieces. Alternate meat, green pepper and tomato on skewers until they are filled. Place on the grill of a 350° smoke oven and cover. Turn skewers once after 5 minutes, basting with marinade or wine. Repeat in another 5 minutes. Test for doneness after 15 minutes. *Serves 4.*

LAMB KIDNEYS EN BROCHETTE

8 lamb kidneys

MARINADE

¼ cup olive oil   ½ teaspoon curry powder
1 cup dry red wine   ½ teaspoon black pepper
1 teaspoon salt   2 cloves garlic, chopped fine

½ pound sliced bacon   Olive or salad oil
16 mushroom caps   Toast strips

Wash kidneys, cut in half, remove outer membrane, white veins and
fat. Mix oil, wine, salt, pepper, garlic and curry powder in a saucepan. Place kidneys in cold marinade and bring slowly to a boil.
Simmer until tender. Remove from marinade and cut each kidney
piece in half again. Cut bacon slices into pieces long enough to
wrap around each kidney piece. Wrap each kidney piece with bacon
and alternate on skewers with mushroom caps. Dip each skewerful
in oil, then place on the grill of a 325° smoke oven, cover, and
cook until bacon is done. Serve on toast strips with heated marinade
as a sauce. *Serves 4.*

LAMB KOZANI

2 pounds shoulder of lamb   1 can small cooked onions

MARINADE

1 onion, minced   ⅓ cup olive or salad oil
1 teaspoon marjoram   2 tablespoons lemon or lime
1 teaspoon thyme   juice
1 teaspoon salt

Cut meat into strips about ½ inch thick and 1 inch wide. Combine
marinade ingredients in a bowl, add meat, and marinate overnight. When ready to cook, thread strips on skewers, looping meat
around small onions. Roast on the grill of a 350° smoke oven,
covered, until meat is brown. This should take about 20 minutes
at the minimum. Shoulder of lamb is tastier if cooked longer than
leg of lamb. *Serves 4.*

ABATS EN BROCHETTE

1 calf heart	½ pound calf's liver
4 lamb kidneys	

MARINADE

2 onions, minced	1 teaspoon sage
½ cup wine vinegar	1 teaspoon salt
⅓ cup olive or salad oil	½ teaspoon black pepper

½ pound bacon

After washing and removing membrane, fat and veins, cut heart, kidneys and liver into 1-inch pieces. Prepare marinade, add meat and allow to marinate 3 hours or more. Cut bacon into 1-inch pieces. Alternate heart, bacon, liver, bacon, kidney, bacon on skewers. Cook on the grill of a 325° smoke oven, covered, until bacon is crisp. Be sure to use plenty of green hardwood smoke with this recipe. *Serves 6.*

BROCHETTE DE BOEUF

2 pounds sirloin tip or lean chuck

MARINADE

1 onion, minced	1 teaspoon orégano
⅓ cup olive or salad oil	½ teaspoon black pepper
½ teaspoon salt	2 cloves garlic, chopped
½ teaspoon celery salt	

1 can small cooked onions (optional)	12 cherry tomatoes (optional)

Cut meat into cubes—chef's choice of size. Combine marinade ingredients and add meat. Leave in refrigerator overnight. If onions and tomatoes are used, alternate them with the meat on skewers; if not, just place meat on skewers, with spaces between in either case. Place skewers on the grill of a 350° smoke oven, covered, and cook for 7 or 8 minutes. Turn and baste with marinade. Cook until done. *Serves 4.*

SHERRY LAMB OR BEEF

2 pounds tender meat
1 cup soy sauce
½ cup salad or olive oil
1 tablespoon ground coriander

1 teaspoon salt
2 cloves garlic, chopped
½ cup sherry

Cut meat into 1- or 2-inch cubes and marinate overnight in remaining ingredients. Add more sherry if meat is not covered. Put meat on skewers, leaving spaces between pieces. Cook in a 325° to 350° smoke oven, covered, for 10 minutes then turn and baste with marinade. Cook another 5 minutes then test for doneness. Brush with marinade just before removing from the smoke oven. *Serves 4.*

TURGUTLU KABABS

2 pounds lamb or beef

MARINADE

1 cup fresh lime juice
1 cup dry white wine

1 cup grated onion
2 cloves garlic, chopped

Salt
Pepper

½ teaspoon saffron

Cut meat into 1- or 2-inch pieces. Marinate overnight in lime juice, wine, grated onion and garlic pieces. Remove meat from marinade and place on skewers. Season with salt, pepper and saffron. Cook on the grill of a 350° smoke oven, covered, until done the way you like it. Test for doneness at 15 minutes. *Serves 4.*

VEAL BOSDAPAN

3-pound veal roast

MARINADE

1 can frozen lemonade
½ cup olive oil
1 tablespoon turmeric
1 teaspoon black pepper
1 teaspoon salt

1 teaspoon monosodium
   glutamate
1 can small cooked onions
1 can pitted large black
   olives
2 green peppers

Cut meat into 1-inch cubes while the lemonade is defrosting in the oil and spices. Marinate at least 4 hours. Alternate meat on skewers with onions, olives and 1-inch pieces of green pepper. Brush with marinade while cooking on the grill of a 325° smoke oven, covered. Test for doneness after 20 minutes of cooking. *Serves 4.*

LEMON BEEF

2 pounds beef steak or sirloin tip

MARINADE

½ cup lemon juice
½ cup salad oil
1 teaspoon salt

½ teaspoon black pepper
2 cloves garlic, crushed

Cut beef into 1½-inch cubes. Prepare marinade and leave the beef in the marinade 4 hours. Skewer and cook on the grill of a 375° smoke oven, covered, until cooked to desired doneness. *Serves 4.*

ORANGE LAMB

MARINADE

½ cup brown sugar
½ teaspoon dry mustard
¼ teaspoon powdered cloves
2 tablespoons minced onion

2 tablespoons lemon juice
Syrup from oranges (see below)

2 pounds leg or shoulder of lamb

2 cans mandarin oranges
1 jar stuffed green olives

Prepare marinade in a bowl. Cut lamb into 1½-inch cubes and marinate for 3 hours if the meat is from the leg, or overnight if from the shoulder. When ready to cook, alternate meat with an orange piece and an olive on skewers. Place on the grill of a 350° smoke oven, and cover. Turn once and baste while cooking about 15 to 20 minutes. *Serves 4.*

AEGEAN VEAL

2 pounds boneless veal
½ cup olive oil
½ cup lemon juice
1 teaspoon black pepper

1 teaspoon thyme
1 can small cooked onions
Salt

Stir 1½-inch veal cubes in a bowl with oil, lemon juice, pepper and thyme. Mix thoroughly. Carefully add the onions without breaking them. Marinate 6 hours. Alternate pieces of meat and onions on skewers. Salt and cook on the grill of a 325° smoke oven, covered. Turn once during 20 to 25 minute cooking period and brush generously with marinade. *Serves 4.*

PINEAPPLE PORK

2 pounds boneless pork loin
½ cup tarragon wine vinegar
½ cup olive oil
1 cup crushed pineapple

½ teaspoon black pepper
1 teaspoon monosodium
   glutamate
1 teaspoon salt

Cut meat into 1-inch cubes. Combine other ingredients and marinate pork in it for 3 hours. Skewer and place on a rack over a broiling pan. Place pan on 325° smoke oven grill in the area of indirect heat. Cover and cook until meat tests for doneness. Baste a few times with marinade. *Serves 4.*

SPICY RED PORK

2 pounds lean, boneless pork
3 cloves garlic, chopped fine
½ cup butter
½ cup olive or salad oil
1 small can tomato sauce
1 teaspoon turmeric

1 teaspoon black pepper
1 teaspoon salt
2 teaspoons curry powder
1 cup sherry
1 can small white onions

Cut meat into 1-inch cubes and place in a bowl. Sauté chopped garlic in butter and olive oil in a good-sized skilled. Add tomato sauce, turmeric, pepper, salt and curry powder. Stir while simmering for 5 minutes. Stir in sherry wine and heat. Pour hot over meat cubes and allow to marinate 2 hours. Alternate cubes of pork on skewers with onions and place on a rack over a broiling pan. Put pan in a 325° smoke oven in the area of indirect heat. Cover and cook until done, turning 2 or 3 times and basting with marinade. *Serves 4.*

GINGER SOY PORK

2 pounds lean, boneless pork
1 teaspoon powdered ginger
1 teaspoon coarse black
   pepper

4 cloves garlic, chopped
1 bottle soy sauce
1 can pineapple chunks or one
   fresh pineapple, chunked

Cut meat into 1-inch cubes and sprinkle with ginger and pepper. Chop garlic fine and scatter over meat. Put meat into the smallest bowl that will hold it and cover with soy sauce. Add a little white wine if more liquid is needed to cover the meat. Marinate at least 2 hours. Turn meat once or twice during the marinating process. Skewer with alternating chunks of pineapple and cook in a 325° oven on a rack, over a pan, in the area of indirect heat. Turn skewers a few times and baste with marinade. Cook until crusty brown and well done. *Serves 4.*

CARAWAY PORK

2 pounds pork tenderloin or
   boneless lean roast
½ pound butter
2 tablespoons lemon juice

2 teaspoons caraway seeds
2 tart apples
1 pound fresh sauerkraut
2 cups dry white wine

Cut meat into 1-inch cubes. Melt butter slowly and add lemon juice and caraway seeds. If you have a mortar, crush the seeds before adding to butter. Alternate cubes of meat with pieces of apple on skewers. Brush well with seasoned butter and cook slowly at 300° to 325° in the indirect heat area of the smoke oven. Skewers should be on a rack over a shallow pan to catch basting juices. Baste a couple of times when turning the skewers.

    Wash the sauerkraut in cold water and cook in wine. Serve the skewered meat on a bed of sauerkraut. Heat the seasoned butter and brush over the meat just before serving. *Serves 4.*

CHICKEN SUPREME

2 pounds chicken breasts
1 cup dry white wine
2 tablespoons curry powder
1 onion, grated

1 teaspoon Tabasco
½ teaspoon black pepper
Oil or butter
Salt

Remove chicken from bones and cut into 1-inch pieces. Marinate 2 hours in wine, curry, onion, Tabasco and pepper. Place on skewers and brush with oil or butter, then salt to taste. Place skewers on a rack over a broiling pan and cook in a 325° smoke oven until golden and well done. Brush with marinade or oil or butter during the cooking process. *Serves 4.*

CHICKEN FOR MELISSA

2 pounds chicken breasts,
    thighs or both
Salt
Pepper

15 mushroom caps
½ pound lean bacon
2 eggs
1 cup dry bread crumbs

Remove chicken from bones and cut into 1-inch pieces. Sprinkle with salt and pepper to taste. Wash mushroom caps and dry on paper towels. Cut bacon into 1-inch pieces. Alternate chicken, bacon and mushroom caps on skewers. Beat eggs and brush on meats and mushroom caps. Sprinkle with bread crumbs. Place skewers on a rack over a broiling pan in a 325° smoke oven and cover. Cook until bacon is crisp and chicken is done to a golden color. *Serves 4.*

BROCHETTES DE FOIES DE POULET

2 pounds chicken livers
Salt
Pepper
½ pound bacon

24 mushrooms
½ cup melted butter or olive
    oil

Cut livers in half. Dry on paper towels, then salt and pepper. Cut bacon into 1-inch pieces. Wash and dry mushrooms. Alternate livers, mushrooms and bacon squares on skewers. Brush with melted butter or olive oil. Cook in a 325° smoke oven over direct heat. Turn once and brush again with melted butter or oil. Remove as soon as bacon is crisp. *Serves 6.*

GRANT STREET CHICKEN

3 pounds chicken breasts
1 cup soy sauce
6 cloves garlic, crushed

1 cup dry sherry
½ cup olive oil

Remove chicken from bones and cut into 1-inch cubes. Marinate in the remaining ingredients at least 3 hours. Skewer chicken and place on a rack over a broiling pan. Cook in a 325° smoke oven with cover on. Baste with marinade at least twice during the cooking process. Cook until brown and well done. *Serves 6.*

ROUND STEAK ROLLS

2 pounds beef round steak

MARINADE

2 cups dry red wine
⅛ cup salad oil

1 onion, minced
1 teaspoon black pepper

½ pound sliced bacon
1 can beef gravy (or your
  own)

Salt
Pepper

Cut round steak into long strips about ¾ inch wide. Marinate overnight. Cut bacon strips in half lengthwise. Place a piece of beef on a piece of bacon and roll into a loose disc, starting in the center. Figure 14 shows the way the bacon and beef strips should be rolled. Run a skewer through the diameter of the circle and loosen the layers of beef and bacon slightly. Boil the marinade in a saucepan until it is reduced by one half. Add the beef gravy and heat. Season the rounds of skewered meat with salt and pepper. Place on the grill of a 350° smoke oven, cover, and cook 5 minutes. Turn and cook 5 more minutes or until the bacon is done. Serve with the hot marinade poured over the rounds of meat. *Serves 4.*

14—Round Steak Rolls. The bacon and beef strips are rolled together and placed on a skewer as shown.

SKEWERED TENDERLOIN WITH GARLIC BUTTER

2 pounds beef tenderloin   4 cloves garlic
16 mushroom caps   ¼ pound butter

Cut beef into 1-inch cubes and alternate on skewers with mushroom caps. Peel and blanch the garlic, and crush or chop fine. Mix thoroughly with butter until soft paste is formed. Heat in a cup or small bowl over hot water until melted. Brush skewered meat and mushroom caps with garlic butter. Place on the grill of a 375° smoke oven, cover and cook 5 minutes. Test for desired doneness. Brush again with hot garlic butter before serving. *Serves 4.*

12

Sausage

On occasion religion has proscribed certain foods and drinks. The Jews outlawed pork; the Hindus, beef; and the Mohammedans, spirits.

But when Christians tried to prohibit sausage, there was trouble that continued for years and did not end until the Church was in full retreat. Sausage has had a rightful place on Christian tables ever since.

The church's sausage war broke out in the days of the Roman empire. The Romans were inordinately fond of a suasage made from pork, chopped pine nuts, cumin, bay leaves and pepper. They always used this sausage with certain rituals, which the Christians regarded as pagan. When the Christians finally came to power in the Roman Empire, they banned sausage eating because of its identification with orgiastic festivals.

Like the American experiment with prohibition centuries later, this led to private—and a certain amount of public—outrage. It also led to bootlegging. As the years went by it became clear, as it did in the United States, that the outlawed item could not be stamped out that way, and indeed the prohibition was worse than sanction. So the Church repealed its ban on sausage.

Sausage's hold on man goes back further than the Roman Empire.

"Let them make sausages of me and serve me up to the students," said Aristophanes in 423 B.C. And the *Odyssey*, which probably was written in the ninth century before Christ, mentions sausage too. No earlier reference is known, but sausage probably goes back ages before that—possibly so far back that the mysteries of sausage making were passed from tribe to tribe so long ago that when history began to be written, sausage appeared native to every land. Even the American Indian, not generally regarded as a gourmet, made sausage.

Essentially, sausage is a mixture of ground meat and spices. Over the years some recipes have become complex, some simple. Most recipes became popular in a region or a city, and the world now knows them by the name of the place where their popularity originated.

Frankfurters of course came from Frankfurt-am-Main in Germany. Bologna is named for Bologna, Italy, and Göteborg for the city in Sweden. Salami is believed to have been named for the Greek city of Salamis on Cyprus. There are hundreds of others, some with only local fame. Emigrants, mostly from Italy and Germany, brought a huge variety of sausage recipes to America.

The trend in recent years, however, has been for large meat packers to take over the market on a nationwide basis. Even in Europe the small butcher has been disappearing, and with him the regional sausage This is a twofold loss. First, it is a loss of variety, and in this day of prepared foods and standard brands, we need more, not less, variety. Second, it is a loss of quality. The products of the big packing houses are excellent, but neither food nor wine produced on a mass scale can equal in taste that made by hand by the small merchant or homeowner

So in this chapter we will give you a number of sausage recipes to keep variety and quality alive. There is perhaps more work connected with sausage making than in other meat dishes. The meat must be ground, the spices mixed in, and perhaps all run through the grinder again. Then there is the stuffing and smoking. But certainly it is no more work than the making of wine, and there are thousands of people, perhaps millions, who consider no effort too great to achieve the perfection of wine. The perfection of sausage is something to be sought too. Your own care will guarantee a flavor that cannot be duplicated elsewhere. After your first success, you most likely will become as stubborn about improved sausage as were the Romans.

Your own care, too, will keep sausage as safe to eat as any food you will ever prepare. We say safe, because carelessly made sausage can make you ill. This has caused many to feel that sausage making is difficult and should only be done by professional food processors. This is not true. Any meat can cause illness if not properly taken care of or not cooked sufficiently. It is well known that ground meat of any kind is more perishable than solid cuts. Sausage is made from ground meat and certain simple precautions must be followed to have good sausage. Let us discuss the two things that cause trouble.

First, there is the parasite trichina in pork that causes trichinosis in humans. This can be caused by an undercooked pork chop, pork roast or any piece of pork that has not been properly prepared. Every cookbook warns that pork must be cooked until well done. The trichinae are rendered harmless at 137° F. If any pork is heated to this temperature it is safe to eat. Heating to 170° will of course make a roast more palatable. The only other method practical for the home sausage maker to make pork absolutely safe is to freeze and store it at 0° for twenty-one days. This is not difficult if you have a home freezer. The ice-cube section of a refrigerator is not cold enough. This is the method used by many meat plants, especially if they are making a dry uncooked sausage such as summer sausage, or cervelat. This was called summer sausage because years ago it was made in the winter and cured and then eaten in the summer.

The second troublemaker is bacteria.

Out of the hundreds of bacteria, three cause nearly all food poisoning: staphylococcus, salmonella and streptococcus. They are the most frequent because they grow at temperatures between 60° and 120°. A fourth bacteria—the most dangerous—is botulinus. This grows only in anaerobic conditions, and botulism is almost always confined to canned foods.

There is a simple way to destroy any toxins. Heat the food to boiling for fifteen minutes. If the food is something you do not want to boil, a pork chop for instance, use a dry heat—oven or fry pan—until the surface fat sizzles and the food cooks. Yeasts and molds do not cause food poisoning. In blue cheese, for example, mold is desirable.

A heavy concentration of curing salt, 5 percent by weight, or the traces of formaldehyde (not harmful to humans) left by wood smoke will prevent the growth of bacteria.

Refrigeration is important in preventing bacteria growth. Cooked or uncooked meat should be stored at 45° or colder. All meat is perishable, so keep it refrigerated.

Cold cuts will keep a day at room temperature and seven days in the refrigerator. Cooked meats will keep for five days in the refrigerator, but only two days at room temperature. Most smoked and cured meats will keep for at least ten days in the refrigerator, but only three days at room temperature. Raw ground meats will keep for only three hours at room temperature and not more than two days in the refrigerator Ground meat is more perishable because the bacteria present on the surface are mixed all through the meat during grinding.

All meat must be kept cold, and it must be cooked to the proper temperature. Sausage is no exception, although there are a few types of dry sausage that have been cured, and sometimes smoked, that are eaten without cooking. A few of these are summer sausage, uncooked salami and pepperoni. These are usually not made by the home sausage maker. Proper drying temperature and humidity are not generally available. All other smoked or fresh pork sausage must be cooked before eating.

Now we will mention a few of the things you will need before you make your first sausage. A sharp meat grinder is essential. If the meat is mashed and crushed rather than cut, you loose juice and texture. You will also need a sausage-stuffer attachment for your grinder or a small sausage stuffer. When grinding a large quantity of meat twice, you should let it stand overnight in the refrigerator between grindings to allow it to cool and permit the seasoning to blend through the sausage. If you are making only a few pounds, this is not necessary. Be sure the meat is kept cold before and after you grind it.

SAUSAGE CASINGS. They come in all sizes, natural and man-made. Ask your butcher to get you some small hog casings or manufactured cellulose casings. The natural casings are salted and must be flushed out in warm water before using. If salted, they will keep indefinitely in the refrigerator until ready to use. The man-made casings are dry and crackly. They can be kept on a kitchen shelf.

All they need is a ten-minute soaking in warm water to be ready for stuffing. They are probably more practical than hog casings for the occasional sausage maker. A muslin casing can easily be made: Sew a strip of folded fabric to form a bag two inches in diameter and about a foot long. These should be damp when used. Soak and then wring out before using.

SAUSAGE STUFFING. Put the stuffer spout in place and grind enough meat to fill. Slip as much of the wet casing as you can or want to on the stuffing tube. Tie the open end with string. Start grinding the meat and it will be forced out of the tube into the casing and begin to fill it up. The weight must be supported slightly above the spout with a couple of fingers of your left hand. This will prevent a crimp in the casing at the spout end and will help you fill the casing solidly without air pockets. When you have filled the casing, tie it in a ring or links, depending on the type of sausage you are making. Small links can be made by just twisting the sausage.

Here are a few points to remember when making sausage:

1. Use only fresh meat and keep it cold before and after sausage making.
2. Keep equipment clean.
3. Store smoked or fresh sausage in the refrigerator.
4. Cook all smoked or fresh sausage before eating.
5. If making dry sausage that contains pork that will not be cooked, freeze the pork and store at $0°$ for twenty-one days before using.

Try sausage patties this way: Dip in beaten egg, roll in crushed corn flakes and fry.

Prunes and sausage complement each other. Split a few prunes and try cooking them in the same pan you fry the sausage in and at the same time.

Roll biscuit dough thin, sprinkle with grated onion and green pepper, and wrap around cooked link sausages. Bake until dough is done. These are delicious and great for the cocktail hour. Fresh sausage can be used if you will form it into small rolls about three inches long and about as thick as your thumb. Bake, parboil or pan fry before putting them in the dough.

GLAZED SAUSAGES

1 pound smoked sausages or
   unstuffed sausage meat
½ cup flour
1 pat butter
   Juice of 1 orange

4 ounces sherry
1 tablespoon berry jelly
½ teaspoon sugar
⅛ teaspoon cinnamon
⅛ teaspoon mace

Form the sausage meat into 4 patties. If you use smoked sausages, remove the meat from the casing. Poach in water for about 10 minutes, then roll in the flour and put into a frying pan with the butter. Brown the sausage. Meanwhile, combine the orange juice with the sherry, jelly, sugar, cinnamon and mace. Add this to the frying pan. Simmer until it thickens and the sausages glazed. When serving, pour the remaining sauce over the meat. *Serves 4.*

BREAKFAST SAUSAGE

1 pound fat pork
2 pounds lean pork
3 teaspoons salt
1½ teaspoons black pepper

¼ teaspoon cayenne pepper
1 teaspoon sage
¼ teaspoon nutmeg
½ teaspoon thyme

Grind the fat and lean pork and mix together. Mix the dry seasonings together and work into the ground meat. Stuff in a muslin casing and smoke at 100° for 4 hours. Keep in refrigerator and slice off patties as needed. Cook as you would any pork sausage.

BEEF SAUSAGE

2 parts lean beef

1 part fresh pork

Seasoning for each pound of meat:

2 teaspoons salt
¼ teaspoon black pepper
⅛ teaspoon red pepper

1 clove garlic, crushed
1/16 teaspoon saltpeter

Chop meat and sprinkle with salt and spices. Grind twice with a fine blade and stuff into casings (large casings are best). Smoke for 2 hours at 100°. To cook, place in boiling water for 12 minutes. This mixture makes tasty meat balls. Cook until done in a 350° smoke oven with some wood smoke.

RINDFLEISCHKOCHWURSTE

2 parts fresh pork fat   3 parts lean beef

Seasoning for each pound of meat:

1 teaspoon salt   ¼ teaspoon coriander
½ teaspoon pepper   1/16 teaspoon saltpeter

Chop meat with a knife; season. Grind once and stuff casings. Let dry for 2 days in a cold place. This need not be smoked, but try some both ways. To cook, poach for 15 minutes.

AUGSBURGERWURSTE

2 parts lean pork   1 part bacon fat

Seasoning for each pound of meat:

1 teaspoon salt   ¼ teaspoon nutmeg
½ teaspoon pepper   1/16 teaspoon saltpeter
¼ teaspoon cloves

Dice pork and bacon fat into small pieces and mix together with seasonings. Stuff casings and smoke in a 100° smokehouse for 4 hours. Poach for 30 minutes and serve.

FRANKFURTERS

1 part pork   2 parts beef

Seasoning for each pound of meat:

1 tablespoon dry cure mix*   1 teaspoon sage
1 tablespoon black pepper   1 clove garlic (optional)

Chop meat with a knife and add the seasonings. Run through a fine grind twice, stuffing the small casings when you grind the second time. Smoke at 100° or less for 2 or 3 hours. Cook in hot water (at least 150°) until frankfurters float. Rinse in hot water and wipe off grease. Store in refrigerator until ready to serve. Heat again in simmering water before eating.

* Eight pounds salt, 2 pounds sugar, and 2 ounces saltpeter (for 100 pounds of meat).

CHICKEN AND PORK SAUSAGE

1 part lean pork   1 part chicken

Seasoning for each pound of meat:

1 teaspoon salt   3 tablespoons Rhine wine
½ teaspoon black pepper   1 egg
¼ teaspoon mace

Chop meat with a knife and mix together with your hands. Spread out evenly on wax paper and add dry seasonings. Add wine and mix well. Run through a medium grinder. Add the egg, lightly beaten, and mix with your hands. Stuff large casings. Cook until done in a smoke oven at 350°. Do not place over the coals. Allow to cool. Slice and serve cold.

SPICY PORK SAUSAGE

2 parts lean pork   1 part bacon fat

Seasoning for each pound of meat:

2 teaspoons salt   ¼ teaspoon coriander
¼ teaspoon black pepper   ¼ teaspoon marjoram
⅛ teaspoon red pepper   ¼ teaspoon thyme
1 clove garlic, crushed   ¼ teaspoon ground bay leaf
1/16 teaspoon saltpeter   ¼ cup red wine
¼ teaspoon savory

Chop meat with a knife. Blend all the spices carefully in a bowl. Season the meat and run through a coarse grind. Add red wine and grind a second time, stuffing the casings. Smoke at 100° in a smoke-house for 2 hours. To cook, poach in boiling water.

SMOKED SAUSAGE

1 part lean beef   6 parts pork

Seasoning for each pound of meat:

1 teaspoon salt   ⅛ teaspoon mace
1 teaspoon black pepper   Red wine
⅛ teaspoon marjoram

Chop meat with a knife and blend with seasonings. Run through a grinder twice. Pack meat in a bowl or crock and allow to cure for a day in the refrigerator. Mix meat with enough red wine to make it pack easily into casings. Hang in smokehouse at 100° or less and smoke for 6 to 8 hours. Refrigerate until ready to cook. Cook until done as you would any pork sausage.

BOLOGNA

3 parts beef   2 parts fat pork

Seasoning for each pound of meat:

1 teaspoon salt   ⅛ teaspoon cayenne pepper
½ teaspoon black pepper   ⅛ teaspoon coriander
¼ teaspoon mace   1 egg

Chop beef with a knife and add salt and pepper. Run through a coarse grind and cool in a crock or bowl for 24 hours. Add cut-up pork and the rest of the dry seasonings. Mix well and grind again. Add the eggs, lightly beaten, to the meat and mix thoroughly. Stuff into large muslin casings and dry for 3 hours. Hang in a smokehouse for 4 hours at 100° or less. Simmer sausages in plenty of water until they float. Cool by plunging into ice-cold water.

CURED BOLOGNA

3 pounds beef   2½ teaspoons black pepper
2 pounds lean pork   ½ teaspoon coriander
⅔ cup dry cure mix*   ½ teaspoon mace

Coarse-grind chopped beef with 2½ tablespoons dry cure. Cut pork into small pieces and mix with 1½ tablespoons dry cure and coarse-grind. Put ground meats, separately, in a cold place to cure for 48 hours. After 48 hours, mix the two meats together very well and add all the seasonings. Run through a fine grinder and stuff in large muslin casings and hang in a cool place for 8 hours. Smoke for 4 hours at 100°. Use plenty of smoke. Place in hot water and simmer until they float. Cool quickly in ice-cold water and hang to dry in a cool place.

* See footnote, p. 171.

KNOCKWURSTE

5 parts lean pork   2 parts pork fat
3 parts beef

Seasoning for each pound of meat:

2 teaspoons salt   ⅛ teaspoon cumin
1 clove garlic, crushed   1/16 teaspoon saltpeter

Chop meat and fat with a knife and mix together with your hands.
Spread out on wax paper and season. Run through a fine grinder.
Stuff the casings and allow to dry for 4 days in a cold place. Smoke
for 4 hours in a smokehouse at 100° or less. To serve, cook in boiling
water for 10 minutes.

FRESH SAUSAGE

1 part lean pork   1 part pork fat

3 teaspoons spiced salt per pound of meat:

1 pound salt   2 teaspoons coriander
4½ tablespoons white pepper   2 teaspoons mace
2 teaspoons allspice   2 teaspoons ground clove
2 teaspoons savory   2 teaspoons sage
2 teaspoons marjoram

Mix pork and pork fat together with 3 teaspoons spiced salt for each
pound of meat. One whole egg per pound of meat will make it
easier to stuff into casings. Smoke lightly and cook in hot water or
use in casserole dishes as you would any sausage. This is good if
formed into small meat balls and cooked in a smoke oven at 350°
until done.

SUMMER SAUSAGE

1 part pork, which has been   2 parts beef
     frozen for 21 days

Seasoning for each pound of meat:

1 tablespoon dry cure mix*   ½ teaspoon white pepper
1 teaspoon black pepper   1 clove garlic, crushed
1 teaspoon sage

* See footnote, p. 171.

This is a dry uncooked sausage. Cut meat into small pieces with a knife and mix. Run through the grinder and spread evenly on wax paper. Add the seasonings and mix well with your hands. Grind again, using the fine blade. Spread meat on wax paper in a cold place to cure for 3 days. Stuff into muslin casings and tie in sausages about 1 foot long. Smoke at 100° for 4 or 5 hours. Hang in a cool place to age for 1 week.

WURSTCHEN TYPE

2 parts lean pork   1 part bacon
1 part veal

Seasoning for each pound of meat:

1 teaspoon salt   ½ teaspoon cardamom
½ teaspoon black pepper   3 tablespoons Rhine wine

Cut up all meat with a knife and mix it all together. Sprinkle on salt and dry spices. Coarse-grind once. Add wine and fine-grind as you stuff casings. Cook for 3 minutes in salted water and cool. To serve, cook in smoke oven at 350° until done. If you want to use later, store in refrigerator after the 3 minutes' cooking in water. Use as you would any pork sausage.

SMOKED GOOSE LIVER SAUSAGE

1 pound lean pork or poultry   ½ teaspoon white pepper
    meat   ¼ teaspoon nutmeg
1 pound goose liver   ¼ teaspoon marjoram
5 tablespoons curing salt   ⅛ teaspoon ground cloves
½ cup water   ½ ounce chopped truffles
½ cup white wine   (optional)
1 teaspoon salt

This is not pâté de foie gras, but it is delicious. The pork should be cured first. Cut up pork (or poultry) and place in bowl. Cover with a brine of ⅓ cup of curing salt, ½ cup water and ½ cup white wine. Refrigerate for 2 days. Grind goose liver and cured pork together. Add salt, truffles and seasonings and mix. Grind and stuff in muslin casings. Cook for 1 hour at 160°. Cool and dry for 8 hours. Smoke 4 hours at 100° and chill. Serve cold.

SMOKED LIVER SAUSAGE

2 pounds pork trimmings,
    heart, liver or tongue
½ pound liver
1 cup beef broth

2½ teaspoons salt
1 teaspoon black pepper
¼ teaspoon red pepper
½ teaspoon allspice

Cook pork trimmings in water, covered, for 2 hours. Add liver and cook for another ½ hour. Remove meat from any bones, and grind. Add a cup of broth and mix thoroughly with salt, pepper and spices. Stuff in a large muslin or beef casing. Smoke for 2 hours at 100°. Simmer until it floats. Plunge in cold water and chill for 30 minutes. Hang up to dry.

CURED GAME SAUSAGE

1 part venison
1 part lean pork

1 part fat pork

Seasoning per pound of meat:

1½ tablespoons dry cure mix*
½ teaspoon black pepper

¼ teaspoon ground cloves
½ teaspoon sage

Cut meat up into ½-inch pieces and mix with curing salt. Store in a covered bowl for 2 days to cure in the refrigerator. Add spices and grind, stuffing into casings. Smoke for 4 hours at 100° or less. Cook the way you would any pork sausage. Instead of smoking, this sausage can be smoke-cooked in a 350° smoke oven and served hot.

* See footnote, p. 171.

13

Variety Meats

If you enjoy the flavor of variety meats, you are lucky indeed. They're usually more economical than other cuts (except calf's liver, which is overpriced) and are loaded with nutrients. Something you like that is good for you and inexpensive is a hard combination to beat.

Variety meats include sweetbreads, brains, heart, liver, tongue, kidneys, tripe, pigs' feet, oxtails and a few others. They come from beef, veal, lamb and pork. Lamb and veal parts can be interchanged in any recipe. Lamb kidneys, for example, can be substituted for veal kidneys.

All variety meats are more perishable than regular cuts and should not be stored more than two days in a refrigerator. They will keep for three or four months at 0° in a freezer.

Here are a few tips on the preparation of the meats mentioned in this chapter.

BRAINS. After washing, remove the membrane and soak in cold water for one hour. Simmer in a court bouillon or salted water for thirty minutes.

COURT BOUILLON

2½ quarts water   ½ bay leaf
2 teaspoons salt   1 onion, chopped
½ teaspoon thyme   4 bruised peppercorns

If you want to use just the salted water, mix 2 teaspoons salt for each 2½ quarts of water. The bouillon or salt water will firm up the brains and turn them whiter. They are delicate and tender and should be soaked and blanched soon after purchase regardless of when you plan to prepare them.

SWEETBREADS. This is the thymus or pancreas of a calf. The meat is delicious and can be prepared in many ways. Sweetbreads should be treated like brains before cooking. Presoak in cold water for an hour, then blanch in salted water, but only for a few minutes.

Sweetbreads and brains are easy to handle if placed on individual small mesh grills that are then placed on the main grill in the smoke oven. Just remove the small grill from the oven when the meat is cooked.

HEART. Beef heart is not recommended for the smoke oven unless sliced, marinated and tenderized. Use calf and lamb heart. They are much more tender.

KIDNEY. Kidneys are delicious. They are much more popular in England and France than they are in the United States. When cooked in a smoke oven they should be split open. Kidneys should be cooked quickly; long cooking toughens them.

TONGUE. This meat is not tender and should be simmered either before or after smoking. Which way depends on how you plan to use it and how you want it to look on the table. Either way, the skin is removed after cooking and the root end is trimmed. Tongue is good hot or cold. Try horseradish or mustard sauce with cold tongue.

LIVER. Liver is the most popular of all variety meats. Its great supply of nutrients is well known and has probably contributed to its popularity. Liver can be ground into pâté, made into loaves or patties, or cooked in slices. There is very little waste. Remove any membrane or tubes before cooking.

Sorry to say, as great as the smoke oven is, there are variety meats that resist the cooking action of charcoal and smoke. Braising and cooking in liquid are the methods best used. However, if you want to experiment, try simmering your choice first in salted water or a sauce. When it's almost done, transfer it to your hot smoke oven for the final blessing. We know you won't hurt it, and who knows? You might come up with a new specialty of the house.

SMOKED BRAINS

1 pound brains	Juice of 1 lemon
⅓ cup melted butter	4 teaspoons capers

Soak brains in cold water for 1 hour and parboil in salted water for 30 minutes. Cut into 4 uniform slices and place on small mesh racks. Toss a few wood chips on the fire and put the meat into a 300° oven. Cook for 15 minutes. Baste a couple of times with the butter, to which has been added the juice of 1 lemon. To serve, turn the small grill over so the meat is placed on a piece of hot buttered toast. Put a teaspoon of capers on each slice and pour on what is left of the butter baste. *Serves 4.*

TONGUE WITH MUSTARD SAUCE

4 pounds veal tongue	1 stalk celery
1 large onion	½ cup vinegar
1 bay leaf	Water to cover
2 cloves garlic	

Place tongue on cut-up onion, bay leaf, garlic and cut-up celery in bottom of soup pot. Pour in vinegar and water to cover. Simmer for 3 hours or until meat is tender. Let cool, skin and trim big end of tongue. Smoke at low heat, around 100°, for 45 minutes. Use plenty of smoke. Add wet wood chips from time to time if smoke stops. Slice and serve with mustard sauce. *Serves 6.*

MUSTARD SAUCE

1 cup Béchamel sauce (see Index)	2 teaspoons dry mustard
	1 teaspoon lemon juice

Heat sauce in double boiler. Add mustard and lemon juice. Mix well and serve hot on sliced smoked tongue.

MARINATED BRAINS

1 pound brains	½ onion, chopped
2 quarts water	1 teaspoon ginger
2 teaspoons vinegar	1 teaspoon thyme
2 teaspoons salt	½ cup sherry
1 cup soy sauce	1 can consommé

Soak the brains and blanch for 30 minutes in water with vinegar
and salt. Allow to cool. Cut into 4 even slices and cover with soy
sauce, onion, ginger, thyme, sherry and consommé. Refrigerate for
1 or 2 hours. Put on small mesh racks and place in oven, but not
directly over coals. Smoke-cook at 300° for about 20 minutes.
Serves 4.

CALF HEART

2 calf hearts	½ teaspoon salt
¼ cup lemon juice	½ teaspoon pepper
¼ cup olive oil	8 slices bacon

Cut hearts in half. Remove membrane and any clots or tubes. Mix
lemon juice, oil, salt and pepper in a cup. Baste each half well and
let stand for 30 minutes. Place cut side down on the grill in a 325°
oven. Cook for 20 minutes. Use a few chips for smoke. Baste once
or twice. Turn hearts over and cover each half with 2 bacon
slices and cook for another 20 minutes. Test for doneness. Serve
plain or with a sauce. *Serves 4.*

SWEETBREADS ASPEN

2 quarts water	8 slices bacon
2 teaspoons salt	½ cup Parmesan cheese
2 sets of sweetbreads	

Chill sweetbreads in ice-cold water for 30 minutes. Blanch in salted
water for a few minutes. Place in cold water again to chill. Remove
and allow to dry. Cut into thick slices and wrap each serving in
2 slices of bacon and fasten with a couple of toothpicks. Cook indirectly in a 325° oven without turning for 30 minutes. Serve hot
with a pat of butter and a healthy sprinkle of grated Parmesan
cheese. *Serves 4.*

SMOKED HEART SLICES

2 pounds calf heart	1 teaspoon rosemary
½ cup wine vinegar	2 tablespoons olive oil
½ cup soy sauce	⅛ pound butter
2 cloves garlic, chopped	Pepper
1 teaspoon salt	

Slice heart into slices about ½ inch thick. Mix vinegar, soy, garlic, salt and rosemary. Pour over slices and marinate for 2 hours. Turn meat over a few times. Remove meat and wipe off marinade. Brush well with olive oil. Put a few wood chips on the coals of a 350° fire. Lay meat on grill and close cover. This is best when nice and brown and a bit on the rare side. Put a pat of butter on each slice and serve hot. Put a good grind of fresh black pepper on each slice. *Serves 4.*

MARINATED LIVER

2 pounds liver	1 onion, chopped
½ cup salad oil	2 cloves garlic, crushed
½ cup red wine	1 teaspoon salt

Cut into serving-sized pieces and marinate for 3 hours in oil, wine, onion, garlic and salt. Lay the liver pieces on the grill of a 325° oven. Put a handful of wood chips on the fire. Baste a few times. Turn after 10 minutes and baste again. Liver should be done in about 20 minutes. Test a piece after the meat has cooked for 15 minutes. Try serving with onion rings fried in butter. *Serves 4 to 6.*

SWEETBREADS BORDELAISE

2 sets sweetbreads	½ pound mushrooms
1 cup Bordelaise sauce	2 tablespoons chopped onion
(see Index)	3 tablespoons butter

Chill sweetbreads in cold water for 30 minutes. Blanch for a few minutes in salted water and allow to cool and dry. Cut into thick slices and place on small mesh grills. Cook in a 325° oven indirectly with a few wood chips for about 30 minutes. While sweetbreads are cooking, heat a cup of Bordelaise sauce in a small saucepan. Sauté thinly sliced mushrooms and onions in butter. When sweetbreads are cooked put on hot plates. Garnish with sautéed mushrooms and pour Bordelaise sauce over each serving. *Serves 4.*

SWEETBREADS WITH HAM

2 sets sweetbreads
2 quarts water
2 teaspoons salt

½ cup melted butter
4 thin slices cooked ham
2 large tomatoes

First chill sweetbreads in cold water for ½ hour. Blanch in 2 quarts of salted water for 15 minutes. Allow to cool. Remove any membrane or tubes. Place the sweetbreads on small mesh grills. Baste with butter and place in a 325° oven. Cook for 10 minutes. Remove and turn over to place a sweetbread serving on each of the 4 slices of ham. Baste again and place on the grill ham side down. Also place 4 tomato slices, basted with butter, on the grill and close the cover. Cook for another 10 to 15 minutes. Baste again with butter and serve hot. *Serves 4.*

LAMB KIDNEYS

2 pounds lamb kidneys
½ cup salad oil
½ cup white wine
½ teaspoon salt

½ teaspoon black pepper
½ teaspoon thyme
¼ pound maître d' butter (see Index)

Remove outer membrane and split kidney almost in half, leaving it hinged like a clam shell on one side. Remove the core. Place kidneys in a container that will just hold them all, and cover with the marinade of oil, wine, salt, pepper and thyme. Marinate for 1 hour. Drain kidneys and pierce each with 2 toothpicks to hold halves open. Arrange on small grills and place in a 350° oven with a few wood chips. Try for doneness after 10 minutes. Remove as soon as they are done. Overcooking toughens them. Serve with a dab of maître d' butter in the hollow of each kidney half. *Serves 4 to 6.*

LIVER BORDELAISE

2 pounds baby beef or calf's liver
½ pound sliced bacon
Salt

Pepper
1 cup Bordelaise sauce (see Index)
2 tablespoons chopped parsley

Cut liver into slices a little wider than the bacon slices and about 5 inches long. Cut the bacon slices into 2 pieces so each piece will just cover each piece of liver. Remove the grill from the oven and arrange the liver slices and season with salt and pepper. Place a bacon slice on top of each piece of liver. Put a handful of wood chips on the fire of a 300° oven and position the liver-laden grill. Smoke-cook until bacon and liver are done. Arrange slices on a hot platter and pour hot Bordelaise sauce over them. Sprinkle lightly with finely choped parsley. *Serves 6.*

BACON LARDED LIVER

2 pounds liver	½ teaspoon garlic salt
½ pound bacon	1 teaspoon dry mustard
½ cup chopped onions	3 feet string
1 teaspoon black pepper	½ cup white wine

Cut bacon into thin strips ¼ inch wide and about 1 inch long. If you have a larding needle, lard the liver with the bacon lardoons. If you don't have a needle, poke the bacon lardoons into holes made with a skewer. Place them about an inch apart, or less, all over the liver. Have them sticking out both sides. Spread one side of the liver with the chopped onions, pepper, garlic salt, and dry mustard. Roll liver up with onion and seasoning on the inside. Tie the roll with 3 strings, 1 on each end and 1 in the middle. One large roll is best if you can buy 1 large slice of liver. Put in a 325° oven on a rack over a broiler pan. Smoke-cook indirectly for about 30 to 45 minutes. When done remove meat and pour wine in pan and stir well. Get all pan juices and browned specks. Pour this hot over the sliced servings. *Serves 4.*

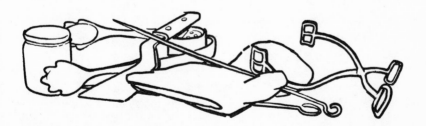

14

Sauces, Marinades, Bastes and Butters

Cervantes was right when he said, "There is no sauce in the world like hunger." He also could have said there is nothing in the world like a good sauce. Making it is an art. Sauce making requires time, patience and complete dedication to the task. It is never an accident. Good sauces cannot be thrown together.

A smoke oven is simple to use. We say anyone can prepare a delicious roast in one. A Sauce Robert, by contrast, does not depend on the equipment, but on the cook. However, the fruit is worth the labor. Leftovers can be lifted out of the ordinary with a sauce. Ordinary meats can be made great. Sauces sharpen the appetite and bring out the best in the food they are served with.

Great cooks such as Escoffier, Carmé and Dumas, who wrote about food, were lyrical about sauces. Escoffier felt that the stock used in making sauces was the most important part of French cooking.

For the sake of definition a sauce is any liquid seasoning that is served with food. A marinade is a liquid seasoning, but is used to season the food before it is cooked. Sometimes it is made into a sauce later.

Although sauce making is a demanding cooking skill, it can be learned. With the use of a few simple tools and a good recipe, anyone of reasonable wit and patience can turn out a commendable sauce. All you need is a good wooden spoon, a wire wisk and a sturdy, heavy, flat-bottom saucepan. Some experts prefer tin-lined copper pans.

The classic sauces fall into two groups: the Great Sauces and the Lesser Sauces. The Great Sauces are basic and are used to make the Lesser or Compound Sauces. Here is a simple classification.

Brown Sauces

Basic Brown (Espagnole)
Demi-glace (basic brown reduced by half or more)
Tomato Sauces

White Sauces

Béchamel
Velouté

Compound Brown Sauces are made with the basic brown sauces. Sauce Robert, Diable, Colbert, Chateaubriand are a few.

Compound White Sauces are made with white stock and basic white sauces. Bercy, Allemande, Béarnaise and Hollandaise are some of the famous ones.

Compound Butters are not really sauces, but are included here because they are used to season meats and hors d'oeuvre. Many of them are easy to prepare.

The basic sauce recipes that follow are simplified in form, and some of the preparations have been shortened from the classic rules laid down by the masters.

In addition to White Stock and Brown Stock, three other important ingredients of many sauces should be mentioned.

Roux. This is the thickening agent used and is often the first step in making a sauce. There are three kinds of roux: brown, blond and white. They are all made with equal parts clarified butter and flour. Some cooks prefer cornstarch. For brown roux, blend the butter and flour together and cook in a saucepan until pale brown. Stir to keep from burning. Brown roux will keep. It is used mostly in brown sauces. Blond roux is cooked only when needed. Don't cook it as long as the brown roux. When the color is pale gold take it off the heat. White roux is over heat just long enough to cook the flour. Avoid any color, but be sure the flour is cooked. Not more than five minutes over medium heat.

Mirepoix. This is a mixture used to enrich some sauces. The most common is made with two parts finely diced carrot, two parts finely chopped onions and one part celery. Simmer slowly in butter with a bay leaf and a pinch of salt and a pinch of thyme. Cook until soft.

BOUQUET GARNI. This is composed of one large bay leaf, six sprigs fresh parsley and one sprig thyme, tied together with thread. Celery and other herbs are often used.

Seasoning is important to sauce, but it must not overpower the food to the point of smothering everything, the way a hot barbecue sauce would smother a thin slice of porterhouse steak. A good sauce should be smooth and free of lumps. It should have a creamy texture without being runny. It should be shiny and free of any grease. When it is right it sparkles. It should never be served cold. If it must be kept hot for a time on the stove, small flecks of butter floated on the surface will help prevent a skin from forming.

Sauces can be frozen. Don't hesitate to make two or three quarts of a sauce that takes hours to prepare, but would keep only a week under ordinary refrigeration. It is as easy to make three quarts as it is three cups.

Allow the sauce to cool and fill small freezer containers within a half inch of the top. Cover and freeze. When you need sauce, remove from container and melt in a double boiler. If you freeze sauce in aluminum containers, defrost in a 300° oven right in the container. If you like smaller quantities of sauce available, freeze in plastic ice-cube trays. When frozen store the cubes in a heavy plastic bag in the freezer. If you are serving a late dinner for two and want just enough Chateaubriand sauce for two steaks, place a couple of sauce cubes in a double boiler to melt while you are starting the fire. A friend reports he even froze Hollandaise sauce. After melting, all it needed was a spoonful of hot water and some beating to restore it. Keep frozen sauces no longer than five months.

Marinades are easy to make and use. Anyone who can read can make a marinade as well as the best chef in town. This is not to discount their importance. A good marinade can tenderize and flavor an ordinary piece of meat right into the gourmet class. Witness pot roast in a red wine marinade. All it takes is good ingredients. Don't use bad-tasting wine just because it's a marinade. You want the wine's flavor, not the alcohol. If it smells so bad that you don't want to drink it, pour it down the drain. Don't put it on your meat. This does not mean we recommend vintage wines for marinating pot roasts. Use a good table wine. If you don't make your own wine buy it by the gallon; it's cheaper. Decant it into five wine or whiskey bottles with screw caps. You won't lose the flavor you would in a half-empty gallon jug. Besides, it looks neater. Used clean champagne bottles with the new plastic "corks" are fine for storing wine. Have one set for red wine and one for white.

Use olive oil or your favorite salad oil. Some recipes will call specifically for olive oil. If you can't stand olive oil, by all means switch.

There are only a few points to remember when making marinades. Always use glass, stainless steel, a crock or enameled containers—never aluminum or sheet metal. Use a container just large enough to hold the meat. This will keep to a minimum the amount of marinade needed to cover the meat.

Try to plan ahead so meat will marinate long enough to season and tenderize. Unless the meat is cut up, as for Oriental cooking, three hours is the minimum for a roast or large steak. Roasts are better if they marinate overnight in the refrigerator. All meats that are in a marinade for over an hour should be in a cool place or in the refrigerator. If the meat wants to float to the surface, put a small plate on it and some sort of weight to keep it below the surface. Turning the meat often is important. This gives the marinade a chance to penetrate all sides evenly. If several pieces are in the bowl, stir them every half hour.

The basic marinade is usually a mixture of oil and acid with a few aromatic vegetables and seasonings. The acid, in the form of wine, vinegar or lemon juice, helps tenderize the meat. The oil improves the flavor, helps the cooking and keeps the meat from drying out. The only advantage of cooked marinade is that it will probably keep longer without refrigeration. Years ago it was used mainly in the summer.

BROWN SAUCES

Here are a few of the classic French sauces that go beautifully with meat cooked in a smoke oven. They are robust enough not to be overpowered if the meat is really smoky. The most famous and useful sauce of all is probably Espagnole. This is used alone or as part of brown sauces such as Bordelaise or Sauce Robert. An inexpensive substitute for Espagnole (and a timesaver) is canned beef gravy. However, if you want to try your hand at Espagnole made from scratch, here is one method. But first you must make a brown stock.

5 pounds bones	1 stalk celery
2 carrots	2 teaspoons salt
2 onions	1 pound beef trimmings
1 clove garlic	1 bouquet garni

Break up 5 pounds veal and beef bones in small pieces. Spread them in a large pan in a hot oven (400°) and cook for 30 minutes. Dump them into a soup kettle with carrots, onions, garlic, celery, salt, beef, bouquet garni and 4 quarts water. Bring to a boil and simmer for 4 hours. Skim all fat and strain liquid. Refrigerated, this stock will keep for 4 days. Freeze it to use later.

SAUCE ESPAGNOLE

4 strips bacon	½ cup flour
1 medium onion, chopped	½ cup white wine
1 carrot, chopped	2 quarts brown stock
1 bay leaf	½ cup tomato purée
½ teaspoon thyme	

Cut bacon into small pieces, dice, and sauté in a deep saucepan. When half done, add chopped onion, carrot, bay leaf and thyme. Cook until onions are golden color. Add flour and stir until everything is cooked nice and brown. Pour off any bacon fat that is left and add ½ cup of wine and 6 cups of brown stock, which has been heated. Cook this slowly until it is reduced about ½. Stir occasionally and skim off fat frequently. When reduced, allow to cool. When cold, skim off any remaining fat. Add tomato purée and the remaining 2 cups of brown stock. Simmer slowly for 1 hour. Remove all grease and strain through a fine sieve or cloth. Store in covered jars in the refrigerator. If you are not going to use it within a week, freeze it in 1-cup containers.

WHITE STOCK

2 pounds veal bones
1 pound chicken giblets
1 pound veal trimmings (if available)
1 carrot
1 onion

1 leek (if available)
2 celery stalks with tops
2 teaspoons salt
1 handful parsley
1 bay leaf

Have the butcher break up the bones into small pieces. Put bones, giblets and veal trimmings and any chicken bones you might have in a soup kettle. Add 5 quarts of water and bring to a boil. Skim until scum no longer forms. Add vegetables and seasonings. Simmer slowly for 3 hours. Cool and remove fat. Strain through a sieve or cloth and store in the refrigerator. It will keep for at least 4 or 5 days. Can be frozen. Use in soups and sauces.

BECHAMEL SAUCE

1 tablespoon chopped onion
2 tablespoons butter
2 tablespoons flour
2 cups hot milk
2 ounces chopped veal (optional)

1 tablespoon butter
½ bay leaf
Pinch white pepper
Pinch nutmeg
Salt

Cook onion for a few minutes in 2 tablespoons butter. Add flour and stir until blended. Slowly add the hot milk. Stir constantly. While this is being done, the veal should simmer slowly in 1 tablespoon of butter with bay leaf, white pepper and nutmeg. Cook veal for a few minutes without browning. Add veal to milk and cook slowly over water in a double boiler for 1 hour. Salt to taste and strain. This sauce can be made without the veal if you use a cup of veal stock in place of 1 of the cups of milk. Cool and save for use in other sauces. May be frozen. Béchamel will keep for about a week in the refrigerator.

EASY BROWN SAUCE

2½ tablespoons butter
2 tablespoons flour
2 cups beef consommé

1 tablespoon tomato sauce or
catsup

Clarify the butter by melting it in a cup placed in hot water. Pour the clear butter into a saucepan with the flour and throw away the sediment left in the cup. Cook the butter and flour until the roux is dark brown. Stir while you gradually add the hot consommé. Cook and stir for a few minutes. Add tomato sauce and blend. Turn heat down and simmer for 30 minutes. Skim off fat and strain. Store in refrigerator or freeze.

HUNTER SAUCE

¼ pound mushrooms
1 tablespoon chopped onion
2 tablespoons butter
½ cup red wine
½ cup Espagnole sauce or
canned beef gravy

2 tablespoons tomato sauce
2 tablespoons butter
1 tablespoon chopped parsley
Dash Tabasco

Thinly slice mushrooms and sauté in butter with onions. Add wine and Sauce Espagnole and reduce by about ½. Add tomato sauce and heat to the boiling point. Add butter, parsley, Tabasco. This is a good sauce for poultry, game, small meat cuts.

SAUCE DIABLE

½ cup white wine
1 tablespoon vinegar
1 tablespoon chopped green
onion
½ teaspoon thyme

¼ teaspoon black pepper
1 cup Sauce Espagnole
3 tablespoons butter
1 teaspoon chopped parsley

Mix wine, vinegar, onion, thyme, pepper. Boil until reduced by ⅔. Stir in 1 cup of Espagnole sauce and cook for a couple of minutes. Remove sauce pan from heat and stir in 3 tablespoons of butter and 1 teaspoon finely chopped parsley.

SAUCE BORDELAISE

1 cup red wine
2 tablespoons chopped green
    onions
½ bay leaf
¼ teaspoon thyme
    Pinch salt

1 cup Sauce Espagnole or
    canned beef gravy
2 tablespoons butter
2 tablespoons chopped parsley
2 ounces beef marrow, diced
    (optional)

Put wine, onions, bay leaf, thyme and salt in a saucepan. Boil until it is reduced by ½. Add 1 cup Sauce Espagnole or gravy and reduce ⅓. Remove from heat and add the butter. Strain and add chopped parsley. Poach marrow in salted water and add to sauce. Serve sauce hot over sliced pot roast, steaks or ground beef.

RED WINE SAUCE

2 tablespoons chopped onions
1 tablespoon butter
2 cups red wine
1 bouquet garni

1½ cups Sauce Espagnole or
    canned beef gravy
1 tablespoon butter

Sauté onions in butter until soft. Add wine and bouquet garni and cook until reduced by ⅔. Add Sauce Espagnole or beef gravy. Boil to reduce by ½. Strain through a sieve. Reheat and add 1 tablespoon butter.

SAUCE FOR PORK

2 tablespoons chopped onion
1 tablespoon butter
    Pinch salt
    Pinch thyme
    Pinch powdered bay leaf
½ cup white wine
1 tablespoon vinegar

1 cup Sauce Espagnole or
    canned beef gravy
1 teaspoon mustard
1 teaspoon parsley
1 teaspoon chervil
    Cayenne pepper

Sauté onions in butter until soft. Season with salt, thyme, and powdered bay leaf. Add wine and vinegar and boil until almost completely reduced. Add Sauce Espagnole and simmer while stirring for a couple of minutes. Add mustard, parsley, and chervil. Pepper with cayenne to taste.

SAUCE VELOUTE

½ cup butter
½ cup flour

1 quart white stock (see Index)

Make a pale roux in a saucepan by combining the butter and flour. Cook and stir with a wooden spoon until the roux is a pale golden color. Stir in the white stock. Bring to a boil, stirring constantly. Turn the heat so the sauce simmers very slowly. Skim frequently and cook for 1 hour. Strain through a sieve or cloth and let cool. This may be cooked longer if you want a thicker sauce.

CHARCUTIERE SAUCE

2 tablespoons chopped onion
1 tablespoon butter
1 tablespoon white wine or wine vinegar

1 cup Sauce Espagnole or canned beef gravy
2 tablespoons diced gherkins
1 teaspoon mustard (optional)

This is an excellent sauce for pork and sausages. Cook onions in butter until soft. Add wine or vinegar and cook for a few minutes. Add Sauce Espagnole and bring to a simmer; add gherkins and mustard. Serve hot with pork.

FISH STOCK

½ cup small bits of mushrooms
1 onion, chopped
1 sprig parsley
1 sprig thyme (or ½ teaspoon dry)
½ bay leaf

4 pounds fish bones and trimmings, heads, etc., of any fresh fish
½ teaspoon lemon juice
1 teaspoon salt
2½ quarts water
1 pint white wine

Put mushrooms, onion, parsley, thyme and bay leaf in bottom of pot and cover with fish bones and trimmings. Sprinkle on lemon juice, salt, water and wine. Bring to a boil and simmer for ½ hour. Skim during cooking. Strain and store in refrigerator or freeze.

FISH ESPAGNOLE

This is made in the same way as the brown Sauce Espagnole, except that a fish stock is used instead of brown stock.

COLBERT SAUCE

⅔ cup Sauce Espagnole or
   canned beef gravy
1 tablespoon lemon juice
¼ pound butter, melted
   Dash nutmeg

Pinch cayenne pepper
½ tablespoon lemon juice
1 tablespoon chopped parsley
1 tablespoon sherry or
   Madeira

This is an all-around sauce. Use it on fish, meats or vegetables. Boil
Sauce Espagnole with 1 tablespoon lemon juice for a moment. Re-
move from heat and add butter. Season with nutmeg and cayenne.
Add lemon juice, parsley and wine. Stir well and serve hot.

SAUCE LYONNAISE

½ cup chopped onions
1 tablespoon butter
1 tablespoon cornstarch

1 tablespoon vinegar
1 cup Sauce Espagnole or
   canned beef gravy

Cook onion in butter until soft. Add cornstarch and stir. Add vinegar and reduce about ½. Add Sauce Espagnole or beef gravy. Cook
and stir for a few minutes. This is an excellent sauce for slices of
cold smoked meat.

SAUCE ALLEMANDE (for fish)

2 egg yolks
1 cup fish stock

1½ cups Fish Velouté Egg
   Sauce (see above)
1 tablespoon butter

Mix egg yolks with fish stock in a saucepan. Add Fish Velouté Egg
Sauce and mix well before cooking. Cook and stir with a wooden
spoon until the sauce thickens. Stir in a tablespoon of butter and
serve as is or strain.

SAUCE ALLEMANDE (for meat)

2 egg yolks
1 cup chicken stock

1½ cups Sauce Velouté (see
   Index)
1 tablespoon butter

Proceed the same as the Sauce Allemande for fish. This is an excellent sauce for variety meats.

FISH VELOUTE EGG SAUCE

2 tablespoons butter
2 tablespoons flour
1 cup fish stock (see Index)

3 egg yolks
1 teaspoon lemon juice
2 hard-boiled eggs, grated

Combine the butter and flour and cook until golden. Stir in fish stock and cook until mixture thickens. Beat 3 egg yolks separately and stir gradually into sauce. Keep stirring but don't let the sauce boil. When well blended and ready to serve, add lemon juice and eggs.

SAUCE MORNAY

1 cup Béchamel Sauce
½ cup fresh cream

½ cup Parmesan cheese
2 tablespoons butter

Reduce Béchamel Sauce by ⅔ and add cream and Parmesan cheese. Stir constantly until well blended.

D'UXELLES (for meat or fish sauces)

¼ pound mushroom pieces
½ onion, chopped fine
1 teaspoon butter

Salt
Pepper
Nutmeg

Clean mushrooms and mince very fine. Put in a cloth and twist to remove all moisture possible. Brown mushrooms and onion in butter and season with salt, pepper and nutmeg. Use as is or put aside to cool for use in sauces. May be frozen.

D'UXELLES SAUCE (for fish)

1 cup white wine
2 tablespoons d'Uxelles

1 cup tomato purée*
1 tablespoon chopped parsley

Combine the wine and d'Uxelles in a saucepan and cook for 10 minutes. Add a cup of tomato purée and boil for a few minutes. Just before serving, stir in a tablespoon of chopped parsley.

* If you have fish stock on hand, use ½ cup of it and reduce the tomato purée to a ½ cup.

SMOKED FISH SAUCE

½ cup white wine
1 tablespoon chopped onion
Salt
Pepper

2 tablespoons brown sauce
6 tablespoons butter
½ teaspoon lemon juice
1 tablespoon chopped parsley

Boil wine and onions until reduced by ¼. Season with salt and pepper. Add brown sauce and heat. Remove pan and add butter. Heat carefully and add lemon juice and chopped parsley. Serve on smoked fish fillets.

WINE SAUCE FOR FISH

½ cup vegetable mirepoix
2 cups red wine
1 clove garlic
1 can consommé

3 tablespoons butter
Pinch cayenne
1 tablespoon chopped parsley

Make a mirepoix with finely chopped carrots, onions and celery seasoned with thyme and bay leaf. Cook it in butter. Add wine and garlic. Reduce by ½. Add consommé and cook to reduce by ½ again. Remove from heat and stir in butter and cayenne. Just before serving, add parsley.

BEARNAISE SAUCE

1 tablespoon chopped green
    onion
1 teaspoon dry tarragon
1 sprig thyme or ½ teaspoon
    dry
½ bay leaf
3 tablespoons wine vinegar

Salt
Pepper
2 egg yolks
¼ pound butter cut into small
    pats
1 tablespoon chopped parsley

Combine the onions, tarragon, thyme, bay leaf, vinegar, salt and pepper. Reduce to a couple of teaspoons in a saucepan and let cool. Put in top of double boiler and mix with egg yolks, which have been mixed with a tablespoon of water. Beat with a whisk over hot but not boiling water. When yolks begin to thicken, add the butter a piece at a time while you continue to use the whisk. Remove from heat and add the chopped parsley.

SAUCE BERCY

1 tablespoon chopped onion   1 cup Béchamel Sauce
1 tablespoon butter   3 tablespoons butter
½ cup white wine   1 tablespoon chopped parsley
½ cup fish stock

Cook onions for a few minutes in butter. Add white wine and fish
stock. Reduce by ½ and add Béchamel Sauce. Heat almost to boiling point and stir in butter and parsley. Spoon over a fish in the
oven to finish off the last 5 minutes of cooking, and serve hot to
pour over fish at the table.

HOLLANDAÏSE SAUCE

4 egg yolks   2 teaspoons lemon juice
2 teaspoons water   Pinch white pepper
¼ pound butter, cut into small   Pinch salt
   pats

Have everything you need ready and at room temperature. Use
a double boiler but don't let the upper part touch the water. Have
the water in the lower pan as hot as you can get it without boiling.
Have the butter cut up in small pats.

Combine the egg yolks and water in the top of the double boiler
over the hot water. Beat until they are well mixed. With your other
hand, add the pieces of butter one at a time. As each piece melts
and blends, add the next, all the time blending with the whisk.
When all butter is melted and blended, remove the pan from the
heat and continue to whisk for a couple of minutes. Add lemon
juice, salt and pepper. Mix over the hot water again for a minute.
If it should curdle, add a teaspoon of hot water and blend until it
goes together again. Keep warm in the double boiler.

SAUCE NICOISE

2 pimientos, chopped very fine   ½ teaspoon tarragon
2 tablespoons catsup   1 cup mayonnaise

Mix pimientos with catsup and tarragon. Blend well with mayonnaise and chill.

AIOLI SAUCE

3 cloves garlic
1 egg yolk
Pinch salt

½ cup olive oil
1 tablespoon lemon juice

Crush garlic in mortar until fine. Add egg yolk and pinch of salt. Mix well. Add oil a little at a time, alternating with lemon juice. Start with a few drops of each. Stop adding oil and juice when the aioli has a nice, thick, creamy consistency. Add a few drops of water if sauce is too thick.

MAYONNAISE

2 egg yolks
White pepper
Salt

2 teaspoons lemon juice
2 cups olive oil

Be sure all ingredients are at room temperature before you begin. Put the yolks in a bowl. Add salt, pepper and a few drops of lemon juice. Mix these ingredients with a whisk or at medium speed with an electric beater. Start adding the oil drop by drop as you beat rather slowly. After 3 or 4 minutes start adding the oil in a fine trickle. Add a few drops of lemon juice from time to time. If the mayonnaise should curdle, beat another egg yolk with some oil in another bowl; add the first mixture to it and beat together.

BASIC TOMATO SAUCE

3 strips bacon
½ cup butter
1 carrot, diced
1 onion, chopped
1 clove garlic
1 quart tomato purée
1 stalk celery, with tops

2 sprigs parsley
1 teaspoon thyme
4 teaspoons flour
1 teaspoon salt
2 teaspoons sugar
2 cups White Stock (see Index)

Cut the bacon up fine and half cook in butter. Add cut-up carrot and onion and cook until soft. Sprinkle with flour and brown. Add garlic, tomato purée, celery, parsley, thyme, salt, sugar and stock. Bring to a boil; then simmer for 2 hours. Force through a strainer and cool. Can be frozen.

SMOKED SALMON SAUCE

1 cucumber	1 tablespoon lemon juice
1 cup sour cream	Salt
2 tablespoons finely chopped	Pepper
green onion	

This simple-to-make sauce is delicious with smoked salmon or smoked tuna. Dice the cucumber and mix in a bowl with the sour cream. Add the green onions and lemon juice. Salt and pepper to taste. Chill.

CUMBERLAND SAUCE

1 teaspoon finely chopped onion	1 cup port wine
	Juice of 1 orange
1 tablespoon orange peel	Juice of 1 lemon
1 tablespoon lemon peel	1 cup red currant jelly
1 teaspoon mustard	Salt and ginger to taste

Chop the onion quite fine. Cut the orange and lemon peel into ⅛-inch strips and then into ½-inch lengths. Add the onion, rind and mustard to the port wine in a saucepan. Cook for about 10 minutes. Stir in the jelly and the orange and lemon juice. Season with salt and ginger to taste. Serve hot or cold on roasted meats.

Bastes

Some meats require basting during cooking. This prevents drying out and adds a surface flavor. Most marinades with oil can also be used as bastes. A few basic all-around bastes are worth mentioning here.

VERMOUTH AND BUTTER. Combine ½ cup of melted butter with ½ cup dry vermouth. This is an excellent all-purpose baste for roasts, turkey, meat patties, and even fish. If you do not have a pastry brush, try a stalk of celery.

LEMON BUTTER BASTE. Combine ½ cup melted butter, 1 tablespoon lemon juice, 1 teaspoon Worcestershire sauce, 1 clove garlic (crushed), and 1 tablespoon olive oil. Heat and blend well. Use on all meats.

HOT BASTE. One cup tomato juice, 3 tablespoons minced onion, 1 teaspoon marjoram, 1 teaspoon chili powder, 3 cloves garlic (crushed), ½ cup wine vinegar, and ½ cup olive or salad oil. Blend or beat with an egg beater and simmer for a few minutes. Force through a sieve and use as an all-purpose baste for meat or fish that has not been marinated.

TERIYAKI MARINADE NO. 1 (for beef)

4 slices ginger, minced
1 onion, minced
2 tablespoons brown sugar

½ cup soy sauce
½ cup sherry

Stir slices of beef into this mixture and let stand for 1 hour. Stir occasionally.

TERIYAKI MARINADE NO. 2 (for pork)

¼ cup sherry
¼ cup pineapple juice
3 tablespoons soy sauce

1 clove garlic, minced
½ teaspoon powdered ginger

Pour over sliced pork and stir well. Let stand for 1 hour.

TERIYAKI MARINADE NO. 3 (for fish)

½ cup soy sauce
½ cup brown sugar

½ teaspoon monosodium
   glutamate
¼ cup dry sherry

Pour over small pieces of fish and let stand in refrigerator for 1 hour.

CHINESE PORK MARINADE NO. 1

1 cup soy sauce
1 cup sherry
1 cup pineapple juice

2 tablespoons brown sugar
2 cloves garlic, crushed
1 tablespoon catsup

Blend ingredients and pour over meat. Marinate in cool place for 2 hours or longer.

CHINESE PORK MARINADE NO. 2

1 cup chicken stock
1 teaspoon salt
2 tablespoons soy sauce

3 teaspoons sugar
⅓ cup honey
2 cloves garlic, crushed

Heat marinade slightly and blend well. Marinate in covered dish in cool place for 2 hours or longer.

CHINESE PORK MARINADE NO. 3

⅓ cup brandy
⅓ cup soy sauce
2 tablespoons brown sugar

1 teaspoon powdered ginger or
1 tablespoon minced fresh
  ginger
⅓ cup finely minced onion

Blend well and pour over meat. Refrigerate or place covered in a cool place for 2 or 3 hours.

PORK RIB MARINADE

4 tablespoons soy sauce
4 tablespoons brown sugar
4 cloves garlic, minced

4 tablespoons chili sauce
½ cup sherry

Cover serving-sized pieces with a blend of ingredients. Add more sherry if meat is not covered.

HOI SIN MARINADE (for chicken)

½ cup brown sugar
⅓ cup hoi sin (sub chili
    sauce)

⅓ cup sherry
⅓ cup soy sauce
3 cloves garlic, crushed

Blend ingredients and pour over individual chicken pieces. Marinate for 3 hours (see Chicken Breasts Hoi Sin).

CHICKEN PARTS MARINADE NO. 1

1 cup sherry
¼ cup soy sauce
2 tablespoons brown sugar

2 tablespoons fresh ginger,
    minced

Heat ingredients almost to a boil, stirring constantly. Pour hot over chicken pieces and stir. Keep in cool place for 1 hour.

CHICKEN PARTS MARINADE NO. 2

2 tablespoons soy sauce
1 tablespoon oil
1 tablespoon brown sugar
1 clove garlic, minced

½ teaspoon monosodium
  glutamate
⅛ teaspoon salt

This is rather a thick marinade and should be used only in quantity enough to completely coat the chicken parts. Let meat stand 30 minutes before cooking.

INDONESIAN SATE MARINADE

1 teaspoon ground caraway
1 teaspoon ground coriander
2 cloves garlic, crushed
2 tablespoons brown sugar

2 tablespoons lemon juice
1 tablespoon turmeric
½ cup coconut milk

Make coconut milk by mixing 1 cup grated coconut with 2 cups boiling water. Let stand for ½ hour. Stir well and squeeze through a cloth to extract milk.

Mix all ingredients well. Use to marinate small cubes of steak to serve as a first course. Marinate for 1 hour.

BEEF MARINADE

1 cup red wine
½ cup olive oil
2 cloves garlic
½ cup grated onion

12 peppercorns, crushed
½ teaspoon orégano
½ teaspoon salt

Blend oil and wine with a blender or use an egg beater. Add garlic, onion, peppercorns, orégano and salt. Mix thoroughly.

ORIENTAL STEAK MARINADE

1 teaspoon sesame oil
⅓ cup honey
⅓ cup soy sauce

2 tablespoons sherry
1 clove garlic, minced

Stir thinly sliced pieces of steak with this marinade and let stand for 1 hour.

SHERRY MARINADE FOR LAMB

1 onion, chopped
1 clove garlic, chopped
1½ teaspoons dry mustard
1½ teaspoons melted butter

1 cup sherry
½ teaspoon black pepper
½ teaspoon salt

Mix all ingredients and pour over individual cuts of lamb such as chops (see Sherry Chops).

MARINADE FOR LAMB

1 cup dry vermouth
1 cup salad oil
1 tablespoon lemon juice
1 small onion, chopped

2 cloves garlic, chopped
1 teaspoon tarragon
8 peppercorns, crushed
½ teaspoon salt

Blend together and pour over meat. Marinate for 4 hours.

MARINADE FOR FISH

1 lemon, sliced
1 onion, chopped
3 tablespoons chopped parsley
2 cloves, crushed
1 bay leaf

1 teaspoon black pepper
¼ cup olive oil
¼ cup tarragon vinegar
1 cup white wine

Put lemon, parsley and onion on the bottom of a dish just large enough to hold the fish. Lay fish on top of the vegetables and sprinkle on the pepper, cloves and bay leaf. Pour the oil, vinegar and enough wine to cover. Marinate for 2 hours in a cool place. Turn every half hour.

LAMB OR CHICKEN MARINADE

1 cup olive oil
1 cup red wine (white for
    chicken)
¼ cup tarragon vinegar
6 cloves

10 peppercorns, crushed
1 teaspoon rosemary
1 tablespoon chopped
    parsley

Mix oil, wine, vinegar with an egg beater or in a blender. Add cloves, peppercorns, rosemary and parsley, and mix well. Pour over meat in a container just large enough to hold meat. Turn frequently.

MARINADE FOR SMALL CUTS OF MEAT AND FISH

Salt
Pepper
1 onion
½ cup chopped parsley

1 bay leaf, broken into 3 pieces
Juice of 2 lemons
1 cup oil

Place pieces of fish or meat in shallow dish and season with salt and pepper. Cover with onion. Sprinkle with parsley and bay leaf. Sprinkle with lemon juice. Pour on the oil. Turn everything over after ½ hour. Fish will be ready in 1 hour, meat in 2.

COOKED MARINADE FOR MEAT

1 onion, chopped
1 carrot, diced
1 stalk celery, chopped
1 sprig parsley
1 clove garlic, chopped

½ teaspoon thyme
1 cup oil
2 cups white wine
½ cup vinegar

Cook vegetables and herbs in 3 tablespoons of the oil until slightly brown. Add wine and vinegar. Simmer for 15 minutes. Add rest of oil and cool. Pour over meat and refrigerate for 2 or 3 hours.

RED WINE MARINADE

1 onion, sliced
½ cup chopped celery
2 tablespoons chopped parsley
6 peppercorns, crushed

1 bay leaf
½ teaspoon thyme
½ quart red wine
1 cup salad oil

Put half the vegetables in the bottom of a bowl. Put the meat in the bowl and cover with the rest of the vegetables and the seasoning. Cover with the wine and oil. Add more wine if meat is not covered. Keep in refrigerator. Marinate for 4 hours if the roast weighs over 4 pounds. Remove meat and wipe dry before putting in the smoke oven.

LAMB MARINADE

½ cup oil
⅓ cup vinegar
1 clove garlic
1 teaspoon soy sauce

½ teaspoon salt
¼ teaspoon black pepper
⅛ teaspoon orégano

Mix well and cover meat. Refrigerate overnight.

Butters

COMPOUND BUTTER. Blend enough anchovy paste or desalted anchovy with butter to achieve the flavor you want. Use with smoked meat or fish.

BERCY BUTTER. Add 1 tablespoon finely chopped green onion to ½ cup white wine. Boil to reduce by ½. Add 2 tablespoons butter and 1 teaspoon chopped parsley. Use on smoked meat or fish.

BROWN BUTTER. Brown 1 cup butter in a small saucepan. Add 1 tablespoon parsley flakes and 1 teaspoon capers. Heat for a minute and add 1 teaspoon of vinegar. Stir and pour on fish or eggs.

KNEADED BUTTER. Blend 4 tablespoons cornstarch with ¼ pound butter. This should be a smooth paste. Use as a thickening agent in sauces where butter and flour are called for.

CAVIAR BUTTER. Makes a little caviar go a long way. Pound 2 ounces caviar with ½ cup of butter. Blend well and force through a sieve. Excellent for canapés.

SHRIMP BUTTER. Pound equal amounts of butter and shrimp by weight in a mortar until mixed into a fine paste. Use on cold-smoked fish or on canapés.

COLBERT BUTTER. Blend ½ cup butter, 1 teaspoon chopped parsley, ½ teaspoon salt, 1 pinch pepper, and squeeze of lemon juice. Mix into a smooth paste. Add ½ teaspoon chopped tarragon and ½ teaspoon of meat extract or 1 tablespoon demi-glace.

CRAYFISH BUTTER. Make a mirepoix of ½ onion and ½ carrot, ½ bay leaf and 1 tablespoon butter. Cook until vegetables are soft. Put 8 to 10 crayfish on vegetables and cook for ½ hour, covered. Add more butter if needed. Remove crayfish and pull off tails to nibble on. Pound claws, shells and all, in a mortar until fine. Return to mirepoix and stir in ¼ pound butter. Stir until butter becomes pink and creamy.

HORSERADISH BUTTER. Use 1 tablespoon fresh grated or prepared horseradish, blended and pounded with ½ cup butter. Force through a sieve. Delicious on smoked meats.

CHIVE BUTTER. Cut 4 tablespoons of chives very fine and cook for a minute in 2 tablespoons white wine or water. Pound them fine in a mortar. Add 4 tablespoons butter and mix well. Good on smoked fish.

LEMON BUTTER. Mix the grated rind of ½ lemon with ½ cup butter and 1 pinch white pepper.

MAÎTRE D' HÔTEL BUTTER. Combine ½ cup butter with 1 tablespoon finely chopped parsley, ½ teaspoon salt, freshly ground pepper and the juice of ½ lemon. This can be used with fish or meats.

MARCHAND DE VIN BUTTER. Put two tablespoons chopped green onions in 1 cup red wine. Boil to reduce by ½. Add 1 tablespoon rich brown stock, 4 tablespoons butter and 1 teaspoon chopped parsley. Combine well, season to taste. Use this with steaks or smoked roast.

MUSTARD BUTTER. Blend 1 tablespoon of mustard with a ½ cup of butter. Add 1 teaspoon finely chopped parsley. Spread cold on hot-smoked fish and let it melt. Great with smoked fish.

SALMON BUTTER. Use the outside pieces. Pound 2 ounces smoked salmon with ½ cup butter in a mortar. Force through a fine sieve. Serve cold. Use with canapés. This is best when made with heavily smoked salmon.

GARLIC BUTTER. Blanch 3 cloves garlic and drain. Crush and pound until smooth. Add ¼ pound butter. Mix well and force through a sieve. Good on steaks.

15

The Oriental Touch

It is no accident that many Chinese, Japanese, Korean and other Asian-born recipes adapt to the smoke oven so readily. Charcoal ovens and grills were born in the Orient and are still used there to a great extent.

All Oriental meat cooking is distinguished by the use of one or the combination of three sauces:

1. the marinade;
2. the basting or cooking sauce;
3. the dipping sauce.

Another characteristic of meat cooking in the Orient is that almost all meat is cut up before cooking, as distinguished from the Western style of cooking meat in large pieces to be carved later. There is an exception: Poultry is sometimes cooked whole and then cut into serving pieces.

There are good reasons for slicing the meat before cooking. It marinates faster, it cooks faster (saving fuel), it goes further if it is to be part of another dish. Thin slivers of meat will flavor food cooked with it better than a large hunk of meat would. Besides, who could eat an unsliced pot roast with chopsticks?

Which meats to use? Although many beef dishes are served in Chinese restaurants, pork is the favorite with the Chinese. Duck and chicken are also very popular. The pork dishes in this chapter are traditional, but a dish such as Flank Steak with Broccoli is an example of adapting Oriental methods to make a new and delicious dish.

The sauces and marinades for Oriental meat dishes contain ingredients that are not always readily available in your neighborhood grocery. Many dishes, however, can be made with what you can buy anywhere if you use a few substitutes.

If you believe what the ad writers say—"getting there is half the fun"—go to a Chinese grocery store. If you live in a city that has a Chinese or Japanese population of any size, there is usually a grocery store catering to their needs. Search it out. It's worth the trip. You will probably see a festoonery of mahogany brown ducks and pieces of pork hanging from hooks in a corner of the store. There are vegetables that look as though they might have grown under the sea. You will see exotic labels on cans and bottles proclaiming oyster sauce, hoi sin sauce, black bean sauce, sesame seed oil, heung new fun (spices of five fragrances), duck sauce, bean curd, fresh ginger roots, bamboo shoots, dried fish bladders and lotus roots. Here are shark fins and preserved duck eggs, bitter melon, bean cake, snow peas and wun ton skins.

If you are interested in food, a trip to a Chinese grocery store is the same as a visit to a new art museum for someone who likes to paint. Ask questions and the owner will be more than happy to help you. He is an apostle of the Oriental cooking way of life and happy to gain a convert.

If you want to try Oriental cooking, the following items are all you will need to prepare any of the recipes in this book. Those marked with an asterisk can probably be found only in a Chinese grocery store.

HOI SIN OR HAISEIN.* A red seasoning sauce for which hot chili sauce can be substituted.

FRESH GINGER ROOT.* This will keep for a long time. Ground ginger can be used as a substitute.

SOY SAUCE.* The imported variety is best.

SESAME OIL.* Smells like toasted sesame seeds. There is no substitute!

Onions, green and dry; garlic, brown sugar, cinnamon, dry sherry, corn starch, honey, monosodium glutamate, sesame seeds, salt and pepper.

If you have ever eaten a side order of pork in a good Chinese restaurant, you will agree when we say that this is one of the world's great hors d'oeuvre. It can be served hot or cold, with hot mustard and toasted sesame seeds, or show up later in the meal as part of another dish that requires tasty pieces of cooked pork. It can be cooked ahead if you plan to serve it cold.

There are probably as many slight variations on this wonderful dish as there are Chinese chefs, but they all have two things in common. The recipe starts with a good lean loin of pork and the meat is never better than when cooked in a smoke oven.

All of the recipes that follow for Chinese pork are for approximately a two-pound loin that has been split the long way into two equal pieces. Splitting the meat this way allows the marinade to cover and work on more of the surface; it also makes it easier to carve the cooked pork into thin tender slices across the grain. The methods of cooking are similar, but with subtle differences. Take your choice and make your own side order of pork. Exact cooking time is difficult to give. The tenderness of the meat, the charcoal fire and the efficiency of your oven all contribute to the cooking time. For Chinese pork, try to maintain a 325° oven and test the meat after forty-five minutes. If the same size fire is always built, and a constant temperature of 325° maintained you will soon learn how long to cook anything to the doneness you want.

CHINESE PORK NO. 1

2 pounds lean loin

MARINADE

1 cup soy sauce	2 tablespoons brown sugar
1 cup sherry	2 cloves garlic, crushed
1 cup pineapple juice	1 tablespoon catsup

Cut meat into long strips about 1 by 2 inches thick. Marinate in refrigerator for at least 2 hours; overnight is better. The meat may be cooked in 3 different ways:

1. directly over coals (in ovens where grill is at least four inches above coals);
2. on a rack over a shallow pan or indirectly;
3. with or without wood smoke.

Meat cooked directly over the coals will be crustier and should be turned once or twice during cooking. The indirect method will take a little longer, but the meat will not have to be turned. Smoke is recommended! Pork and wood smoke are a happy combination. This should be well done in a 325° oven in less than 1 hour. Test for doneness at 30 minutes. Experiment with this classic; it is worth the effort to find the combination that best suits your taste. *Serves 4.*

CHINESE PORK NO. 2

2 pounds lean loin
1 cup soy sauce
2 tablespoons catsup (or hoi sin sauce)

1 clove garlic, crushed
½ teaspoon monosodium glutamate

Split the loin into 2 long pieces. Mix marinade well, and because of the small quantity the meat should be turned frequently. Marinate for at least 3 hours. *Serves 4.*

CHINESE PORK NO. 3

2 pounds lean loin
1 cup chicken stock or prepared base
1 teaspoon salt

3 teaspoons sugar
2 tablespoons soy sauce
⅓ cup honey
2 cloves garlic, crushed

Split loin into 2 long pieces. Heat sauce slightly and blend well. Marinate meat for 1 hour. Use the remaining marinade to baste the meat every 15 minutes. *Serves 4.*

CHINESE PORK NO. 4

2 pounds lean pork
½ cup soy sauce
⅓ cup sherry
½ cup sugar
3 cloves garlic, crushed

2 tablespoons minced fresh ginger or 1 teaspoon powdered ginger
1 small box sesame seeds

Cut pork into strips about 2 inches thick. Marinate overnight. Sprinkle seeds over meat and coat evenly. Turn once during cooking. Be sure to use wood smoke with this recipe. *Serves 4.*

CHINESE PORK NO. 5

½ cup sherry   1 teaspoon salt
¼ cup sugar   ⅓ cup finely chopped onion
¼ teaspoon cinnamon   2 pounds pork shoulder (lean)
½ cup soy sauce

Mix marinade well. Cut meat into 2-inch-thick pieces, as long as possible. Place in a bowl and cover with marinade. Turn every ½ hour for 2 hours. This is good sliced thin when cold. *Serves 4.*

CHINESE PORK NO. 6

2 pounds pork loin   1 teaspoon cinnamon
2 tablespoons soy sauce   1 teaspoon salt
3 tablespoons honey   ½ cup sesame seeds (optional)

Split meat into 2 long strips. Blend all other ingredients except sesame seeds. Rub the pork thoroughly with the mixture, sprinkle with sesame seeds and let stand for 2 hours. *Serves 4.*

CHINESE PORK NO. 7

2 pounds lean pork loin   2 tablespoons brown sugar
⅓ cup brandy   1 teaspoon powdered ginger
⅓ cup soy sauce   ⅓ cup finely minced onion

Cut meat into 2 pieces about 1 inch thick. Blend ingredients and marinate meat for 2 hours. Baste frequently with marinade during cooking. *Serves 4.*

CHINESE PORK NO. 8

2 pounds pork loin   2 cloves garlic, crushed
⅓ cup soy sauce   2 slices fresh ginger, minced
2 tablespoons sherry   1 teaspoon dry mustard

Split loin in half the long way. Rub with salt and let stand for 1 hour. Blend marinade well and pour over meat. Turn occasionally and let stand for 1 hour. Cook directly over coals with plenty of wood smoke. *Serves 4.*

CHINESE PORK NO. 9

2 pounds pork loin or lean
    pork
¼ cup dry mustard
4 slices fresh ginger, minced

2 tablespoons honey
2 tablespoons soy sauce
2 tablespoons sherry

Cut loin into 2 pieces; or cut a shoulder into pieces about 2 inches thick. Mix other ingredients into a smooth paste. Rub paste into meat and let stand for 2 hours. Cook at 325° until done. *Serves 4.*

SMOKED RIBS NO. 1

4 pounds spareribs
4 tablespoons soy sauce
4 tablespoons brown sugar
4 cloves garlic, minced

4 tablespoons catsup or chili
    sauce
½ cup sherry

Cut ribs into serving-sized pieces and marinate for 1 hour. Roast with wood smoke in a 325° oven. Test for doneness. *Serves 4.*

SMOKED RIBS NO. 2

4 pounds spareribs
2 cups soy sauce
1 cup sherry

3 tablespoons honey
3 cloves garlic, crushed

Cut ribs into handy serving pieces and marinate for 1 hour. Roast for about 1 hour at 325°. Turn once and baste with marinade. *Serves 4.*

ORIENTAL SHORT RIBS

3 pounds lean ribs
⅔ cup soy sauce
⅛ cup sherry
2 tablespoons brown sugar

2 cloves garlic, crushed
½ teaspoon monosodium
    glutamate
½ teaspoon powdered ginger

Trim as much fat as possible from ribs and marinate for 2 hours. Place directly over coals in a 350° oven. We prefer this without wood smoke. Cook for about 30 minutes. *Serves 4.*

BEEF TERIYAKI

2 pounds round steak, thinly
   sliced
4 slices fresh ginger, minced
1 onion, grated

2 tablespoons brown sugar
½ cup soy sauce
½ cup sherry

Slice beef in ¼-inch slices. Marinate for 1 hour. Have oven adjusted
to 350°. Remove cover, take out grill and replace cover. Lay pieces
of meat on grill. If you can't get them all on, wait and run a second
batch through. Remove cover, throw on a handful of hardwood
chips, and replace grill and cover. This will cook in about 5 minutes. *Serves 4.*

TENDERLOIN TERIYAKI

1½ pounds tenderloin
 3 tablespoons sherry

2 tablespoons soy sauce
2 slices fresh ginger, minced

Slice steak into ¼-inch slices and mix with marinade. Let stand for
1 hour. Have smoker at 350° with a bed of coals that covers the
grate. Remove grill and replace cover to keep oven hot. Lay steak
slices on grill, getting as many on as possible without overlapping.
Remove cover, place grill in place and recover. Three to 5 minutes
should be enough time. Don't overcook. *Serves 4.*

FLANK STEAK AND VEGETABLES

2 pounds flank steak
3 tablespoons soy sauce
2 tablespoons sherry
1 tablespoon brown sugar

1 teaspoon salt
¼ teaspoon fresh pepper
1 clove garlic

Slice steak diagonally into thin strips. Mix with mixture of ingredients and marinate for 1 hour. Meanwhile, steam-cook enough
peas or broccoli for 4 people. Cut broccoli into 1-inch pieces. Put
meat strips on roasting rack over shallow pan and place in 350°
oven. When meat is done, lift the rack and dump the meat and
steamed vegetables together in the pan. If dry, add 1 teaspoon
cooking oil. Stir-fry for a few minutes and serve on hot plates.
Serves 4.

PORK TERIYAKI

2 pounds lean shoulder or
    tenderloin
¼ cup sherry
¼ cup pineapple juice

3 tablespoons soy sauce
1 clove garlic, minced
½ teaspoon powdered ginger

Slice meat into about ¼-inch slices and marinate for 2 hours. Place on grill in a 325° oven with wood smoke and roast for about 20 minutes. Test for doneness. Serve with soy sauce and toasted sesame seeds. *Serves 4.*

CATHAY BEEF

1½ pounds steak
1 teaspoon sesame oil
⅓ cup honey

⅓ cup soy sauce
2 tablespoons sherry
1 clove garlic, minced

Slice meat into ¼-inch slices and stir in bowl with marinade. Let stand for 1 hour. Stir a few times so all meat is evenly marinated. Place on grill and roast directly over coals for about 5 minutes. *Serves 4.*

LION'S HEAD

1 pound ground pork
½ pound ground beef
6 fresh mushrooms, chopped
6 to 8 water chestnuts, peeled
    and chopped
1 cup chopped onions
1 tablespoon cornstarch
2 eggs, beaten

2 teaspoons sherry
2 tablespoons soy sauce
½ teaspoon salt
¼ teaspoon pepper
2 tablespoons sugar
2 pounds celery cabbage
1½ cups chicken stock

Mix together all ingredients except cabbage and chicken stock. Mix well and form into 4 large balls. If too soft, add bread crumbs. Place balls in 350° oven with plenty of smoke and roast for at least 30 minutes. Cut cabbage into 4-inch pieces and place in large pan. (If celery cabbage isn't available, use regular cabbage.) Place meat balls on top. Pour on chicken stock and cover. Simmer until cabbage is cooked (about 30 minutes). Heat 4 plates, and arrange a bed of cabbage on each plate with a meat ball on top. Serve meat juice on the side. *Serves 4.*

CHINESE POT ROAST

4 pounds pot roast
2 cloves garlic, minced
⅛ cup soy sauce
1 teaspoon salt

¼ teaspoon pepper
1 teaspoon minced ginger
3 tablespoons sherry

Mix together and spread on meat and let stand for 4 hours (overnight is better). Roast in smoke oven at 300° for about 1½ hours. Allow to cool for 10 minutes. Serve in thin slices cut across the grain. *Serves 4.*

PLUM SAUCE DUCK

1 five pound duck
1 cup plum sauce

½ cup sherry
½ cup soy sauce

Cut duck up in 2-inch pieces and marinate for 1 hour in mixture of plum sauce, sherry and soy sauce. (Plum sauce can be bought fresh in some Chinese grocery stores, where it is made up daily and sold in little paper cartons. If plum sauce is not available in your Chinese grocery store, use plum jam.) Put pieces on grill. Place over a shallow pan and roast at 350°. Baste a couple of times and test for doneness after about 45 minutes. *Serves 4.*

CHINESE DUCK

1 5-pound duck
3 slices ginger
2 tablespoons soy sauce
2 tablespoons sherry
⅛ teaspoon powdered cloves

⅛ teaspoon powdered aniseed
⅛ teaspoon black pepper
2 cloves garlic, crushed
1 tablespoon cornstarch

BASTE

2 tablespoons honey
2 tablespoons soy sauce

1 tablespoon sherry

Mix all ingredients except cornstarch and baste. Heat to blend. Mix cornstarch with cold water and blend with sauce to thicken it. Sew neck opening tightly and spoon mixture into duck cavity; sew up opening. Steam the bird on a rack in a tightly covered pot for

1 hour. Remove duck and start the fire. By the time your charcoal is going well and the oven is 350°, the duck will be dry enough to paint with a baste of honey, soy sauce and sherry. Place duck on a rack over a shallow pan and close the oven for 10 minutes. Give the bird another quick coat of the baste. Cooking time should be about 1 hour. Baste 3 or 4 times and turn the duck to assure even coloring. To serve, cut up into segments Chinese style. *Serves 4.*

ROAST TURKEY CHINESE STYLE

1 10-pound turkey	½ cup brown sugar
2 cups sherry	1 tablespoon salt
2 cups soy sauce	2 teaspoons ginger powder
1 large onion, minced	

This recipe calls for a large, uncovered kettle that will hold the turkey almost entirely submerged. Mix the last 6 ingredients, pour into kettle with turkey breast down, and water to a safe simmering level. Bring to a boil and simmer for 1 hour. If pot is small, turn the bird a few times. While the turkey simmers, get a good fire going in the smoke oven with plenty of charcoal so it will maintain a good, even 325° for 2 or 3 hours. Place the bird on a roasting rack over a shallow pan, add a handful of green wood to the coals, and put the turkey in the oven. After 15 minutes, pour a couple of cups of the liquid over the turkey. Baste every 15 or 20 minutes. Roasting time should be about 2½ hours. Check at 2 hours if you aren't using a meat thermometer. Serve hot or cold. If you want a well-smoked bird, add green wood when you baste.

GINGER-SHERRY CHICKEN

2 small fryers	2 tablespoons brown sugar
1 cup sherry	2 tablespoons fresh ginger,
¼ cup soy sauce	minced

Cut chicken parts into 2-inch pieces. Bring sherry, soy sauce, brown sugar and ginger almost to a boil and stir well to blend. Pour over chicken pieces and stir. Marinate for 1 hour. Stir a few times. Drain chicken and arrange pieces on wire mesh over a shallow pan. Cook in a 350° oven until brown and well done. Serve hot or cold. *Serves 4.*

CHICKEN BREASTS HOI SIN

6 large chicken breasts
⅓ cup hoi sin sauce or hot
   chili sauce
⅓ cup sherry

⅓ cup soy sauce
¼ cup brown sugar
3 cloves garlic, crushed

Cut chicken breasts in half. Mix other ingredients and add to chicken to marinate for 3 or 4 hours. Place on rack over a broiling pan and roast in a 350° oven for about 1 hour. Baste frequently with remaining sauce. A little wood smoke before you baste the first time improves the flavor. Thighs and drumsticks may also be used in this recipe. *Serves 6.*

CHICKEN CARAWAY

2 fryers
⅓ cup soy sauce
⅓ cup sherry

2 cloves garlic, crushed
1 box of caraway seeds
Cornstarch

Cut chicken into 2-inch pieces, Chinese style. Mix soy sauce, sherry and garlic into a mixture and stir with chicken pieces. Marinate for 1 hour. Stir a few times. Drain chicken and place on a piece of mesh screen if your grill is too widely spaced. Dust pieces with cornstarch and caraway seeds. Roast directly over coals in a 300° oven. Test one of the thicker pieces for doneness after 30 minutes. *Serves 4.*

CHINESE ROAST CHICKEN

1 large roasting chicken
3 tablespoons sherry
3 tablespoons honey
2 cloves garlic, crushed

1 tablespoon minced fresh
   ginger
½ cup minced onion
1 teaspoon salt

Rub chicken inside and out with a mixture of all the ingredients. Let stand for 1 hour. Cook chicken on roasting rack over shallow pan in a 350° oven. It should be done in about an hour. Test by moving one of the legs to see if it's loose and moves easily. Baste 3 or 4 times with the sauce. Cut chicken into serving pieces; arrange on hot platter. Heat remaining sauce and pour over chicken. *Serves 4.*

SMOKED CHICKEN

1 4-pound chicken
½ cup soy sauce
1 teaspoon salt

¾ cup honey
1 tablespoon salt mixed with
3 cups water

Rub chicken with some of the soy sauce and salt. Let stand for 30 minutes. Bring the salted water to a boil and simmer the chicken, covered, for 20 minutes. Allow to cool and dry off. This may be refrigerated overnight. Mix honey and rest of soy sauce into a basting sauce. Cook chicken on a roasting rack over a pan in a 350° oven for about one hour. Baste 3 or 4 times with soy and honey mixture. Cut chicken into small pieces and arrange on a hot platter. *Serves 4.*

BULLGOGI

3 pounds lean beef
1 cup salad oil
¼ cup sugar
3 tablespoons soy sauce
1 small onion, chopped

2 cloves garlic, chopped
4 tablespoons sesame seed
Salt
Pepper

Slice the beef in thin strips. Combine the other ingredients and marinate the meat overnight, placing covered bowl in the refrigerator. Remove the meat and cook in a 300° oven. The time will vary, depending on the thickness of the slices. About 5 minutes is usually long enough. Watch the first ones closely, so that you determine the correct time. This dish is of Korean origin and is usually served with rice and a spicy cabbage salad. *Serves 6.*

CHICKEN BREAST SATE

4 chicken breasts
½ cup soy sauce
1 tablespoon crushed garlic
2 tablespoons brown sugar

1 teaspoon ground coriander
1 tablespoon lemon juice
1 teaspoon salt
½ teaspoon ground pepper

Cut meat into ¾-inch cubes and marinate in mixture for 1 hour. Place meat on skewers and roast in 350° smoke oven directly over coals for about 10 minutes. Try these first without any green wood smoke. Serve as a first course with hot sate sauce. *Serves 4.*

CHUCK STEAK RIBBONS

4 pounds lean chuck steaks, or
  a pot roast split into 2
  pieces about 1 inch thick
⅔ cup soy sauce
⅓ cup sherry
2 tablespoons brown sugar
2 cloves garlic, minced

1 teaspoon monosodium
  glutamate
3 tablespoons toasted sesame
  seeds
½ teaspoon ginger powder
1 tablespoon sesame seed oil

Trim the fat off the meat, remove any bones, and slice into ¼-inch slices as long as you can make them. Place the meat strips in a bowl with all the ingredients and stir well. Let stand for 2 hours—all day would be better. Have an even bed of coals ready. Remove the grill and lay the meat strips out full length; put them as close together as possible. Don't worry if you can't get them all on, because they cook quickly and you can make a second run. Replace the grill, close the cover and be ready to serve the meat in about 5 minutes. It is best to cook this recipe twice during a dinner, thus assuring a second helping of hot meat. It is best, and more tender, when piping hot. *Serves 4.*

INDONESIAN SATES

Sate is a skewered meat dish that is not a shish kabab (there are no vegetables or mushrooms) that works perfectly in a smoke oven, with or without smoke. The Indonesians cook it by turning the skewered meat a few times over a charcoal fire. The smoke oven eliminates the turning.

The spices and flavorings used in sates are similar to other Oriental foods, but turmeric, coconut and coconut milk are three distinctly Indonesian touches. Turmeric comes in a powder form and is made from an aromatic root of the ginger family. Its golden color makes it a substitute for saffron in many dishes. The sweet flavor of turmeric blends well with the hot pepper and lemon juice used in sate recipes. The lemon juice in most dishes is a convenient substitute for tamarind juice. Tamarind is a tropical fruit. The juice the Indonesians use as flavoring is made by soaking shelled tamarind seeds in water. A marmalade can also be made from tamarind. If you wish to try your hand at tamarind juice, soak a third of a cup of shelled tamarind in a cup of water until dissolved and force through a sieve. Keep refrigerated.

You can prepare the classic sate in two ways. Both use meat cut into ¾-inch squares. In the first method you boil the meat in the marinade and then put it on the coals to get crusty and a bit of smoke flavor. The second method calls for a cold marinade over the meat for an hour or so before being skewered and roasted.

Lamb, beef, pork and chicken are all used with the same marinades. Sates are usually served with a hot sauce called *saos sate*. The sauce usually has onion flakes floating on top and is served hot. Sates are probably best used as a first course for a meal rather than as the main meat dish.

PLAIN SATE

1 pound chicken breasts, or sirloin steak, or top round steak	Salt Pepper

Cut meat into ¾-inch cubes. Season with salt and pepper. Let stand for 20 minutes. Put 5 or 6 pieces with some space between on each skewer. Use a small amount of green wood on the fire and place skewered meat directly over coals for about 10 minutes. Test for doneness.

SAUCE FOR SATE

½ cup melted butter ½ cup soy sauce Juice of 1 lemon	Ground red pepper 2 tablespoons dehydrated onion flakes

Melt butter in small frying pan and add soy sauce, lemon juice and ½ teaspoon red pepper (or to taste). Heat onion flakes in a small amount of butter. Simmer sauce for 3 minutes and float onion flakes on top of sauce as you bring it to the table.

STEAK SATE

2 pounds sirloin steak
1 teaspoon ground caraway
1 teaspoon ground coriander
2 cloves garlic, crushed

2 tablespoons brown sugar
2 tablespoons lemon juice
½ cup coconut milk*
2 tablespoons soy sauce

Mix ingredients well and marinate ¾-inch cubes of meat for 1 hour.
Place on skewers and cook directly over coals for about 10 minutes in a 350° oven. This marinade can also be used for pork or boned chicken. Pork takes to wood smoke better in this recipe than either chicken or beef. *Serves 4.*

* Coconut milk is made by mixing 1 part finely grated coconut with 2 parts boiling water. Let stand for 30 minutes. Stir well or run through a blender for a few seconds. Squeeze through a cloth to extract milk.

LAMB SATE

2 pounds lamb shoulder, or
    lamb that will make lean
    ¾-inch cubes
2 cloves garlic, crushed
2 tablespoons minced onion
1 tablespoon ground caraway
    seed

1 tablespoon ground coriander
2 tablespoons turmeric
½ cup soy sauce
2 slices fresh ginger, minced
½ cup brown sugar
½ cup coconut milk*

Bring ingredients to a boil and simmer ¾-inch meat cubes for 30 minutes. Drain meat and reserve the sauce. Place meat on skewers and roast in 350° smoke oven for about 10 minutes. Serve with sauce prepared from the marinade.

Thicken the marinade with cornstarch mixed with a little cold water. Sauce should be served hot with meat. *Serves 4 to 6.*

* See Steak Sate recipe for making coconut milk.

16

Curing

The curing of meat is something of a mystery. Its origin is unknown, and even after centuries of doing it we still don't fully understand it. We can guess that man first noticed that seeds that fell onto rocks and dried in the sun were good to eat some time later, while those that fell in damp places spoiled. From that he probably tried drying fruit, fish and other flesh in the sun. Sometimes it worked. Gradually he found a system to preserve food, even if he did not know why it worked.

Then someone discovered that heavily salted meat could be preserved. This must have been a haphazard process at first, for salt is inconsistent. Its action varies with different foods. To this day the principles involved are not understood completely. It must have been frustrating in those days, when even the salt varied in content.

Today at least we have salt that is uniform in strength and the knowledge that butter, for example, will keep better if about 2 percent of it is salt. We know too that fermentation sometimes plays a part in food preservation—as in sauerkraut and pickles. Sugar sometimes helps. It is used partly for this in jam and jelly and in the candying of fruit.

These days canning, freezing, even bombardment by gamma rays are used to preserve food, but we are concerned here only with the historic ways: salt and dehydration.

Micro-organisms cause most spoilage. They need water to grow. Enzyme action and other damaging chemical reactions also are retarded or prevented when the water content is low.

We start with this simple principle. For our removal of water, we will use the smokehouse. Not only does it drive water out of the meat slowly and evenly, but it also imparts a taste that man loves.

Some of us have forgotten—or never had had the chance to find out—how good home-smoked meat is. There is a generation or two that has not been exposed to it. For them, an announcement:

With a homemade smokehouse and a few hand-mixed ingredients you can outflavor, outsmoke and outcure a million-dollar meat plant. You can make pastrami or Canadian bacon no supermarket could afford. You can kipper your own salmon or make mouth-watering lox.

A smokehouse (Figure 15; also see Chapter 2) is essential because the cold-smoking process must be used. This means temperatures sometimes must be kept at 90° for two or three days. It is difficult to do this for more than a few hours in a regular smoke oven.

15—Examples of the smokehouse, which is essential for cold-smoking.

A smokehouse doesn't have to be big or unsightly. But you do need one in which the coals are at some distance from the meat and the temperature in the meat chamber can be kept below 100°.

The smoke itself will not preserve meat. That is accomplished by the salt and the drying. The smoke adds flavor and color.

Salt is the essential ingredient. You want just the right amount of salt and just the right amount of time for it to penetrate the meat. Too much salt can hurt the flavor of meat and harden the muscles. Too little salt, or too little time, can spoil the meat.

Sugar sometimes is used to stop the hardening effect of salt and to improve the flavor and texture. Brown sugar or even molasses can be used, depending on the flavor you want.

Saltpeter is also used often, but only in small quantities to fix the red color of lean meat.

Spices are often added for flavor.

Table salt can be used in an emergency, but it is better generally to buy a good grade of barrel salt. There are establishments in many cities where you can buy packages of curing mix—the salt, sugar and saltpeter in the correct proportions. If you are going to mix your own, have this book handy so you can refer to the correct proportions.

There also are two ways of applying the salt: Rubbing it onto the meat in heavy quantities, or putting the meat in a brine. The dry method generally produces a saltier flavor and heavier shrinkage, but is sometimes more useful. The brining method results in a milder flavor and less shrinkage.

CURING SMALL CUTS

Make a brine by dissolving ½ cup salt, ¼ cup sugar, ½ teaspoon saltpeter and ½ teaspoon pepper in a quart of water. Pour this over a lean pork loin in a glass or plastic container. Weight the meat to keep it submerged. Leave it in a refrigerator for 7 days. When it is removed, dry it well, then smoke in a 325° oven until the meat thermometer reads 150° to 180°. Use heavy smoke. If you do not wish to cook it at once, dry it, wrap it and leave it in the refrigerator for use later as a roast, or cut up for pork chops.

SPARE RIBS

Put the ribs in a glass or plastic container. Pour over them a brine made by dissolving ½ cup salt, ¼ cup sugar, ½ teaspoon saltpeter and ½ teaspoon pepper in a quart of water. Refrigerate three days. Dry the ribs well and smoke-cook them at 300° with plenty of green wood until done.

HOME-SMOKED BACON

This is the way to make what is called Canadian bacon. It is necessary to keep the meat cool—36° to 40°—while it is being cured. This means you will have to use your refrigerator if you are preparing the meat at home.

Take an untreated 10-pound loin of pork and cut it into 1-pound pieces. Wash them and place in an enameled tray or glass container wide enough to hold the bacon and shallow enough to go in the refrigerator. Over the bacon pour this mixture:

2 quarts water	¼ cup sugar
¾ cup salt	1 teaspoon saltpeter

Weight the bacon to keep it under the surface of the brine. A heavy dish will do. Check the brine each day. If it smells sour or becomes sirupy or cloudy, remove the meat and wash it. Throw away the brine, wash the container thoroughly and sterilize it with boiling water. Make a new brining mix and renew the process, using the same piece of bacon. The bacon should be in the brine 15 days. Larger bacon pieces should be in brine 2 to 2½ days per pound.

Remove the meat and stir the brine two or three times during the curing.

When the meat is removed from the brine after 15 days, soak it in tepid water 30 minutes to an hour to remove the excess salt near the surface.

Wrap stout cord or clean wire around the bacon so it is held securely and hang it to drain 24 hours before smoking. It can be hung in the smokehouse if the meat compartment is screened and free from flies and insects. The pieces should not touch each other. A skewer running through each strip of bacon will keep it from curling. Rub the bacon with black pepper if you like a little pungency in your bacon.

When you start the smoking process, keep the temperature down. Smother the fire with green hardwood chips or sawdust. If the temperature is maintained between 110° and 120°, 30 to 40 hours of continuous smoking will be enough. If the weather is cool, you can let the fire go out at night and renew it the next day. Six hours a day for five days will do a good job. If you can keep the temperature between 90° and 100°, you will have less shrinkage and have excellent color and flavor.

TWO-DAY SMOKED LOINS

Here is a treat, but you must plan it 48 hours ahead. Make a brine of 2 quarts water, 1 cup salt, ½ cup brown sugar, 1 teaspoon black pepper and 1 teaspoon allspice. Submerge the meat in the brine for 24 hours, keeping it in a refrigerator. Wipe the meat dry and place in front of a fan or a heat outlet for a few hours until the meat is thoroughly dry. Cold-smoke it for 2 hours, using heavy smoke. Start some coals outside the smoker, and add them to the oven after 2 hours of cold-smoking. With the heat at 300° the loins can be cooked until done. Baste it with honey for a beautiful crust.

PORK CHOPS

In 2 cups water, dissolve ¼ cup salt, 2 tablespoons sugar and ¼ teaspoon pepper. Pour this over a few pork chops in a glass or enamel container. Submerge the chops with a weight and leave them in the brine for 24 hours. Dry them and smoke-cook until done.

PASTRAMI

For a 4- to 5-pound cut of brisket or lean chuck, cut about 1½ inches thick, make the following mixture:

1 cup salt	3 cloves garlic, crushed
½ cup sugar	½ teaspoon ground cloves
1 teaspoon saltpeter	1 teaspoon black pepper
1 tablespoon dry ginger	2 quarts water
1 tablespoon crushed coriander	

Submerge the meat in a glass, enamel or plastic container. Use a weight to keep the meat under the surface of the brine. Keep it in a refrigerator and turn the meat every 2 days. After a week, remove it and hang to dry for 24 hours. Cold-smoke it for 2 hours at 100° or less, then add coals, started outside the smoker, and cook another 2 hours at 300° or until done. Serve hot or cold.

HOME-SMOKED HAM

There are three easy methods of curing hams: brining, the dry mix, and the combination cure.

BRINING

If the ham is under 10 pounds, put it in an enamel or glass container deep enough to hold a submerged ham and shallow enough to go in the refrigerator. The ham should be between 36° and 40° while it is curing.

Make the brine of these ingredients:

2 quarts water	¼ cup sugar
¾ cup salt	1 teaspoon saltpeter

Submerge the ham in the brine, keeping it down with a weight on a plate. Check the brine daily to see that it does not turn sour, cloudy or sirupy. If it does, remove the meat at once and rinse it. Throw away the brine, clean and sterilize the container and make a new mixture. Replace the ham and continue the curing. Ham should be in the mixture 3 to 3½ days for each pound, but any ham, including the lighter ones, should stay there at least 28 days. If you plan to use the ham at once, it can be removed early. It will not be as salty, nor will it keep as well. While it is curing, remove the ham and stir the mixture every 7 days.

When the ham is removed for smoking, wash it, soak it an hour in tepid water, and then hang to dry for 24 hours.

String a stout cord or clean wire through the shank of the ham to hang it in the smokehouse. Smother the fire with hardwood sawdust or chips. If the fire is directly below the meat, put a sheet of metal over the fire so that direct heat does not reach the ham. Keep the temperature low. If you can keep the heat between 110° and 120°, the ham will be well cured in 30 to 40 hours. If the weather is cool, you can let the fire die each night and rebuild it the next day. A ham can be cured as long as a month this way.

A Smithfield ham then will be aged 8 to 12 months. It can be left in the smokehouse if the meat compartment does not become too warm and insects cannot get at it. Give it a light smoking occasionally. When stored elsewhere, use a dry, well-ventilated room for a week. Then wrap it in heavy paper and place it in a box and cover it with clean dry salt. Sometimes on a farm the ham is wrapped, then buried in a bin of grain. Or it can be wrapped in cheesecloth, then in heavy paper. Let the hanging cord protrude from the wrapping. Place the ham in a starched cloth sack. The starch will exclude the air. Tie the sack tight around the cord and hang the ham in a dry, ventilated room. If mold develops, rub or cut the moldy area away. The rest of the ham should be all right.

DRY MIX

The dry-mix method of curing ham often is used in the South, where temperatures are warmer and it is advisable to cure the ham as quickly as possible. The dry-mix method is faster. It usually produces a saltier ham and results in more shrinkage. For a ham weighing 10 pounds or less mix carefully ¾ cup salt, ¼ cup sugar and 1 teaspoon saltpeter. Distribute the saltpeter evenly so that the meat is not disproportionately flavored. Take half of the mixture and rub all surfaces of the ham thoroughly. Force some of it around the bone. Place it in a box, a shallow crock or other dry container. Store it in a cold (36° to 40°) place. If you do not have a box or crock small enough to fit in a cold place, you can place the ham in the refrigerator uncovered, but it will shrink more. After 5 days, rub on the second half of the curing mixture. A big ham should be cured 2 days to the pound. Any ham, however, should be dry-cured for 25 days. So a ham 10 pounds or under will be cured 3½ weeks.

When it is removed for smoking, wash it in tepid water to remove surplus salt. Hang it for 24 hours before smoking.

COMBINATION CURE

The combination cure requires a meat pump, which is a large syringe. The curing solution is the same as in the brining method. The solution is drawn into the pump and the needle inserted along a bone. The solution is forced into the meat in the bone area. After pumping five 2-ounce shots into a 10-pound ham, the dry cure is rubbed on and the cure is finished in the dry manner.

CORNED BEEF

Beef can be cured as easily as pork. It has more lean meat, though, and tends to become harder and develop a saltier flavor than pork. Nor will it keep as long as pork.

Nevertheless, corned beef is a delicious and easy-to-make dish. The cheaper, fatter cuts make excellent corned beef—flank, plate, chuck or rump. The brisket is used often.

If you have 10 pounds or less of meat, take a pound of salt and rub it thoroughly into the meat. Sprinkle some salt on the bottom of a sound box or a crock that has been cleaned and sterilized. Sprinkle a little more salt on top and let the meat stand in a cold place (36° to 40°) for 24 hours.

Prepare a brine by dissolving ⅓ cup sugar, 1 teaspoon saltpeter and 1 teaspoon baking soda in 1½ quarts water. Put the meat in an enamel or glass container and pour the brine over the salted meat. Use a weighted plate to keep the meat submerged. Keep it at 36° to 40° for 30 to 40 days. Inspect the brine daily to make sure it does not become cloudy or sour. If it does, make a new brine and—after sterilizing the container—resume the curing. When the meat is removed for smoking, wash it in tepid water to remove surface salt. Hang the meet to dry for 24 hours, then smoke it.

If you want to eat it at once, you can cook it in a smoke oven at 300° as you would any other cut of beef. It will acquire a smoky taste while cooking if you use hardwood sawdust or chips on the coals. Smoke it about 30 minutes per pound. It will be done sooner if it is a shallow cut of meat. If you want to smoke it for later use, keep the temperature under 100° and use smoke for 6 hours. Keep it in the refrigerator until ready to use. Then simmer it 2 hours and serve.

CHICKEN GIBLETS

Try curing hearts, livers and gizzards for 8 hours in brine made of 1 cup water, 1 cup wine, ¼ cup salt, 2 tablespoons sugar and ¼ teaspoon pepper. Use a jar or bowl and keep it in the refrigerator until time to cook. Line 4 or 5 on a skewer, or place them on a fine mesh grill (hardware cloth makes a good grill for this). Cook them in a smoke oven and serve as an appetizer.

BIG BIRDS

Turkeys, geese, ducks and chicken can be cured in a brine made by dissolving 1½ cups salt, ½ cup sugar and 2 teaspoons saltpeter in a gallon of water. Put the dressed bird in a crock, large plastic container or enameled bucket. Not aluminum! Completely cover with brine and store in the refrigerator at 36° to 40° for 4 days if you are going to cook the bird at once. If you are not going to cook the bird at once, leave it in the brine for a week. When it is cured, hang it to dry. Drying can be speeded with paper towels and a fan.

Cold-smoke the bird about 5 hours with the temperature under 100°. Put it in a smoke oven and roast with hardwood smoke until done at 300° to 350° If you are in a hurry, you can smoke-cook the bird without the preliminary cold smoke. It is good, but not quite as tangy. Serve hot or in cold slices.

FISH

A special note of caution here to anyone planning to smoke fish. Fish are partially cured by brining. After they are removed from the brine, it is important to dry them carefully before starting the smoke process. If they are still moist, they are likely to steam and soften in the smoking. The color and the surface will not be as good.

INDIAN CURED FISH

This is the way to cure fish to last 2 or 3 years. Fillet the fish so that there are no bones or skin. If it is a large fish, such as a chinook salmon, cut the meat into long strips. Brine them overnight in a solution of 1 gallon water and 5 cups salt. Hang them in a well-ventilated place, free of insects, for 24 hours.

Now the strips go into the smokehouse for 2 weeks. Keep a light smoke moving through the compartment at a low temperature— around 90°. If the fire goes out at night, rebuild it as early as possible the next day. After 2 weeks of this treatment, the fish will stay in good condition for a period up to 3 years. If in storage a surface mold appears, scrub it off with salty water and smoke another 24 hours.

SUGAR-CURED FISH

Fish cured this way are sweeter in flavor. The keeping quality is excellent if you give them a long smoke. Even with a short smoke, the fish will keep for weeks.

Make a curing mix composed of equal parts of salt and sugar. If you are doing a large trout, take a couple of handfuls of the mix for each fish. Split the fish open so that they lay flat. Rub the mix well into the fish. Place them in a crock or barrel with the skin side down. Sprinkle each layer with black peppercorns. Turn the skin side up for the top layer.

Leave the fish overnight in a cold place. In the morning, wash the fish in running water for 30 minutes. Stack the fish and apply pressure to the stack to squeeze out as much moisture as possible. Dry the fish with towels.

Hang them in a well-ventilated place until thoroughly dry. When you put them in the smokehouse, hang them separately or place them on wire trays so that they do not touch each other. Start a very small fire. You do not want the temperature to get over 85° to 90° for the first 3 hours. By that time a smoke skin will have formed on the fish and the temperature can be raised to 110° for an hour or so. Next raise the temperature to 120° and smoke another hour or 2. The smoking can be continued if you want to keep the fish indefinitely, but they will keep for several weeks from this point.

FISHERMAN'S SPECIAL

Here's one for the angler who makes an unexpectedly heavy catch at an isolated lake or stream. He doesn't want the fish to go to waste, but he has no ice and no way to get the fish to cold storage at once. If he has salt, the fish can be saved.

The head and viscera should be removed. Cut above the backbone almost to the tail. Cut under the backbone and break the backbone off, leaving only a little of the tail section uncut. The fish should now lie flat in one piece. Score it lengthwise from head to tail on the fleshy side. Make the cuts about 1 inch apart and ¼ inch deep. Wash the fish and wipe it dry. Mix 1 ounce pepper in 1 pound salt. Rub the fish inside and out with the salt mixture. Store it in a cool place overnight, protecting it from insects and animals.

Rinse the fish the next morning. Fasten 2 or 3 stiff twigs across the back of the fish to keep it spread open. Sharpen the ends of the twigs and poke them through the skin. Hang the fish in a shaded, breezy place until the surface is dry and a thin film forms. The fish should be dry in 3 hours.

Meanwhile dig a shallow fire pit and build a bed of coals in it. Use hardwood only. Wood from conifers, aspen or cottonwood affects the taste adversely. Also cut a number of sticks 4 to 5 feet long with the smaller end forked.

Press the thick ends of the sticks into the ground several feet from the fire, angling the forked top toward the fire. Hook a fish on the forked end. Take 3 longer sticks and build a tripod above the fish sticks. Cover the tripod with canvas or with a thatch of boughs and grass to trap the smoke. Before closing the top, toss some green twigs and leaves on the coals to create smoke. Put more green wood on the coals periodically. Smoke the fish for 6 to 18 hours, depending on the size of the fish and the amount of dehydration you want.

After the fish cools, wrap it in clean leaves and store in a cool, dry place. The fish will keep two weeks to a month.

SPICE-CURED FISH

Dissolve 2½ cups salt in 2 quarts water. Place the container on ice and chill the brine well. Place whole sides of fish (such as steelhead or large trout) in the brine 60 to 90 minutes. The cold stops the oil from leaving the fish.

While the fish are in the brine, make the following dry mix:

2 pounds salt	2 tablespoons crushed bay
1 pound brown sugar	leaves
2 tablespoons saltpeter	2 tablespoons crushed allspice
2 tablespoons pepper	2 tablespoons crushed cloves

Put the mix in a shallow pan. Remove the fish from the brine, drain for ½ hour, then place in the dry mix. Rub the mix on the fish lightly and leave the fish there overnight. In the morning wash the mix off the fish, dry them several hours, then put them in the smokehouse. Keep the heat under 100°. Use smoke as heavy as possible and keep it up for 24 to 48 hours. Remove the fish and brush with vegetable oil.

KIPPERED SALMON

Cut the filleted fish into chunks and soak for several hours in a brine made by dissolving 2½ cups salt in 2 quarts water. Remove the fish, blot the chunks dry and allow to air-dry for 2 to 3 hours. Put the pieces on a wire rack in a smokehouse and smoke lightly with low heat—85° to 90°—for 10 hours. Add coals now and raise the temperature to 180°. Put green wood or sawdust on liberally for 2 hours.

Appendix: Seasonings

The Greeks believed that snakes nibbled on fennel to sharpen their vision. They also thought that anise, added to a drink, would prevent fatigue, and that birds could be stupefied and caught easily if fed boiled garlic seed.

Hippocrates, the father of medicine, had other notions: Anise stops sneezing, coriander prevents heartburn, thyme expels phlegm, too much mint has a deleterious effect on a man's love life, and onion is good for the sight and bad for the body, while garlic is bad for the sight and good for the body.

Modern science is finding that spices have a preserving effect. The ancient Egyptians knew it too: They used spices in embalming bodies.

Hippocrates and other Greeks had their varying thoughts on anise, but the Romans were convinced it was an aphrodisiac. The Romans were also wild for cassia, the sweet-tasting, aromatic bark from a tree that is native to China and Indonesia. We call it cinnamon. The true cinnamon is a native of Ceylon. Like cassia, it is bark from a member of the laurel family, but the true cinnamon is buff-colored and milder in taste than cassia, which is reddish-brown in color. True cinnamon is popular in the many parts of the world, but we import ten times as much cassia as true cinnamon.

The Roman preoccupation with spices was only a part of man's long love affair with condiments. It goes back to prehistoric times. The earliest writings refer to spice. The ancient Assyrians knew cardamom, cumin, dill, fennel, orégano, thyme, saffron and sesame. Since not all of these were native to their land, there must already have been a spice trade.

The course of history has been affected by spices. America was discovered by Columbus because he was trying to find a short cut to Asian spices. World powers have sprung from spice. For centuries, whatever nation controlled the spice trade was the strongest in the Western world.

In Europe there once was no way to keep herds of cattle through the winter because there was not enough feed for them, so most farm animals were killed in the fall and the meat salted. Some of it spoiled, and the rest was not too tasty. In the winter, there were no fresh vegetables, corn, sugar, potatoes, tea, coffee, chocolate or lemon. The winter table in Europe was dreary.

What a dash of pepper, cinnamon or ginger did for them! This explains why spices were so important, and how it happened that spices came to be worth their weight in gold and silver.

The Arabs, Portugal, Spain, England and Holland took turns rising to world power through the spice trade. A pound of pepper could be bought for a few pennies in the tropics, and later sold for a hundred times more. To control the trade, though, meant that a nation had to control a remarkable section of the world—the spice coast of India and Ceylon, Indonesia and those fantastic islands, the Moluccas—the Spice Islands. They had trees and plants not appearing in the rest of the world. Whoever controlled their output controlled fortunes.

The monopolies were broken, however, when merchants began transplanting spices to other areas of the world. It was found, for example, that clove, a native of the Spice Islands, would flourish in Zanzibar, which is now the world's leading producer of clove. Nutmeg used to be found exclusively in the Spice Islands. Now the biggest source is Grenada in the West Indies.

The East Indies are still the largest source of pepper, but it is also grown all around the world. Some plants found exclusively in America have also been transplanted. The chili peppers of Central America, for example, are now grown in Africa, India, the East Indies and Japan.

With the breaking of monopolies, and with development of cheaper transportation, the price of spices has come down drastically. In the Middle Ages in Europe only lords and wealthy merchants could afford spices. Now they are used universally. It's almost unthinkable to cook without spices.

A quiet controversary goes on about the definition of spices. Some insist that the word should not include the herbs, the mild plants of the temperate zones, while others believe it should include all seasonings, including salt.

Certainly salt has been one of the most important of food seasonings. It not only improves the taste of food, but also is necessary for health. It has been used as money in Africa and Asia. (Even pepper has been used as money in Europe and the United States.) Peppercorn rent is a term still recognized by some, stemming back to the days when rent was paid with pepper pods. It was more common, though, for salt to be used as a means of exchange. In fact, our word for pay comes from salt. The Roman soldiers were given a daily portion of salt. It was called *salarium,* and from that comes our word "salary."

There are no hard and fast rules for the use of seasonings. One person may like garlic on fish; another cannot stand it. An experiment with cinnamon on pork may please one person, and drive the next out of the house.

A spice can be tried with any food. Your own taste will determine whether you like the combination.

Our spice chart (over) is not a rulebook for the use of seasonings, but lists the more common seasonings and their more common usages.

	Beef	Fish	Fowl	Lamb	Pork	Shellfish	Stuffing	Sauces
Allspice	X			X	X		X	X
Basil	X		X	X	X			X
Caraway			X					X
Cardamom							X	
Cinnamon							X	
Cloves	X	X			X		X	X
Coriander	X					X	X	X
Dill	X	X		X			X	X
Fennel		X						X
Garlic	X	X	X	X	X	X	X	X
Ginger	X	X	X	X	X	X	X	X
Marjoram	X	X	X	X	X		X	X
Mustard	X	X	X	X	X			X
Nutmeg		X	X				X	X
Orégano	X	X	X	X	X		X	X
Parsley	X	X		X		X	X	X
Rosemary	X		X	X	X		X	X
Sage		X	X		X		X	
Savory			X					X
Tarragon		X	X			X		X
Thyme		X	X		X		X	X
Turmeric		X		X				X

Index

Index

THE AUTHORS AND THEIR BOOK

MATT KRAMER was born in Missoula, Montana, but has spent most of his life in Oregon. He is a veteran reporter for the Associated Press, now living and working in Salem, Oregon. Mr. Kramer's hobbies include cooking, camping trips, and making his own wine.

ROGER SHEPPARD is a native of Minnesota. He works in advertising in Portland, Oregon, where he has lived since 1939. Mr. Sheppard studied journalism at the University of Oregon. He has at various times been a part-time sculptor and metalworker.

This cookbook is the result of a smoke-cooking contest which the authors have been carrying on for five years. They each started with one smoke cooker and limited barbecue experience, but gradually picked up more elaborate equipment, experience and polish, and a rich assortment of successful smoke-cooking recipes. Finding that only a few scattered pages had ever been written on the subject, the authors were encouraged to combine their best efforts in a practical cookbook devoted entirely to smoke cooking.

SMOKE COOKING was set in type by the Harry Sweetman Typesetting Corporation, South Hackensack, New Jersey. The text type is Caledonia, which was designed by William Addison Dwiggins and was cut by the Mergenthaler Linotype Company in 1938. "Caledonia" is the ancient Roman word for Scotland, and denotes that the type face was intended to have a Scottish-Roman character.